Accounting at War

Accounting is frequently portrayed as a value-free mechanism for allocating resources and ensuring they are employed in the most efficient manner. Contrary to this popular opinion, the research presented in *Accounting at War* demonstrates that accounting for military forces is primarily a political practice. Throughout history, military force has been so pervasive that no community of any degree of complexity has succeeded in surviving without an army.

Through to the present day, for all nation states, accounting for the military and its operations has primarily served broader political purposes. From the Crimean War to the War on Terror, accounting has been used to assert civilian control over the military, instill rational business practices on war, and create the visibilities and invisibilities necessary to legitimize the use of force.

Accounting at War emphasizes the significant power that financial and accounting controls gave to political elites and the impact of these controls on military performance. *Accounting at War* examines the effects of these controls in wars such as the Crimean, South African and Vietnam Wars. *Accounting at War* also emphasizes how accounting has provided the means to rationalize and normalize violence, which has often contributed to the acceleration and expansion of war.

Aimed at researchers and academics in the fields of accounting, accounting history, political management and sociology, *Accounting at War* represents a unique and critical perspective to this cutting-edge research field.

Warwick Funnell is Professor of Accounting and Public Sector Accountability and Head of Accounting and Finance Group at Kent Business School, UK.

Michele Chwastiak is Associate Professor of Accounting at the Anderson School of Management, University of New Mexico, USA.

Routledge New Works in Accounting History

Series Editor: John Richard Edwards, Richard Fleischman, Garry Carnegie, Salvador Carmona

This innovative series contains volumes on accounting history, auditing, bibliography, development of accounting principles and standards, education and ethics, financial reporting, law and regulations, management accounting and the theoretical works of leading scholars. Providing students, teachers and researchers with the opportunity to learn more about the discipline of accountancy and its past, this series is a vital addition to any accounting library.

For a full list of titles in this series, please visit www.routledge.com

Accounting at War

The Politics of Military Finance

**Warwick Funnell and
Michele Chwastiak**

LONDON AND NEW YORK

First published 2015
by Routledge

2 Park Square, Milton Park, Abingdon, Oxfordshire OX14 4RN
711 Third Avenue, New York, NY 10017

Routledge is an imprint of the Taylor & Francis Group, an informa business

First issued in paperback 2018

Library of Congress Cataloging-in-Publication Data
Funnell, Warwick.
   Accounting at war : the politics of military finance / Warwick Funnell, Michele Chwastiak.
      pages cm. — (Routledge new works in accounting history)
   Includes bibliographical references and index.
   1. War—Economic aspects—Case studies.   2. Armed forces—Accounting—Political aspects.   3. Accounting—History.   4. War finance—History.   I. Chwastiak, Michele.   II. Title.   III. Title: Politics of military finance.
   UA710.F864 2015
   355.6'22—dc23
   2014048311

ISBN: 978-1-138-85979-1 (hbk)
ISBN: 978-1-138-61673-8 (pbk)

Typeset in Sabon
by Apex CoVantage, LLC

Contents

1 Introduction

Accounting is frequently portrayed within mainstream thought as a value-free mechanism for allocating resources and ensuring they are employed in the most efficient way possible. According to this view, accounting is a pragmatic response to the need for organizations to account for resources, and is credited with embodying the principles of objectivity, rationality and usefulness. In contrast, critical accounting theorists do not view accounting as an impartial means for distributing capital. Rather, accounting is perceived as serving the interests of the political and economic elite by embodying assumptions that sustain the status quo distribution of wealth and power in society. For example, accounting is premised on the belief that companies exist to maximize profit. Such an assumption places the concerns of stockholders above those of workers and ensures that wages will be held to a minimum.

The way in which things are counted will always produce both winners and losers and, therefore, accounting policies and practices are products of political struggle. While mainstream accounting theorists mask the political competition by regarding policies as a natural response to market needs, critical theorists focus on the interested nature of all accounting innovations. Even within the public sector, where politics is the rule, calculative practices have frequently supplanted informed judgment to lend an appearance of objectivity to decision making. Yet, calculative practices have an inherent bias in that they only consider those aspects of a problem that can be represented quantitatively. One result is that issues of fairness, justice, equity and even survivability are lost.

Ultimately all political power is dependent upon control over public finances for, at its most basic level, control over finances ensures the ability to marshal and use military force, either against external foes or to stifle internal discontent, to maintain political dominance. This nexus between political hegemony and public finances lay at the heart of the constitutional battles between Parliament and the Executive in the evolution of the English Constitution (Clode, 1869). From the late 17th century until the 20th century the constitutional intent of making the Executive financially accountable to Parliament for the expenditure of monies appropriated by Parliament, while progressively less prominent, still continued to provide the core rationale for reforms to government accounting and Executive accountability which relied upon the simple charge-discharge form of accounts long favored by the Exchequer.

Accounting at War demonstrates the interested and political nature of accounting. From the Crimean War in the 19th century to the War on Terror in the 21st century, accounting has been used to assert civilian control over the military, instill rational business practices on war and create the visibilities and invisibilities necessary to legitimize the use of force. While accounting's ostensible objectivity and rationality were frequently used to validate such actions, the chapters in *Accounting at War* show that accounting was used strategically and in ways that benefitted some at the cost to others.

The constitutional battles in the 17th century between the British Parliament and the Crown etched indelibly on the English, and later the Americans, the potential for a national army to oppress the ordinary citizens whom it ostensibly served. It was believed that, in order to prevent the use of force against the internal population, civilians needed to exert command over the military. Civilians discovered that they could constrain the military and protect their liberty by controlling military finances and that accounting was the mechanism through which this could be accomplished. Centuries later accounting would still be used by civilians to reign in the military, such as during the 1960s when the U.S. Secretary of Defense strategically employed budgeting to centralize decision making in his office.

During the 20th century, political elites started using accounting as a tool to manage political crises. Thus, in the early 20th century when Britain's empire was threatened by the advance of the German and U.S. economies, to restore Britain's high standing in the world the political elites engaged in a movement of national efficiency that harnessed the rising reputation of cost accounting to inculcate a business culture in the administration of war. While such a move did not necessarily produce efficiency gains, it created an aura of action which was needed to again legitimize Britain as a strong empire. Further, in the U.S., Planning, Programming and Budgeting (PPB) was introduced into the Department of Defense during the 1960s as a mechanism for supposedly allocating resources efficiently. While PPB eventually proved to be inadequate for such a mission, it did provide a discourse through which nuclear war could be discussed rationally, thus normalizing that which had been the unthinkable. Thus, in the U.S. accounting has assisted political and economic elites with legitimizing the use of force by creating the visibilities and invisibilities necessary to do so. Most notoriously, accounting assisted the Nazis with the systematic attempt to exterminate the Jewish people by denying their humanity. In ignoring the social and human costs of war, accounting has made war a more viable option for the U.S. political elites. Accounting also allowed corporations to participate in the state crime of "extraordinary rendition" by transforming it into just another opportunity to generate profit.

The Crimean, South African and Vietnam Wars exposed the contradictions between the policies enforced through accounting and the reality of conflict which produced unintended consequences. Accounting was partially to blame for soldiers dying from deprivation in the Crimea and for troops killing their commanding officers in Vietnam. The inconsistencies between strict financial controls and military needs, as well as accounting's partial, interested representation of war and reality, proved that accounting was not a reliable or disinterested means for accomplishing the goals of armed conflict.

Accounting at War elaborates upon the above themes. Chapter 2, Accounting and the Crimean War, traces the evolution of financial control of the British army from the Revolution in 1688 to the Crimean War. All financial matters were made the exclusive responsibility of civilians, which also meant the centralization in civilian departments of state of all matters related to providing for the needs of armies. The result was that 90% of the British casualties during the Crimean War were due to disease, exposure and deprivation, not combat. The high mortality of British soldiers during the Crimean War was a direct consequence of the rigid, politically motivated financial and accounting controls which denied the military the ability to influence decisions about their needs.

Chapter 3, Accounting on the Frontline in the South African War, is concerned with how the South African War (1899–1902) exposed significant defects in the administration of the British army and its performance in the field of battle arising from the political motivations. The findings of several inquiries convinced the British Government that the civilian army administrators, especially those responsible for supplying the army, had given insufficient attention to the military benefits which might be obtained from the methods and experience of business. For the first time in government, problems with military efficiency were blamed on the absence of cost accounting systems throughout the War Office and on the field of battle.

Chapter 4, Military Accounting and the Business of War, examines the efforts at the beginning of the 20th century to inculcate in the British army the values and practices of business, in which accounting was to be accorded a prominent place. Costly failures during the South African War and World War I were shown to be partly associated with ineffective and deceptive accounting systems, which served political purposes and were administered by the civilians in the War Office. These failures assumed a high political profile, for they were regarded also as symptomatic of a deterioration in the efficiency of British business and government which had left Britain vulnerable to the aggressive energies of Germany and the United States. To retrieve Britain's greatness, a movement of national efficiency sought to raise efficiency levels in all areas of British national life. Fundamental to the reforms that they advocated were a strong British empire and an efficient, strong army. Thus, to achieve these broad political purposes, military administrators were urged to apply the methods of commerce to the business of war.

Chapter 5, Taming the Untamable: The Normalization of Nuclear War, demonstrates the profound political consequences accounting can have by examining the emergence of Planning, Programming and Budgeting in the United States as an ostensibly value-free tool for allocating defense resources during the 1960s. PPB assisted with normalizing the preparation for nuclear war by converting the "unthinkable" into a technical and mundane resource allocation problem, as well as the internal inconsistencies generated by placing an economically rational frame of representation on a dialectical and political process. This allowed PPB to be strategically deployed by the Secretary of Defense to centralize decisions over resource allocations within his office.

Chapter 6, The Vietnam War, Performance Measures and Representations of Reality, identifies the role which Planning, Programming and Budgeting played in changing visibilities in the Department of Defense in such a way that the U.S. leaders argued that the Vietnam War could be won through the proper management of resources. It also demonstrates how this representation of the war clashed with the U.S. soldiers' experience of combat, creating contradictions that contributed to the downfall of the U.S. command in Vietnam. The chapter shows that while accounting has played a role in disciplining labor and productive processes in capitalist organizations by constructing new ways of being, it has not succeeded in imposing rational control on the turmoil of war. Further, when accounting is used to measure performance in situations for which it is ill suited, unintended tragic consequences have resulted.

Chapter 7, The Holocaust, Accounting and the Denial of Humanity, further confirms the way in which accounting has the ability to create particular visibilities as a tool of political ideologies, which render invisible other aspects of existence and experience. Nowhere is this more obvious than in the treatment of the Jewish people during the period now known as the Holocaust during World War II. Accounting numbers were substituted for qualitative attributes of individuals, thereby denying them their humanity and individuality, and making them invisible to Germans not directly involved in the attempted annihilation of all European Jews. The Nazis also endeavored to use accounting to purify their expropriation and disposal of the vast amount of property taken from the Jewish people.

Chapter 8, Rendering Death and Destruction Visible: Counting the Costs of War, examines the costs that are included and those that are excluded from the U.S. war budget, and why it is in the best interests of the U.S. political elite to undercost warfare. It provides a social accounting for war that goes beyond the economic by further documenting the human and social consequences of conflict. In so doing, it demonstrates the potential of social reporting for emancipation. If the U.S. Government was required to disclose the social and human costs of war, the horror would be revealed, making it difficult to rationalize violence as a means to an end.

Chapter 9, Commodifying State Crime: Accounting for "Extraordinary Rendition," probes the role accounting played in transforming state crime into just another business opportunity. In 2001, the Central Intelligence Agency (CIA) set up an "extraordinary rendition" program in which supposed al Qaeda agents were secretly kidnapped and flown to countries known for torturing prisoners, or to CIA controlled "black sites" where "enhanced interrogation techniques" were employed. In 2009, two of the subcontractors for the CIA's privatized rendition fights, Richmor and Sportsflight, went to court over a contract dispute. Based on the testimony and evidence in the case, this chapter examines the role accounting played in transforming a state crime into a commodity that could be costed and argued about. Accounting did so by elevating profit, performance, minutia and normal business routines as the most important considerations, and kidnapping and torture as irrelevant and effectively invisible.

2 Accounting and the Crimean War

INTRODUCTION

The extent of the ineptitude which characterized the conduct of the Crimean War (1854–1856) by the British was such that it "has become a byword for disaster, gross mismanagement and incompetent leadership" (Judd, 1973, p. 29) which, according to Barnett (1970, p. 283), has made it "one of the compulsive subjects of British historical writing". It was, wrote Florence Nightingale, "calamity unparalleled in the history of calamity" (cited in Woodham-Smith, 1977, p. 15). The causes of the calamities which befell the British army were initially attributed to individuals until it became recognized that, whilst deficiencies of individuals certainly contributed to the failure experienced, the major cause could be traced to financial considerations.

Undoubtedly the greatest influence in shaping the British people's attitude towards the war was the series of articles in *The Times* newspaper by William Russell, the first modern war correspondent. For the first time, the public became intimately familiar with the conditions of war under which the soldier was expected to live and fight and judged them unacceptable (see Laffin, 1964, p. 137). As early as December 23, 1854 Russell described how the "noblest army England ever sent from these shores has been sacrificed to the grossest mismanagement. Incompetency, lethargy, aristocratic hauteur, official indifference, favor, routine, perverseness, and stupidity reign, revel and riot in the camp before Sabastopol . . ." (quoted in Reid, 1911, p. 3).

Successive British governments, without exception, were content to leave military matters in the hands of an aristocratic, wealthy and amateur elite who were interested in the army for its sport and social value (Stanmore, 1906, Vol. I, p. 310). An army ruled over by the aristocracy was accepted as being constitutionally safe. As a result of "the ties of relationship with the rank, wealth, and more advanced intelligence of the country, . . . [they] can be relied upon under all circumstances to maintain order and obey the laws" (*Blackwoods Edinburgh Magazine*, November 1857, p. 583). Writing to Sydney Herbert in March 1855, Florence Nightingale decried the incompetence of the army's aristocratic officers. She complained that "the real hardship of this place . . . is that we have to do with men who are neither gentlemen nor men of education nor even men of business . . . whose only object is to keep themselves out of blame" (quoted in Woodham-Smith, 1977, p. 162).

The incompetence of British military officers decried by Florence Nightingale exacerbated what was a more serious problem. By 1855 it had become clear to the British public that the army in the Crimea had been sacrificed primarily because of financial considerations: "Parsimony, as regard military establishments, was the order of the day" (*Blackwoods Edinburgh Magazine,* January 1856, p. 115; Trevelyan, 1922, p. 305; Russell, 1858, p. 30). Sir Charles Stephenson, in a letter to his brother on March 5, 1855, fumed that "the late Government have a heavy account to answer for. They have been to this army . . . a greater enemy to us than the Russians; . . . they have, in short, done what I deem it impossible for a Russian army to do— annihilated the British army . . ." (Stephenson, 1915, p. 10). Constitutional fears of a standing army manifest themselves in a preference for cheeseparing economy, obsessive surveillance of finance through accounting reports and a grossly centralized and minutely regulated financial administration in the hands of civilians, especially those at the Treasury.

DISTRUST OF STANDING ARMIES

The army's sworn allegiance to the ruling monarch as its commander meant that Parliament regarded armies on English soil as a potential threat to Parliament's sometimes uncertain position in the government of the Nation and an inducement to extravagance (*Edinburgh Review,* Vol. CXXXIII, January to April 1871, p. 240). This apprehension was reconfirmed in the early 19th century by George Fox who noted that while he respected the army he was not prepared to

> sacrifice to them that jealousy which it is the duty of the House of Commons to entertain of *every set of men so* immediately connected with the Crown. To the Crown they must look for promotion; by the Crown they may be dismissed. . . . Such being the situation of all Military Officers, they are fit and necessary objects of the jealousy and vigilance of the House. . . .
>
> (quoted in Clode, 1869, Vol. I, pp. 271–272)

While armies raised for war on the Continent or elsewhere were seen as necessary, the presence of a large standing army in England during peace could only be regarded suspiciously and with apprehension by a Parliament jealous of its own hard-won prerogatives of government ("Observation of Lord Panmure", February 1855, *Panmure Papers,* 1908, p. 46). An army in peace, an army with little to occupy its time and energies, was viewed askance by Parliament, ever worried about the machinations of a

Crown resentful and reflective of its long lost hegemony in government (see Trevelyan, 1960, pp. 54–55). A standing army was seen as fatal to liberty in peace "when there is no other employment for them, but to insult and oppress their fellow subjects . . ." (Sir Thomas Hanmer, Hansard,[1] December 6, 1717).

The House of Commons resolved in January 1673 that a standing army could be nothing other than "a great grievance and vexation to the people" (quoted in Clode, 1869, Vol. I, p. 62). Fletcher of Saltoun, in his published treatise *A Discourse on Government with Relation to Militias* (1698), referred to the unease felt by the Nation "when a standing mercenary army is kept up in time of peace; for he that is armed is always master of him that is unarmed" (quoted in Omond, 1933, p. 46).

To Parliament an efficient and effective fighting force was a potential source of the means of oppression and tyranny. There thus arose a curious paradox, apparently acceptable to the majority of society, of political security and desirable military inefficiency which was to prejudice the performance of the army and Britain until the 20th century (*Blackwoods Edinburgh Magazine,* November 1857, p. 575). The country was prepared to tolerate this curious position, arguing, as *The Times* (February 11, 1854), that "our free constitution is a source to us both of strength and weakness. The strength is perpetual, the weakness periodical". Parliamentary political supremacy, military amateurism and inefficiency thus became synonymous. This paradox led Lord Salisbury to announce, "I do not believe in the perfection of the British Constitution as an instrument of War" (1900, quoted in Ehrman, 1969, p. 85).

Opposition to a standing army can be viewed in terms of glaring self-interest and economic sense: it was better to have an inexpensive, though ineffective, militia, and devote more resources to a constitutionally benign but aggressively potent navy than run the constitutional gauntlet of a large professional standing army. "Our Navy must be our first and greatest defense", wrote Sidney Herbert, the Secretary of State of War, in a confidential Memorandum to Cabinet on December 13, 1859 (cited in Stanmore, 1906, Vol. II, p. 274). Further, there would always be time to arm and supplement the militia. As a consequence, the Nation "never looked upon the Army as a force which was to be kept available for foreign aggression" ("Observations of Lord Panmure", February 1855, *Panmure Papers,* 1908, p. 46).

During the English Civil War, beginning in 1642, a large and well-led army was raised by Parliament. However, at the cessation of hostilities in 1647, Parliament discovered that it had created a monster, in the form of the army, that threatened to devour its master (see Churchill, 1962, Vol. II, p. 210). Davies (1954, p. 26) refers to the New Model Army as "a political force of the first magnitude". It was astutely realized, but too late, that "a victorious army, out of inployment, is very inclinable to assume power over their Principals" (a contemporary 17th-century observer, as quoted in Williams, 1965, p. 75). Parliament soon saw it had placed itself in a position no less unfavorable than that of the king. From 1647 to 1660 the military were supreme in the land under the dictatorship of Oliver Cromwell (Barnett, 1970, p. 102).

Cromwell was only too well aware of the exposed position of the army and attempted, though manifestly unsuccessfully, to marshal behind him a durable base of support and acceptance. Despite his efforts, at no time was Cromwell able to masquerade successfully the army as constitutionally compatible with English history and life. In 1857, at the end of the Crimean War, *Blackwoods Edinburgh Magazine* (Vol. LXXXII, November 1857, p. 5891) could still confidently pronounce that "the army can never become among us more than an adjunct to our national institutions—a mere excrescence growing out of them." In the meantime the public became the army's hawkeyed adversary.

The Civil War and its military dictatorship aftermath etched indelibly on English minds the potential for oppression by a national army harnessed by a despot (see Trevelyan, 1960, p. 55; Gordon, 1935, p. 24). As a consequence the army in Britain became

> an exotic . . . unknown to the old Constitution of the country; required or supposed to be required, only for the defence of its foreign possessions; disliked by the inhabitants, particularly of the higher orders, some of whom never allow one of their family to serve in it. . . . The officers and soldiers of the army are an object of dislike and suspicion to the inhabitants. . . .
>
> (Duke of Wellington, *Dispatches V*, pp. 592–593,
> Memorandum on April 22, 1829, as quoted
> in Hanham, 1969, p. 359)

After the Restoration, James II in 1660, unable to pay for a large army from parliamentary grants, had directed "money for and to the use of the Crown by Pretence of Prerogative for other time and in other manner than the same was granted by Parliament . . ." (*Declaration of Right,* 1689). This allowed him to maintain a large army of 34,000 men by 1688; an army which, according to Barnett (1970, p. 122), "badly frightened the nation— far more than Cromwell's. It has been so plainly designed to coerce" (see also Einzig, 1959). The army was far larger than any previous monarch had been able to maintain in peace and thus a far more dangerous portent of arbitrary autocratic power based on military intimidation.

Consequently, after the Glorious Revolution in 1688, the *Bill of Rights,* sworn to by William and Mary of Orange who had been brought from Holland, categorically denounced monarchy devoid of parliamentary control: "[Almighty God] deliver this kingdom from Popery and Arbitrary Power". The *Bill of Rights* recognized the authority of Parliament once and for all over the Crown by establishing a constitutional monarchy. The king was now a servant of the State and, henceforth, Parliament "was free to harry monarchs, topple ministries, cut supplies, refuse taxation . . ." (Plumb,

1967, p. 73). Most importantly, to "secure the Rights and Liberties of the Lords Spiritual and Temporal and Commons" from being invaded and overpowered by military force, the incumbents to the throne were made to agree, as a condition of their assumption of the monarchy, that Parliament was supreme in law making and that only Parliament could raise an army (*Bill of Rights* as quoted in the *Quarterly Review,* Vol. 146, July to October 1878, p. 237).

Each year the *Mutiny Act* required the Crown to reaffirm its allegiance to the principle of parliamentary control of the army as enunciated in the *Bill of Rights* (1689 1 William and Mary c. 5 & 6 S.R.55). The *Mutiny Act* required the monarch to affirm that "it is illegal for the Queen (King) to keep a standing army in time of peace". The annual *Mutiny Act* also represented, in part, the ultimate compromise reached between Crown and Parliament in the contest for control of the army. The army became a constitutional force, though not a parliamentary army, the existence of which depended on votes of supply made by Parliament. Its loyalty, however, remained the province of the monarch until the late 19th century. This was seen as a great strength because by taking command of the army from Parliament it could never become an instrument in parliamentary tyranny (Duke of Cambridge to Queen Victoria, quoted in Wilson, 1973, p. 51). A cornerstone of the British Constitution in the late 17th century was therefore the supremacy of Parliament in all matters related to the administration, though not command, of the army.

INFLUENCES ON 19TH-CENTURY ATTITUDES TOWARD THE ARMY

No institutions were more important to the progress of the British Nation in the 19th century than the army and the navy ('B', 1899, p. 64); neither were any departments of state more closely controlled. "Practical politics" demanded the supremacy of Parliament, mostly through "a ruthless and dominant Treasury . . .", in all matters related to the granting of finance to the military and accounting for approved expenditures (Midleton, 1939, p. 123). These constitutional protections against military pretensions were inseparable. There still remained in the 19th century a lurking and what might be regarded as paranoid antipathy towards the army derived from constitutional fears (see *Blackwoods Edinburgh Magazine,* Vol. LXXXII, November 1857, p. 575). The Nation appeared unable to free itself completely of the specter of rampant military might. The appointment, for example, of Sir Redvers Buller, a general in the British army, to a civilian position in Ireland in 1886 created great consternation, with many regarding the appointment as "a standing innovation in our Constitution, a serious blow to civil and religious liberty" (as summarized by Lord Randolph Churchill 1886, in Churchill, 1906, Vol. 1, p. 142). Recognizing the civilian lordship of the army as found in Parliament's authority, and its representative the Secretary-at-War, Lord Hardinge in 1832 indicated with satisfaction that

> the Secretary-at-War is in a constitutional point of view, the proper person to draw up the Mutiny Bill. . . . He is bound to stand between the civil subject and the military, and it is his duty to see that the civil part of the community are properly protected. . . .
>
> (referred to by the Royal Commission Appointed to
Inquire into the Civil and Professional Administration
of the Navy and Military Departments and the Relation
of Those Departments to Each Other and to the Treasury
[Hartington Commission] 1890, p. XXIV)

Despite pockets of reaction, by 1854, when Britain went to war with Russia, constitutional antagonism between the Crown and Parliament had long ceased to be the main force which sustained parliamentary determination that military spending would be closely hedged by parliamentary imposed controls ("Observations of Lord Panmure", February 1855, *Panmure Papers*, 1908, pp. 46–47). Instead, moral rather than constitutional indignation of military might had strengthened in the mid-19th century. Both William Gladstone, who occupied the office of Chancellor of the Exchequer on two occasions and that of Prime Minister three times, and the Secretary of State of War, Sidney Herbert, were noted for their devout Christian outlook which found it difficult to accommodate enthusiasm for forces of destruction and death, even on a national scale (see Woodham-Smith, 1977, p. 59). Gladstone regarded the army as amoral and, possibly more importantly, a vicious waste of money, while to the radical politician Richard Cobden a national army was a curse (Sweetman, 1971, p. 84). Palmerston could still gather support and sympathy when in 1854 he persisted in referring to the militia as a civilian bulwark against the military (Anderson, 1967, p. 58, footnote 1). By the mid-19th century Parliament's relations with the army were heavily influenced more by a national obsession with economic parsimony and unease with what was seen as an incorrigibly spendthrift army. "Parliament", noted Gordon, "had exchanged new panics for old"; dislike for the costs of maintaining a standing army sufficient to ensure the Nation's safety instead of fear of the army itself (1935, p. 56).

CONSTITUTIONAL SECURITY AND THE ROLE OF FINANCE IN THE CONTROL OF THE ARMY

Finance and control of the military had always been indissolubly linked in the constitutional struggles between the Crown and Parliament. Sidney Herbert reminded his colleagues that "the Minister who holds the purse-strings of the Army . . . will always have the power in his hands" (Select Committee on Military Organisation, 1860, Question 6372). Nothing was more important, argued Clode (1869, Vol. 1, p. 110), in maintaining civilian liberty than the question of army finance. The army must never be allowed near the public purse for, warned Clode (1869, Vol. 1, p. 186; also see p. 265), "a country ceases to be free when its Treasure is under the influence of the army". Consequently, control of army finances had been based upon constitutional apprehension and jealousies. Parliament had recognized very early that the ability to raise and control finance was the foundation of authority in government and for the legislature the most effective instrument against Executive tyranny (Carter, 1972, p. 111; Hughes, 1934, p. 122). "Vast, almost beyond description", commented the *Quarterly Review* (Vol. 166, January to April 1888, p. 515), "is the power . . . of a Minister who controls the finances of a great country . . .". Thus, it was not surprising that "from the very outset after the Revolution Parliament endeavored to establish and maintain close financial control over the fighting services in general and over the army in particular" (Einzig, 1959, p. 118).

To give the army ready access to the public treasure was leaving the way clear to a reversion to the anarchy and oppression of the Interregnum, the period from the execution of Charles I in 1649 to the restoration of Charles II in 1660. Parliament was especially ruthless with "vipers in its own bosom" who attempted to deny and circumvent Parliament's wishes in respect of the army. For example, articles of impeachment were prepared in 1686 against the parliamentarian Edward Seymour for providing money for the support of the army after a date Parliament had stipulated for its disbandment. No offender was beyond Parliament's rage, even Lord Treasurers (see Clode, 1869, Vol. I, pp. 66–67).

Liberty, described by Peter Wentworth in 1576 as a thing of "value beyond all inestimable treasure" (quoted in Elton, 1963, p. 317), was seen by Parliament as inseparable from control of the army and its financing. Gladstone referred to the control of finance as a powerful lever for English liberty (cited on the title page to Einzig, 1959; also p. 18). Control of the public purse was not infrequently regarded as being sacred (*Westminister Review*, January to April 1876, New Series, p. 167). Members of Parliament had a tendency to become unsettled when the Crown appeared to be given too much money with not enough apparent restrictions. Affirmation in the 1689 constitutional settlement of the Englishman's right not to be taxed without his consent and Parliament's right to be solely responsible for raising taxes cemented a long established practice dating from the Model Parliament of Edward I in 1297 and the *Magna Carta* (Elton, 1963, p. 67): "No scutage nor aid shall be imposed on our Kingdom, unless by common counsel of our Kingdom" (Chapter 12 of *Magna Carta*).

Through the mechanism of appropriation Parliament was guaranteed the opportunity to review proposed expenditures of the Executive. The first recorded instance of appropriation by Parliament was in 1353 for military purposes. Use of appropriation procedures by Parliament continued to be spasmodic until systematized after the Revolution of 1688 (Chubb, 1952, pp. 7–8). The Revolution, Sir James Mackintosh reminded the Commons, ushered in

> a new system in the history of finance, for it was not until then that the system was established of appropriating all parliamentary grants, by the authority of parliament, to services previously approved by parliament, which gave reality and energy to all the constitutional principles respecting the power of the purse, created a constant and irresistible control over the public purse in this House. . . .
>
> (quoted in Clode, 1869, Vol. 1, p. 95)

From the 1688 Revolution to at least the 19th century the primary goal of the process of parliamentary financial approval was to satisfy Parliament that the army raised by the Crown (under the annual Mutiny Acts) did not exceed the judicious level approved by Parliament through annual appropriations (Einzig, 1959, p. 143). Indeed, concluded Lord Welby, "the great financial charge made at the Revolution related to the charge of the Navy and Army" (Select Committee on National Expenditure, 1902, Appendix 13, p. 228). Not until the middle of the 19th century were there further significant advances in parliamentary financial controls over the army with the passage of the 1846 Audit Act. Under the system of appropriation which evolved after 1846 the army's administration became locked into an organizational and reporting pattern according to the form and content of the departmental estimates submitted to Parliament each year (see the Committee of Administration of, and Accounting for, Army Expenditure [Lawrence Committee], 1924, p. 718; *Regulations for the Commissariat and Transport Staff*, 1881, Section 1, subsection III, para. 46–48).

THE IMPACT OF APPROPRIATION AND AUDIT

It was on the basis of the divisions or votes in the estimates, as laid down by Parliament, that Parliament appropriated monies for military uses and upon which Parliament after 1846 expected the military administration to report (see the *1846 Audit Act,* Sections II, VI; *1866 Audit Act,* Sections 23, 24). From 1846 in the Appropriation Accounts submitted to Parliament actual expenditures were to be matched against grants and differences had to be explained (see *1846 Audit Act,* Section VI; *1866 Audit Act,* Sections 26, 27). To enable the army to meet these requirements the process of categorizing expenditures according to votes and vote headings had to commence at the earliest recording of expenditure. This was no more clearly demonstrated than with the Commissariat, the Treasury-controlled department responsible for supplying the army with its material needs. When Commissariat Officers entered receipts and issues in their cash books they were to place a number beside each entry which corresponded to the vote under which the issue of funds or receipt was made (see *Regulations and Instructions for the Guidance of Officers of the Purveyors Department of the Army 1861*, para. 116, 126, 142). The vouchers pertaining to these entries would be bundled according to the vote numbers as used in the Commissariat officer's cash book, and the estimates, and then forwarded to that section of the War Office to which the relevant expenditures related. The accounts were then recast into the required parliamentary form at the War Office by the Accountant-General's Department (Royal Commission into Transport and Supply Departments [Strathnairn Committee], 1867, Question 2679, p. 208).

Administering votes separately within the War Office meant that separate administrative departments, reflecting the organization of votes, developed. This produced a fragmentation of administration with the numerous departments, for all practical purposes autonomous of each other and not tied together by a central coordinating authority, issuing their own plethora of regulations and operating their own systems of administration and accounting (see the Select Committee into Army and Ordnance Expenditure, 1849, Questions 8789 to 8798, pp. 593–594). This departmental organization within the War Office, which was a response to "political considerations" (Committee on War Office Organization [Dawkins Committee], 1901, p. 182) was, however, shown both in the Crimean and South African Wars to be inconsistent with military efficiency and economy. It was inevitable, concluded the Royal Commission on Civil Establishments in 1887, that administration of the army on anything but sound administrative and military lines would be hampered by delays and confusion engendered by the uncertain authority and differing departmental opinions, all of which were motivated originally by constitutional suspicion (see the Hartington Commission, 1890, Appendix C, p. 60).

A further substantial shortcoming of the mechanism of appropriation and required reporting, from the point of view of assuring an efficient and effective military force and aiding parliamentary surveillance of expenditure, was the concentration on cash and the emphasis on appropriating to "subjects" of expenditure. The Appropriation Account in the *1846 Audit Act* was envisaged as nothing more than a cash account; bookkeeping on a single entry basis for stewardship purposes. Recognition in the body of the Appropriation Accounts of non-cash items was precluded (*1846 Audit Act*, Section III). Parliament was very guarded in the 19th century (and earlier) in the use of accrual accounting. Accrual accounting was attributed by Parliament with the ability to obscure Parliament's superintendence of government expenditure ("Report of the Commissioners Appointed to Inquire into and to State the Mode of keeping the Official Accounts", *British*

Parliamentary Papers, 1829, VI, 290, p. 89). It was apparent to Parliament that accrual accounting introduced what was regarded as unnecessary complication and increased the opportunities for malversation in public finance. Cash accounts, on the other hand, had the virtue of simplicity, which was widely held to be of

> great importance for the security of the public; it assists punctuality, and it prevents also the hiding out of any improper payment; misdirection or misappropriation of money is much more easy under a complex system, under which the accounts are continually in arrear.
> (Evidence of Sir William Power before the Strathnairn Committee, 1867, Question 2673, p. 208)

Cash accounts were "in a form", remarked Sir Charles Trevelyan, "which permits no mystification or disguise" (Evidence before the Strathnairn Committee, 1867, Question 2684, p. 209). However, contemporary opinion on the preferability of cash accounting in government was far from unanimous, least of all amongst the government and Parliament's own committees. Parliament failed to see that accounts constructed on accrual accounting principles would in fact give a clearer picture of military spending. The military could easily overcome cash shortages towards the end of any financial year, and thereby exceed parliamentary appropriations, by ordering material to be paid for out of next year's appropriations. Accounts disclosing cash items only would miss this information.

Appropriation and accounting were directed towards major headings of expenditure or subjects such as supplies and salaries. Such a system was entirely consistent with a concern primarily for financial accountability but not with efficient, economical and effective administration of government departments (see Evidence of Sir Ralph Knox, Accountant-General before the Select Committee on Army and Navy Expenditure, 1887, Question 31, p. 12 of evidence). Knowledgeable witnesses before the Select Committee on Army and Ordnance Expenditure in 1849 roundly condemned accounts for being organized under vote headings and, therefore, for being oblivious to the efficient use of money granted by Parliament (Question 8638, W.G. Anderson, Audit Office). According to Sir Charles Harris, a senior finance official in the War Office, this could only be achieved by appropriating to "objects" or purposes (Evidence before the Select Committee on National Expenditure, 1918).

Accounts formulated on an "object" basis had the ability to tease out and analyze departmental functions, results and costs; something not possible nor sought under the traditional "subject" mode of appropriation accounting (see the Evidence of Sir Ralph Knox before the Select Committee on Army and Navy Expenditure, 1887, Questions 34 and 1134). Accordingly, the Accounts Branch at the War Office took little interest in military expenditure apart from a thorough examination of the legality and regularity of expenditures (Evidence of Sir Ralph Knox before the Select Committee on Army and Navy Expenditure, 1887, Question 31, p. 12). Certainly it did not interfere in the *administration* of votes within military departments (Evidence before the Select Committee on Army and Navy Expenditure 1887, Questions 426, p. 39, and 428, p. 40).

Another weakness of accounts and estimates based on subjects of expenditure was the difficulty of ascertaining the total cost of particular government services, for example the cost of mounting military maneuvers. Instead of the salaries and cost of supplies required for a particular military maneuver being accumulated specifically for that maneuver, the costs would remain part of the total for all salaries for the army and contribute towards the total supply cost for a year. As Chairman of the Army and Navy Expenditure Committee in 1887, Lord Randolph Churchill asked the Accountant-General of the Army whether it was possible to determine, from the military estimates, a simple matter such as the increase in expenditure for certain services. This, assured the Accountant-General, "would have been extremely difficult" (quoted in Churchill, 1906, Vol. II, p. 320).

To disregard, as the form of the accounts encouraged, whether the money spent achieved its avowed purpose or did so at the least cost was, argued Sir Charles Harris (1911, pp. 65, 67), not financial control but an inducement to financial delinquency. Towards the end of the 19th century, army finance expert Lieut. Churchill denounced the army's financial and accounting systems. It was difficult to imagine, he claimed, a system that could possibly be worse (1895, p. 36; see also Ormsby, 1908a, p. 836). These were also the sentiments of the Select Committee on Army and Navy Expenditure (1887, Questions 34, 953–979, 1134) and Leo Amery (1902, Vol. 2, p. 41), who referred to the whole system of parliamentary financial control which had operated throughout the 19th century as anachronistic, consisting of "cumbrous safeguards". Sir Charles Harris (1911, p. 64), after many years' service at all levels in army accounting, confessed that "we in the army hardly know what accounts are" for management purposes (Ellison, 1918, "Cost Accounting Committee Address", p. 5). This had been tragically confirmed half a century earlier in the Crimean War.

SUPPLY AND WAR IN THE CRIMEA

With the weakening of the Ottoman Empire in the 19th century, Russia sought to annex territory controlled by Turkey around the Black Sea, most especially the Crimean peninsula. For Russia to expand south, however, was seen by the British as a threat to their pre-eminence in the Mediterranean and possibly in India and Western Europe. Access to ice-free ports in the Black Sea presented for the Royal Navy a particular concern. When hostilities broke out in 1853 between the Russians and the Turks, which had been triggered by ongoing disputes about the protection of Christian sites in the

Holy Land, then under the control of the Turks, Britain and France rallied to Turkey's defense. When negotiations failed in August 1854 Britain and France invaded the Crimea.

The British Government in 1854 sent to the Crimea an army with a primitive means of maintenance to invade the territory of a foe of unknown strength (Barker, 1971, p. 878; Russell 1858, pp. 62, 66). Preparation for supply was so inadequate, lamented Alison (1869, p. 6), that at the first experience of hardship the army's "magnificent . . . battalions . . . melted away like snow". Supply preparations for the Crimean War were essentially the same as with those preceding any other conflict since the Revolution of 1688. All were characterized by "belated preparation; frantic effort; disappointment . . ." (Midleton, 1939, p. 138; Gordon, 1935, p. 33). Apart from army personnel from the Peninsular Wars who were still alive, there was pathetically little to guide in planning for supply at the time of the Crimean War (see Le Mesurier, 1796, p. 27). There was, as Major-General Fuller observed, "almost complete silence upon the problem of supply. Not in *ten thousand books* written on war . . . [was] there to be found one on this subject" (Shaw, 1939, Preface on p. 9). Few supply personnel ever wrote about their experiences, even after the valuable lessons learnt in the Napoleonic Wars. After all, decided Shaw (1939, p. 24), if a supply officer did put his experiences on paper, "who would read them". Generally, apart from the Peninsular Wars (see Glover, 1963), there had always been a lack of foresight, no coherent and cohesive attempts at planning for the maintenance of the army and tremendous ignorance born out of national indifference to the army, lassitude, and traditional British Government obstructiveness where the pressing demands of the situation took second place to inflexible and even moronic regulations (Moncrieff, 1909, p. 380).

Supply of the essentials of life to the army was the responsibility of the Commissariat. The Commissariat was a civil department under the direct control of the Treasury, to which the Commissariat directed all its allegiance, until December 1854 when it passed into the hands of the War Department, where it remained under civilian control and Treasury regulations continued unabated (Griffiths, 1900, p. 216; Biddulph, 1904, p. 8). The Commissariat was also the banker for the army and the agent of the Treasury responsible for supplying money to all branches of the military, for the safe-keeping of specie, the issue of money and for concluding when necessary any contracts for supplies (see Report on the Organisation of the Permanent Civil Service, 1854, Vol. XXXII, pp. 300–301, "Treasury Minute 22 December 1854 on Transfer of Commissariat to the War Department"). For every penny spent and every pound of supplies issued detailed accounting records had to be kept for which the men of the Commissariat were held personally responsible (Evidence of Commissariat-General Archer before the Commissioners Appointed to Inquire into the Practicability and Expediency of Consolidating the Different Departments connected with the Civil Administration of the Army [Howick Commission], 1837, p. 34). Given the lack of adequate staff and training and the width of activities encompassed by the Commissariat, there were unquestionably far "too many responsibilities, too many accounts and too many masters" (Appendix VI to Evidence before the Strathnairn Committee, 1867, Question 2739, p. 247). The Commissariat-General's office at Varna in the Crimea was always so busy with its paperwork and accounts as to resemble, for Russell (1858, p. 81), "a bank in the city in the height of business".

Administration of supply was based on a "ruinous succession of checks and balances" (*Edinburgh Review,* 1855, p. 538). The Commissariat's task of maintaining the troops in the field was difficult enough, yet the Commissariat "was so tied down with orders, and so cramped with surveillance, that its energies were greatly diminished" (Russell, 1858, p. 62). Minute documentation was required to support and evidence each transaction conducted by the Commissariat, its members being charged "with every article received. . . . In short, there is not an article of Entry or Issue but must be exactly immediately accounted for . . ." (Le Mesurier, 1796, Part IV; Ward, 1957, p. 73).

The Commissariat's officers knew only too well that by being held personally accountable for all receipts and issues, contravention of Treasury regulations could prove a very costly exercise. Besides, they were trained as Officers of a Treasury-controlled department never to spend money on their own initiative, no matter how egregious the circumstances (see Woodham-Smith, 1977, p. 116). This was tragically demonstrated by the plight of the Medical Officer of the hospital ship *Charity.* On the ship he had a large number of cholera cases, whose suffering was aggravated by the absence of warm surroundings. To improve conditions the Medical Officer sought to acquire some stoves from the Commissariat. Despite the obvious urgency of the situation the Medical Officer was confronted with the following exchange with a member of the Commissariat:

> COMMISSARY: You must make your requisition in due form, send it to headquarters, and get it signed properly, and returned, and then I will let you have the stoves.
> MEDICAL OFFICER: But my men may die meantime.
> COMMISSARY: I can't help that; I must have the requisition.
> MEDICAL OFFICER: It is my firm belief that there are men now in a dangerous state whom another night will certainly kill.
> COMMISSARY: I really can do nothing; I must have a requisition properly signed before I can give one of those stoves away (reported by Russell, 1858, p. 253).

Airey related the similar fate of 9,000 greatcoats received in December 1854. These coats, instead of being issued, were left in the stores for over two months while the men were literally freezing to death in their hundreds. As Airey (1913, p. 468) disapprovingly indicates, "the reasons officially given for non-use of these coats was that the Regulations only authorized an issue every three years, so troops were not therefore entitled to an issue". Florence Nightingale referred with disgust to the similar paralyzing effect of regulations and accounting surveillance in the hospital wards at Scutari. There, she wrote,

> each department had a series of 'warrants' naming definite articles. The Purveyor only gives such amounts of articles as are justifiable under his 'warrants', by which he is governed, and is not responsible for those wants of the soldier . . . which are in excess of the warrants, whatever may be the evidence before him, either in the requisition of the medical officer or the personal observations, it would appear, he was bound to make of what was close under his eyes.
>
> (quoted in Woodham-Smith, 1977, p. 115)

On one occasion, February 15, 1855, Florence Nightingale went to ask for shirts. She was straightway informed there were no shirts available. Upon being confronted with Florence Nightingale's accusation that she knew of 27,000 shirts delivered four days previously, the supply officer retreated into the laager of his department's regulations. He was unable to unpack them, he assured her, despite the pressing need of the men, "without a board", that is, an inspection, a detailed accounting check and written authorization (Woodham-Smith, 1977, p. 152). Thus, procrastination in the Commissariat and the resulting mortality was inordinately generated by accounting regulations, most of which had been carried over from the Peninsular War, which interposed themselves in every facet of the soldier's life. The army and its associated services were "tied and bound in the coils of excessively complex and minute regulations", judged the Committee on the War Office Reconstitution (Esher Committee) (1904, Part 2, p. 9 of the report). Rules and regulations designed for another place, another time and conceivably for other purposes soon became dangerous anachronisms which retarded efficient operations of all military and civilian branches of the army.

While ever the officers of the Commissariat, as befitted agents of the Treasury, were assessed primarily on how well they met Treasury regulations and kept records and accounts in the pursuit of "petty economy", they refused or were unable to move outside the guidelines for supply as laid down in the regulations (see Florence Nightingale's views in Woodham-Smith, 1977, p. 114). This had been observed much earlier than the Crimean War by the Howick Commission, which was prompted to conclude in 1837 that "the Board of Treasury seems particularly unfitted by its constitution for . . . managing the supply of the Army" (Howick Commission, p. 13 of the report). According to Florence Nightingale, the Commissariat's officers fixed "their attention upon their bookkeeping as the primary object of life" (quoted in Moncrieff, 1909, p. 381). This did not change when the War Department took over the Commissariat in December 1854. Mr. Augustus Stafford, on the basis of his experiences in the Crimea, told the Roebuck Committee (1856) that, not only in the supply departments but throughout all departments, there was a fear of responsibility and exceeding regulations (see Woodham-Smith, 1977, p. 130).

The provision of fuel for cooking is a particularly good illustration of the inflexibility generated by financial regulations and the expectation of personal accountability which afflicted the civilian Commissariat from top to bottom. Commissariat-General Filder, following the precedent set in the Peninsular Wars which had not been revoked subsequently, refused to acquire and issue wood for heating and cooking despite the desperate need of the men,[2] even though it was plentiful only one day's sailing from the Crimea. Filder would not overstep regulations "by a hair's breadth" (*Edinburgh Review*, Vol. CI, April 1855, p. 566). The Roebuck Committee found that Commissariat officers generally had no choice but to follow the given financial and accounting instructions that were "enforced, suitable for a time of peace, but inapplicable to a period of war, and operating unjustly on soldiers" (see Royal Commission Appointed to Inquire into the Supplies of the British Army in the Crimea McNeil and Tulloch Commission, 1856, p. 281).

The rules and financial regulations of the Commissariat were ultimately designed to create accountability, uniformity and ensure a tight control over spending (see Durell, 1917, p. 475; Dawkins Committee, 1901, p. 182). Tragically, as the Howick Commission recognized 18 years *before* the Crimean War, "conflicts of opinion, diversities . . . and delays exceedingly injurious to the public service" also result (quoted in Gordon, 1935, p. 44). Regulations and highly detailed, numerous accounting reports enabled "remote-controlled" Treasury supervision; they were, if not the physical presence of the Treasury, its surrogate, the functional equivalent of direct oral orders. As such, behavior which contradicted Treasury regulations could have been readily and threateningly interpreted as denying the wishes and directions of the office from which they emanated and those of Parliament.

In the Crimean army the web of financial regulations, rules and procedures which served to hem in the Commissariat officer became not only the servant of the superior but of the ranks also. They were used as a defensive fortress into which the supply officer could remove himself (see Woodham-Smith, 1977, p. 117, for examples). Regulations determined by central authorities as the keystone to a highly centralized system of administration and financial control became not, as expected, a link in a chain of responsibility but rather a component in a chain of irresponsibility. They "were the death of common sense" (Woodham-Smith, 1977, p. 113). Regulations effectively enabled the officers of the Commissariat to divorce themselves from the failures of the campaign by the plea that instructions were followed exactly as given (see, for example, the evidence of Commissariat-General Filder before the McNeil and Tulloch Commission, 1856). The officers' defense was that they could not be held responsible for anything outside what they perceived as their given mandate. Financial and accounting regulations as finely detailed as those hedging the British army's supply services therefore encouraged and produced apathy which resulted in the majority of deaths during the war.

According to the Commissioners of the McNeil and Tulloch Commission, the Commissariat, displaying an apparent indifference for the suffering of the army, made little effort to promote improvement. Minimal effort was required, stressed the Commissioners, to meet the outmoded supply requirements and regulations of past campaigns and maintain a general store of supplies shipped from England, the distribution of which "to the members in each division, merely involves the simplest operation of arithmetic" (McNeil and Tulloch Commission, 1856, p. 13). To do much else must necessarily be

> attended with extra trouble, greater complication of accounts, and no small personal exertion. It is . . . natural . . . that those who have the charge of supplying the troops should cling to the system which tends so materially to relieve their difficulties.
>
> (McNeil and Tulloch Commission, 1856, p. 13)

ARMY ACCOUNTING AND THE ROYAL COMMISSION INTO ARMY SUPPLIES

The indignation of the British at home, (for example, see Lord Clarendon's letter to Lord Panmure, December 23, 1855, *Panmure Papers,* 1908, p. 31), convinced as they were that British casualties were attributable in no small measure to supply inadequacies, indifference and the worst incompetence, determined the government to establish a Royal Commission to enquire into the supply arrangements in the Crimea. Accordingly letters patent were issued in 1855 and the McNeill and Tulloch Commission set off for the Crimea. Among the directions to the Commissioners they were charged with examining "the mode of accounting, and if the system be in your opinion unnecessarily complicated for a period of actual warfare, you will suggest such means of simplification as may occur to you" (McNeill and Tulloch Commission, 1856, p. 3). Accounting procedures followed in the field were directly derived from the need for the army to ultimately account to Parliament for money appropriated to military uses. All accounting practice in the Commissariat was subordinated to and fed through the Treasury into parliamentary needs.

As it transpired, the Commissioners did not find what was referred to as the "unclassified" system[3] of accounting used in supply in any way unduly complicated (see Evidence before the Strathnairn Committee, 1867, Question 2677, p. 208). On the contrary the Commissariat's system of accounting showed itself to be well adapted for service in the field, and hardly to admit of being more simple . . . [for the] accounts of the Commissariat Officers attached to Divisions and Brigades consist . . . merely of consecutive entries, or jottings, of all receipts and issues . . . accompanied by the requisite vouchers.

(Great Britain, 1856, p. 43; see also *Notes on Keeping Army Service Corps Books and Accounts,* 1919)

Largely because of the uncertainties and urgency of a major campaign, the McNeil and Tulloch Commission discovered that the accounts constructed in the field were generally so inaccurate "that but little reliance could be placed upon the accuracy of the . . . returns" (Great Britain, 1856, p. 31). The Commissariat accounts invariably could not be reconciled with the Quartermaster-General's books; frequently the discrepancies in some important items could be measured in the thousands. For example, the Quartermaster-General had issued up to the time of the McNeil and Tulloch investigation 36,231 greatcoats, which were duly entered as received by the Commissariat's officers. Yet the accounts of the latter disclosed a total of greatcoats issued and in stores of 23,880, a shortfall of 12,351.

The comments of McNeil and Tulloch were scathing. The Commissioners were expressing dismay that, in the chaos of a protracted war with its extraordinary demands, despite the immense number of financial and store regulations which manacled the Commissariat and the pettifogging attention to documentation through accounts, resulting in intense surveillance, the accounting results were far from acceptable. The records could not be used with any degree of certainty or confidence. Yet it seemed impossible that the end product of such a closely scrutinized and laborious system could be so worthless or, even worse still, dangerously deceptive. However, little else could be expected despite improvement to and simplification in the accounting procedures, argued Sir Charles Trevelyan, because the system of accounting and supply was itself defective (Appendix VII to the Evidence before the Strathnairn Committee, 1867, p. 266).

Given the accountability requirements of Parliament it was not inconsistent for the Commissariat to see the purpose of accounting records in terms of surveillance and responsibility and not as the means to achieve military victory. The accounts were for an outside body, the Treasury, which had no immediate interest in the details of war, only its cost. The accounts were never intended to ensure the efficient management of military campaigns. Meeting the often urgent requirements necessary for the very existence of those engaged in battle was considered mostly after Treasury requirements had been met. Evaluation of military performance did not consider anything outside that which could be disclosed in the accounts and other reports stipulated by Treasury regulations. The approach was entirely consistent with that adopted earlier by the Treasury, again through the Commissariat, during its superintendence of the relief effort during the Irish

Famine of 1845–1847. The results then were equally tragic (see Funnell, 2001), although possibly no less surprising given that this was also the responsibility of Sir Charles Trevelyan. The ostracized position of the Commissariat from the army, composed as it was of civilians, only served to reinforce the callous attention to regulations and the ignoring of the pleas of the combatants.

Not only was the Commissariat forced to muddle its way through the goods as they arrived but also they had to deal with, what was patently clear to the Commissariat officers the most important part of their job, the mountains of paperwork. In other words, the Commissariat and the Treasury "fiddled" while the army "burned" (see Ward, 1957, p. 73). Early supply manuals, and subsequent manuals, displayed a disproportionate concern for bookwork, accounts and correspondence in comparison to attention given to the mechanics of supply. "Yet that in itself", admits Glover (1963, p. 257), when reflecting upon the 1796 supply manual of Havilland Le Mesurier, "was the natural result of a system under which the Commissary was so much more directly responsible to a Treasury which insisted on accurate accounting than to a Commander-in-Chief who merely wanted his men and horses to be properly fed". As the military's banker and the Treasury's representative in the field of battle it was above everything else the duty of the Commissariat to "call to the attention of the officer commanding . . . every instance in which a payment may be authorized, at variance with established regulations, or with any particular direction of the Treasury Board, as well as to report on the subject to the Treasury" (Treasury Regulations cited in Clode, 1869, Vol. I, p. 195). The Commissariat discharged its functions firstly for the Treasury, its real master, and not for the British army. Fear of an unsatisfactory audit result and consequent Treasury disciplinary measures proved to be the immediate motives in the actions of the Commissariat. From the Commissariat-General down, the advantages of a well-fed and healthy army seem to have been lost on the Commissariat (see Moncrieff, 1909, p. 380).

OBJECTIONS TO THE EXTREME CENTRALIZATION OF MILITARY FINANCE

The most serious objections to a highly centralized military finance function were cogently expressed by the venerated military finance expert Sir Charles Harris (1931, p. 320) who alluded to the

> congestion of regulations and correspondence about details [which] . . . submerges offices, multiplies routine clerks and absorbs the time and energy of men who ought to be free for constructive thought. . . . [There results] a paralysing effect on the whole race of officials who soon learn to think that their sole duty is to secure exact compliance with

regulations or to submit to higher authority for a fresh ruling, with the result that their sense of responsibility and power to act for themselves suffer atrophy. On these lines work is done over and over again in the offices through which it passes on its way up to the centre.

(see also Durell, 1917, pp. 258, 475)

Control that is highly centralized is intended to closely regulate subordinate action. Centralization can, additionally, give rise to a multitude of obstacles and hazards not originally intended (see, for example, the Evidence of Sir Ralph Knox before the Brodrick Committee, 1898, Question 1499, p. 219). Thus, fluidity of operation is denied as the actions of subordinates are retarded by the control hurdles they must negotiate (see Bunbury, 1924, p. 132). There results a "maximum of friction with a minimum of efficiency" (Esher Committee, 1904, Part 2, p. 15 of the report); a consistent outcome of control mechanisms which measured performance not by results but instead by "success in an intricate game of artificial hazards (or regulations) and forfeits having little connection with practical requirements or ends" (Harris, 1931, p. 315).

Concentration of financial authority at the War Office was dangerous to the well-being and performance of the army. An over-abundance of detail and "interminable" written reports could not but help occupy the efforts and time of superiors, both civil and military, at the War Office (see the Evidence of Field Marshall Lord Roberts before the Brodrick Committee, 1898). In these circumstances time for policy examination or consideration of broader military issues, time to rise above the quickening accumulation of minutia and gain the breadth of understanding necessary for a successful and cohesive military program, was always at a premium (Dawkins Committee, 1901, p. 182).

There was, unfortunately, little encouragement that the present system would change in principle. While "you have a questioning House of Commons you cannot get rid of returns", concluded General Sir Evelyn Wood, "you must always be prepared for them" (Evidence before the Brodrick Committee, 1898, Question 1090, p. 200). The demands of Parliament were ever to be the sole arbiter of what was sufficient or excessive. The Dawkins Committee recognized that persistent and possibly mischievous parliamentary demands for financial details, which reinforced the need for a centralized financial department where information was concentrated and could be assembled more quickly, were excessive ("Report of the Committee on War Office Organisation [Dawkins Committee]", 1901, Vol. XL, p. 2 of the report).

Reference to undesirable military repercussions flowing from centralized financial administration was made well before the Esher Committee so scathingly criticized the system in 1904 (for example, see the Howick Commission, 1837). The *Edinburgh Review* in 1896 saw a number of evils flowing from "intolerable centralisations": it destroyed initiative, rendered "incompetence undiscoverable" and "strangled progress" (Vol. CLXXXIII,

January to April, pp. 185, 203). Buxton in 1883 (pp. 212–213) saw excessive centralization of finance as the single greatest impediment to an efficient and effective army. Pursuing the point, he argued, and the Brodrick Committee later agreed, that much of the work carried out by the central administration could and should be done at the headquarters of districts or corps who would certainly do the work better and faster. Not only would the work be done better, argued Buxton (1883, pp. 162, 213), but also costs would be lower as officials in subordinate centers could thoroughly work through all matters and only send the "sifted form" to the central office. The great bulk of petty and distracting detail could be thereby eliminated, which would allow more time and effort to be devoted to more important strategic matters (see the Brodrick Committee, 1898, p. 130, para. 9 of the report). To hasten the process, the Brodrick Committee recommended that over 105 army returns and reports be either modified or abolished (listed in the Committee's Final Report of 1898, p. 132, para. 3).

While a centralized financial administration made individuals sensitive to the importance of records and documentation and the need to meet the requirements of regulations, it produced an increasing

> unwillingness on the part of the officers to act on their own responsibility. . . . [So that] in the course of time, the spirit of initiative throughout the army may suffer. Hence . . . the most frightful cause of disaster in time of war—namely, the collapse of the officer trained for many years to be frightened to death of a sixpence when he is suddenly called upon to decide on a matter in which thousands of pounds may be involved.
>
> (*Commonwealth Parliamentary Papers*, Vol. II, 1914, pp. 149–150; also Lawrence Committee, 1924, p. 715)

Officers became "afraid of their own shadows in administrative matters, and dare not incur the smallest expenditure, even for the purpose of saving money . . ." (*Fortnightly Review*, Vol. CCLII, New Series, December 1887, p. 773). Concentration of financial control in the hands of civilians by robbing military officers of the opportunities and training needed to flex their muscles of financial initiative and innovation was also ultimately very expensive (see Esher Committee, 1904, Part II, p. 16 of the report; Grimwood, 1919, May, p. 157). It was unrealistic and unreasonable, announced the critics of highly centralized financial control, to expect army officers denied financial responsibility in the relative calm of peace, and who were stifled by a prodigious number of regulations, to know how to handle large sums of money in the tumult of war (*Fortnights Review*, Vol. CCLII, New Series, December 1887, p. 773): "We tie up in tight folds, during peace, the limbs of . . . officials. . . . When war comes, the bonds are suddenly cast off" (*Edinburgh Review*, Vol. CLXI, January to April 1885, p. 211).

Not only was the military officer inexperienced in handling public money but, with a few exceptions, overwhelmingly deficient in skills essential to accounting for public funds (see Furse, 1894, p. 95). Calls for officer training to include the study of army finance and accounting, however, were not wanting (see Churchill, 1895, p. 36; Evidence of Field Marshall Lord Roberts before the Brodrick Committee 1898, Question 170, p. 164). Officer training had followed the same rigid, and largely outmoded pattern throughout the 19th century. Training typically included: mathematics, geometry, drawing, surveying, horsemanship, artillery, French, German, history, geography, chemistry, geology, astronomy and natural history (*Blackwoods Edinburgh Magazine,* November 1857, pp. 576–577). By the time of the South African War in 1899, however, little had improved in this regard (Amery, 1907, Vol. VI, p. 621). Certainly, the Esher Committee readily agreed that by

> insuring a rigid adherence to elaborate regulations, the Finance Department doubtless effects small savings, but does not and cannot receive real economy. . . . The theory that military officers of all ranks are by the fact of wearing a uniform, shorn of all business instincts has inevitably tended to induce laxity which it is supposed to prevent. . . . There can be no doubt that in proportion as officers are accustomed to financial responsibilities the economy which they alone can secure will be effected.
>
> (quoted by Sir Ian Hamilton, *Commonwealth Parliamentary Papers,* Vol. II, 1903, p. 150)

Waste was not the only consequence of undernourishing the military officers' financial skills. Understandably during war those individuals with their new financial responsibilities thrust upon them became cautious and indecisive. In an organization obsessed with personal accountability when it came to public money, seizing the financial initiative was to be placed under what appeared to be the capricious mercy of financial administrators. Under these conditions the supply of the army, which unavoidably depends on a very efficient army chest, could only suffer. So important was an efficient system of military finance to the military effort that Dundas wrote that "all modern wars are a contention of the purse" (Dundas to Pitt, July 9, 1794, quoted in Rose, 1914, p. 271). According to Le Mesurier, finance held the army together; it was the "sinews" of war (1796, Part X, as reproduced in Glover, 1963, p. 280).

THE MERITS OF DECENTRALIZED FINANCIAL ADMINISTRATION

While accounts and financial reports were more often than not employed in a punitive fashion, as a means to bolster central control, the government and its departments were forced to rely on rigid control by regulation (see Buxton, 1883, pp. 206–212). In matters of professional technique this amounted to, assured Sir John Keane, the non-professional telling the professional how best to do his job. Present control therefore takes somewhat this form: 'You must do it this way whatever the conditions' instead of 'You do it the best way your knowledge and experience suggests and be judged by results'. . . . [With] the present form of accounts no other control is possible.

(Chairman's closing address to the Lecture at the
LSE by Grimwood, 1919, May, p. 158)

Inflexibility, obstinately enforcing and adhering to regulations governing expenditure was, stressed Harris, more likely to be counterproductive to economy. Drawing on his own wealth of experience, Harris indicates that extravagant waste was common in military expenditure despite Herculean attempts to prevent it occurring. Little or no room, as intended, was left to officers to make financial decisions independent of financial regulations. The assumption under the circumstances was that there was always a financial regulation to cover every situation. Independent evaluation of circumstances was irrelevant and too uncertain. Detailed financial regulations were, however, more certain. The Secretary of State for War, in his evidence before the 1892 Public Accounts Committee, was openly hostile to the existing system of financial control, which persistently attempted "to force the administration of the Army into mechanical consistency with minute rules which . . . involve perpetual reference to the Treasury on petty matters. . . . Such a system is not likely to lead to either economy or efficiency" (quoted in Chubb, 1952, p. 72).

Pedantic discipleship to financial regulations which worked "through a system of cash accounts" (Lawrence Committee, 1924, p. 714), created a false sense of security. It created the impression all was well with the army and its readiness for war (Chubb, 1952, p. 72; Durell, 1917, pp. 474, 478). It was only when the strains on both financial and military systems were increased, as during war, that the inherent defects of the system made themselves apparent and then in the worst possible ways (Lawrence Committee, 1924, p. 714).

Subordinates could always plead, in the absence of evidence to the contrary, that no matter what the military results were, they were merely following the painfully detailed instructions laid down for them. Certainly anyone entrusted with materials and/or money was required to be accountable. Their accountability began and ended, however, with a careful rendition of the destination or location of what had once been in, or was at present in, their trust through the seemingly endless reports and returns required by the regulations which emanated from the civilian finance department at the War Office. The results of the use of resources was not of consequence to the responsible official, who was assessed on the basis of "inputs", not the outputs related to those inputs.

Sir Charles Harris was prominent amongst a growing number who advocated that accounting reports based on objects of expenditure were the proper vehicle for encouraging financial initiative and financial responsibility and, therefore, more efficient and effective financial control. Harris sought a system of responsibility accounting which would give officers not only the authority but the responsibility to decide "how, when, where and to what effect resources were to be used" (Evidence before the Sub-Committee on the Form of Public Accounts, Select Committee on National Expenditure, 1918, Questions 220 and 248). Churchill went so far as say that the more of these types of accounts there were the better the military would be served (Evidence before the Brodrick Committee, 1898, Question 544, p. 177). Accounts of this nature, as later argued by Colonel Sir John Keane, enabled

> responsibility to be delegated to those subordinates who know the details and who alone can adjust them to actual requirements. By means of the account you can allow a free hand and judge by results. The delegation of power which . . . accounting makes possible develops those invaluable human qualities of enterprise and resource.
>
> (Chairman's concluding address to the Lecture by Grimwood, 1919, May, p. 158; see also Dicksee's comments on accounts, Dicksee, 1915, p. 43)

CONCLUSION

Constitutional broils of the 17th century in which the army played a prominent and, what was widely seen as a distasteful and treacherous part, had produced national and parliamentary apprehensiveness towards a standing army. This had determined Parliament to use the powers at its disposal to exercise administrative control over the army to meet the influence of the Crown in the command of the army. In particular, Parliament, uncertain still in some measure of its authority and jealous of the esteem held for the Crown by society at large, was determined to exercise a rigid control over the army's spending.

The financial and administrative controls over the army which had been originally prompted by constitutional difficulties remained in force throughout the 19th century despite a shift in parliamentary attitudes. Although Parliament was no longer obsessed with creating constitutional brakes on the army, as the retrenchment priorities of Parliament and the Nation ebbed and flowed with the rapid colonial expansion of the late 19th century, the finances of the military and its administration assumed ever greater importance. As a result of Gladstone's reforms of central government from the middle decades of the 19th century and his obsession with government retrenchment, accounting controls assume an ever greater importance in ensuring effective and efficient parliamentary control of the army.

The financial impotence of the army was compounded by the constitutional requirement that the army continue to account to Parliament for its spending solely and rigidly on the basis of the divisions or heads in the army estimates by which Parliament appropriated monies for military uses (see the *1846 Audit Act*, Sections II, VI). This forced army administration and accounting to be organized according to constitutional conventions of accountability to allow spending to be easily traced rather than organized in a manner which would best promote military efficiency. The primary aim was financial accountability according to the narrowest of legalistic stewardship intentions, including a concern for economy. Government accounting systems had never been designed with the intention to promote military effectiveness. Despite numerous reforms of the British army in the later decades of the 19th century, army officers remained excluded from matters of finance. At the outbreak of the South African War the army again found itself unprepared and vulnerable.

This chapter is based on the paper, "Pathological Responses to Accounting Controls: The British Commissariat in the Crimea 1854–1856", which originally appeared in *Critical Perspectives on Accounting*, 1 (1990), pp. 319–335. The author would like to thank the publisher, Elsevier, for permission to use this material.

NOTES

1. "Hansard" is the term which refers to the record of debates in the British Parliament.
2. All available wood in the Crimea had been consumed well before the end of 1854. Not only trees and buildings had found their way into the cooking fires of the soldiers but almost all vegetation that was combustible. Russell (1858, p. 115) reported that the countryside was destitute of timber. Warner (February 2, 1855) expressed more than a little concern to his father at the absence of fuel and how that in the place of timber "one has to collect . . . dry roots to burn". The situation was so desperate that the men frequently crawled out under the enemy's fire to get enough roots to cook their meals (Russell, 1858, p. 263).
3. The accounts were unclassified in that the only essential headings of expenditure used were those reflecting the headings of Votes as appropriated by Parliament.

3 Accounting on the Frontline in the South African War

INTRODUCTION

Throughout the latter half of the 19th century most British government spending was still for military purposes. Despite the unprecedented social reforms of this period, which saw the British Government assume increasing responsibility for the well-being of its citizens, the financial needs of the army and navy continued to dwarf all other government spending and even that of the largest British businesses (Watt, 1988, 160; Mackinder, 1907, 2). Thus, irrespective of the political importance of the army, its financial demands were of necessity a prominent concern of all British governments. This was especially so in a political environment at various times dominated by either Gladstone's strict, parsimonious morality in public spending or the expansionist demands of empire in the latter decades of the 19th century.

Regardless of the extent of the financial burden of the army upon the Nation, until the arrival of the 20th century there had been only spasmodic appreciation by British governments of the potential for accounting practices used in the management of large businesses to enhance military operations in the field. Rarely was it appreciated beyond a few knowledgeable individuals in the Finance Department at the War Office that cost information could be a potent tool for army administrators to organize and manage in the interests of improved military performance, that is, success in battle. This began to change when investigations of serious administrative failures during and immediately after the South African War (1899–1902) concluded that the contributions of accounting to successful military operations had been consistently and carelessly forsaken. This accusation took on some prominence in a war which one participant described as "more essentially a supply and transport . . . [war] than any in which the British (or any other) Army has ever been engaged" ('Frugalitas', 1905, 10).

It took the exposure of the manifest shortcomings of the Army Service Corps during the South African War, upon whom the army depended for its essential supplies, for the government and army administrators to appreciate finally the relevance of accounting knowledge that went beyond the purely mechanical tasks of checking payments and completing a vast array of accounting returns on behalf of civilian financial overseers in the War Office. So important were the administrative reforms arising from the army's experiences in the South African War that it is generally regarded by military historians as a watershed in military administration[1] and the reason why the British army was better prepared at the outbreak of World War I (Watt, 1988, 156). Not until after the South African War was the British Government, through the reforms of Secretary of State for War Richard Haldane, prepared to permit the organic changes to army administration urged for the previous half a century by the army and its supporters which were required to ensure that the army would be able to run its own affairs and do so efficiently.

The experiences of the British army in the South African War ushered in some of the most far-reaching and enduring changes in the history of British military administration, not the least of which was a salutary appreciation of the contribution of cost accounting to military success in battle. Subsequent reform of military administration was propelled by the findings of the Esher Committee in 1904; the Royal Commission Appointed to Inquire into the Military Preparations and Other Matters Connected With the War in South Africa (Elgin Commission), also in 1904; and the Royal Commission on War Stores in South Africa (War Stores Commission) in 1906. The very extensive reports and minutes of evidence of the Elgin and War Stores Commissions, which relate the detailed evidence provided by both military personnel who had served in South Africa and senior individuals in government and military administration, contain a rich store of historical material concerning military accounting practices before and during the war.

Failures in the Crimean War spawned numerous failed attempts to reform military administration over the next 50 years. The focus of the most important of these reforms was how best to manage, in the interests of military preparedness, the relationship between the military and the civilians who controlled military finances. Each attempt at administrative reform from the Crimean War to the reforms prompted by the recommendations of the Esher Committee in 1904, the importance of which Barnett (2000, 359) believes "can hardly be exaggerated", involved a progressive diminution of the place that civilians as the representatives of parliamentary control would occupy in military finances (for details of the reforms see Biddulph, 1904, pp. 1–14). At the outbreak of war in South Africa in 1899 military finance still remained firmly within civilian hands at the War Office, thereby denying the army the opportunity to gain in peace the experience with financial responsibility that they would need to manage large-scale modern wars efficiently and economically. The way in which the financial ignorance and impotence of the British army exaggerated the deficiencies in army accounting during the South African War and the consequences of this for military success are examined in this chapter. Not only were most army administrators in the field of battle financial novices, they found themselves also bereft of experienced financial staff and reliable accounting systems which could provide the information that they desperately needed to ensure that they had at their command an army which was as efficient and economical as necessary to achieve victory.

Administrative failures of the British army during the South African War convinced British Governments of the insufficiency of policies, administrative structures and accounting systems developed for the conditions of peace, which kept the army at war in a state of financial ignorance. Most importantly for the conduct of World War I, the South African War awakened in government a keen appreciation of the importance to military success of well-developed, frequently rehearsed, habitual systems of cost accounting in the field. Although the British army was not a pioneer in the development of cost accounting techniques, its experiences unambiguously established that the management technologies of business also had an important role to play in government administration, particularly contributing towards military success.

"PRACTICAL POLITICS", ACCOUNTING AND MILITARY EFFICIENCY

The Constitutional Requirement of Financial Ignorance

On the eve of the South African War ultimate authority in all matters military, whether administrative or command, still resided with the Secretary of State for War as Parliament's representative and the Financial Secretary at the War Office. As the highest public officer responsible for the army it was for the Secretary of State "to know for what purpose they required an army, and to insist that the army should be efficient to fulfill that purpose" (Amery, 1902, Vol. I, p. 44). Throughout all the attempts at reform of the army between the Crimean War and the South African War, the Secretary of State for War retained undiminished the constitutional and practical control of army finances and remained the parliamentary officer through which the army's accounts, prepared by the Finance Department at the War Office and audited by the Comptroller and Auditor General, were transmitted to Parliament (see Sir Charles Trevelyan, Assistant Secretary at the Treasury, to the Duke of Newcastle, March 1, 1854, Trevelyan Papers CET 33; Midleton, 1939, pp. 126).

The Finance Department at the War Office had been established in 1870 as part of the administrative reforms of Lord Cardwell, Secretary of State for War between 1868–1874 (Gordon, 1935, pp. 57–68; Spiers, 1992, p. 2). It was staffed entirely by civilians and administered by a senior civil servant, the Accountant-General, who was answerable to the Financial Secretary, a junior member of Parliament who in turn advised the Secretary of State for War on matters of military finance (*Quarterly Review,* Vol. 129, July to October 1870, p. 262). The Cardwell reforms in 1870 had removed finally any lingering ambiguities that the army was answerable to Parliament and not to the head of the Executive government. Cardwell divided the War Office into three sections: the Commander-in-Chief, who was responsible for military personnel; the Surveyor-General of Ordnance, who provided the military's material needs; and Finance. The Finance Department received and disbursed all sums payable and receivable on behalf of the army and supervised the army's accounts, including audit, according to Treasury regulations. In addition to control over cash, the Financial Secretary and his department were also charged with: review of expenditure proposed in annual estimates and the compilation of estimates; financial review of proposals for new expenditure; control of manufacturing departments of the army; and supervision of contracts through the Director of Army Contracts (Royal Commission Appointed to Inquire into the Civil Establishments [Ridley Commission], 1887, p. xxi).

The Financial Secretary was to be the main source of advice to the Secretary of State for War on all financial matters pertaining to the army, thereby placing him in a position to control the efficiency of the army and the economy of its administration (War Stores Commission, 1906, Minutes of Evidence, Question 499, p. 27). Ultimately, as the Crimean War had tragically demonstrated, civilian control of military finances emanating from the Secretary of State for War also had the potential to have a significant impact on military success. There was no place in these arrangements, determined entirely by constitutional imperatives, for the army either to be an equal player or an authoritative contributor. The financial ignorance which this system of financial administration forced upon army administrators, army commanders in the field and army personnel responsible for supplying the army with its material needs, none of whom in South Africa had spent any time at the War Office or had been consulted by the War Office, was only too obvious in the South African War.

The military regularly complained that their exclusion from financial matters pertaining to the army's preparedness most often meant that demands for funds only rarely received the serious consideration that the army believed they deserved (Esher Committee, 1904, p. 150). Soon after assuming the position of Commander in Chief of the army in 1895, Lord Wolseley referred to the tendency of civilians, either in government or in army administration, still to prefer the certainties and the easy economies of peace when planning for the army's material needs, the lessons of the Crimean War apparently long forgotten. At the same time, these civilians pick "up some rudimentary notions of war . . . to see how the supposed wants of war could be best provided for under conditions and establishments . . . created for peace" (quoted in Maurice and Arthur, 1924, p. 291). The result, according to the military, was that the civilians and the military tended to want to take the army in opposite directions.

Military complaints about insufficient funding during the 19th century were not unusual for the military. Victory, according to the military, was always threatened by parsimonious governments in peace, which only released the purse strings when war had been declared. Even then, the bounty of war could not suddenly compensate for the suspicion and neglect of the army during peace, which saw it unable to directly control its finances. To the Nation the financial demands of soldiers had long been notoriously insatiable. No amount of money was ever enough to meet the ghosts of war conjured by the military: "If you believe the doctors", parodied Lord Salisbury at the turn of the 20th century, "nothing is wholesome: if you believe the theologians, nothing is innocent: if you believe the soldiers, nothing is safe" (quoted in Huntington, 1972, p. 66). In the early 19th century Henry Pell had warned that

> if you adopt the opinion of military men, naturally anxious for the complete security of every available point; naturally anxious to throw upon you the whole responsibility for loss in the event of war suddenly breaking out . . . you would overwhelm this country with taxes in time of peace.
> (cited in Morely, 1903, Vol. II, p. 47)

While governments, wary of military demands and growing militarism on the Continent, resisted extravagant military spending during the long periods of relative calm enjoyed in the latter half of the 19th century, the growing obligations of an invigorated empire meant that military spending climbed steadily throughout the latter decades of the century. Military spending received a significant boost after the early 1880s from the staunch imperialist Lord Salisbury when prime minister (1886–1892, 1895–1902), much to the disgust of Gladstone and Lord Randolph Churchill, the latter who resigned as Chancellor of the Exchequer in protest at Salisbury's refusal to reduce military spending in 1887 (Churchill, 1906, Vol. II, pp. 230, 235, 239). Military spending was constrained, however, by both the unpopularity of income taxation, which remained below 8d in the pound throughout the latter half of the 19th century (Mitchell, 1988, p. 645), and the unprecedented demands on government finances arising from widespread social and economic reform (Semmel, 1960). Despite this, between 1880 and 1898, when expenditure on social programs, including public works, education, law and education had increased by 40%, the expenditure for military purposes increased 75% from £25.2m to £44.1m (Mitchell, 1988, pp. 588–589; Esher Committee, 1904, p. 131). Ultimately the extreme demands of war meant that even this level of funding was insufficient to ensure victory in South Africa, when funding had to be increased rapidly from £44.1m in 1898 to £123.3m in 1902. Thus, problems with military performance during the war could not be explained by the military being starved of funding during the war. Rather, the numerous parliamentary committees and commissions of inquiry unleashed by military inadequacies in South Africa argued that the reasons were to be found in the system of military administration which the constitution had demanded but which isolated the military from control of its finances. While ever the government's primary motive in its relations with the army was to ensure that it did not present a political threat, governments did not really understand the systems of financial administration and accounting that were needed to ensure success until the tragedies of war exposed the embedded deficiencies.

In practice, disdain for the ability of the army to manage itself and the demands of "practical politics" meant that until the first decade of the 20th century military administration remained centralized within the numerous, civilian-controlled departments at the War Office from which emanated a plethora of regulations to cover every conceivable situation but which only served to engender confusion and delay (Wright, 1956, p. 464; Amery, 1903, p. 158). Ralph Knox, Accountant-General at the War Office, complained to the Ridley Commission in 1887 (First Report, Question 3068, p. 205) that "Treasury control is increasing every day, and I cannot say that I think that it has been any advantage to the public service, rather the reverse. . . . [W]e have been driven into excessive expenditure by over-regulation" (for similar conclusions see the Esher Committee, 1904, p. 137). Sir Redvers Buller, whose reputation was to be ruined by the South African War (see Fortescue, 1931, Vol. I; Melville, 1923), scathingly castigated the

> whole system of reports and regulations and warrants under which the British Army now serves . . . [for it] has grown up entirely for the benefit of War Office clerks and to find work at the War Office rather than to find control for the Army. . . . [They] do not like to let go out of their hands any power derived from the constant tying-up of Generals more and more by regulation. The result of their making those regulations in such detail is that unless they follow out that practice they have nothing to do.
>
> (Committee to Consider Decentralisation of War Office Business [Brodrick Committee], 1898, Minutes of Evidence, Question 950, p. 194)

The Brodrick Committee in 1898 was unforgiving in its criticism of the suspicious paternalism of army administrators and of the Accountant-General in particular. There was no prospect of improvement, assured the Brodrick Committee (1898, p. 130), when the accounting systems in place stipulated that commanding officers in peace had to apply to the War Office for permission to pay funeral costs when they were more than £2 and where clothing repairs exceeded 3s.6d. Under these circumstances, pleaded the Brodrick Committee, it would be "preferable to face the certainty of occasional mistakes, rather than by a machine-like system of this character, to deny the sense of responsibility and check all inducement to economy". Indeed, the inability of army administrators to control their own finances in peace prevented them from either wanting to assume or being able to assume financial responsibility, thereby suppressing any initiative. The consequences of this in war were entirely predictable to the military, namely "the collapse of the officer trained for many years to be frightened to death of a sixpence when he is suddenly called upon to decide on a matter in which thousands of pounds may be involved" (Field Marshall Hamilton, Commonwealth Parliamentary Papers, Vol. II, 1914, pp. 149–150). To the army, financial authority in military hands and military victory were coterminous.

Cost Accounts and Military Efficiency

The constitutional intent of the appropriation accounts forced upon army accounting an exclusive concern for the "subjects" of expenditure, for example salaries, instead of "objects" or specific purposes to be achieved, for example the cost of maintaining a battalion or a field hospital. As a result of this accounting myopia and enforced exclusivity, Colonel Keane and Major Churchill of the Army Pay Corps, when later reflecting upon a system the intention of which had changed little during their time in the Corps, "dismissed army accounts as valueless for control; of no use for ensuring efficient and economic administration" (Grimwood, 1919, Concluding Address at the LSE, LSE Archives; Churchill, 1895, p. 38; Funnell, 1997). Sir Ralph Knox, at one time the Accountant-General at the War Office appreciated that

> accounts formulated on an 'object' basis had the ability to tease out and analyse departmental functions, results and costs; something not possible nor sought under the traditional 'subject' mode of appropriation accounting.
> (Evidence of Sir Ralph Knox before the Select Committee on Army and Navy Expenditure, 1887, First Report, Questions 34 and 1134; Harris, 1911, p. 64; Crosland, 1918, p. 8)

Sir Charles Harris, reflecting upon "thirty years' experience of the actual working of the present system of external control of War Office expenditure, in peace and war", and army accounting expert Lieutenant Churchill insisted in their evidence before the Select Committee on National Expenditure that the army's accounting system had long been a constitutional anachronism which would continue to subvert attempts to give the army greater autonomy from civilian financial control and, crucially, to jeopardize the certainty of victory in modern wars (Report of the Select Committee on National Expenditure, 1918, p. 391; Harris, 1911, pp. 65, 67; Churchill, 1895, p. 36). They appreciated that for the military embroiled in deadly combat far from their civilian masters in the War Office, the importance of reliable accounting systems in ensuring the best possible use of scarce resources could become a matter of life and death (see also Amery, 1909, p. 618; Ormsby, 1908a, pp. 836, 841). The Lawrence Committee (1924, para. 5 of the report) later confirmed that without "a proper system of accounting it is impossible to obtain the best and most economical administration results", upon which victory would depend. Accounts that merely checked ledgers and vouchers were worthless (Young, 1906, p. 1284). Yet these silences in army accounts were entirely consistent with the very narrow range of visibilities permitted by the cash-based appropriation accounting meant to serve constitutional, that is, political, and not operational management, purposes for the military (Loft, 1986, p. 140; Ormsby, 1908b, p. 1533).

Sir Charles Harris was firmly convinced that modern commercial accounting systems, in which cost accounting might be accorded a place of some prominence, offered the best means to enhance military success by promoting economy and efficiency in military spending, rather than by using detailed and numerous regulations emanating from the War Office to govern every procedure for the sake of procedure (Harris, 1911; *The Balance*,[2] Vol. 2, Spring, 1924). After coming first in the civil service competitive examinations, in 1887 Harris had been appointed as a clerk at the War Office, where he remained until 1924, when he became Joint Secretary of the War Office. Early in his civil service career Harris had been auditor of factory accounts for Ordnance Factories, rising to Assistant Financial Secretary at the War Office in 1908 and gaining membership of the War Council in 1920. Haldane (1929, p. 186) described him as a "very remarkable man" who was "profoundly convinced" that there was great waste in the army.

According to Harris, cost accounts "should become the main channel of administration and the main channel of parliamentary control" (Select Committee on National Expenditure, 1918, Minutes of Evidence, Question 220 and 248, pp. 334–336; Harris, 1911). Convincing parliamentarians of the viability of Harris's hypothesized dual function of cost accounting was later to be a major impediment to the acceptance of cost accounting in government departments at the time of the army's cost accounting experiment between 1919 and 1925 (Ormsby, 1908b, p. 1535). The British Government's experiences with armaments manufacturers during World War I would seem to indicate that Harris's appreciation of the benefits of cost accounting for the army, expressed both before and after World War I (see, for example Harris, 1911), was well ahead of that generally pertaining to government and many businesses. Loft (1986, pp. 146, 148) describes most manufacturers at the outbreak of World War I as ignorant of the cost of their products. Indeed, according to *The Accountant* (March 1, 1919, p. 150) many manufacturers at the outbreak of war would have regarded the need for cost accounts as "ridiculous". One contributor to *The Accountant* in 1900 (June 30, p. 600) complained that it was "surprising how many manufacturers pay little attention" to cost accounts, while the *Journal of Accounting* in 1909 referred to cost accounting being in a "formative state" (April, 1909, p. 234). During World War I Dicksee (1915, p. 19) also criticized senior business managers for being "quite ignorant of the uses that accounts might have . . .".

Before World War I, Captain Young (1906) of the Indian Ordnance Department advocated the adoption of a system of responsibility accounting based upon cost accounts for the entire army. He argued that if economy of operation were to be made the concern of individuals in the army, then accounts would have to identify the cost of operations under each individual's control. These accounts, suggested a senior army officer much later when cost accounts had yet to be adopted by the military, would enable

> responsibility to be delegated to those subordinates who know the details and who alone can adjust them to actual requirements. By means of the account you can allow a free hand and judge by results. The delegation of power which . . . accounting makes possible develops those invaluable human qualities of enterprise and resource.
>
> (Sir John Keane quoted in
> Grimwood, 1919, p. 158)

Information collected by the accounting system advocated by Captain Young could then be used as a form of standard costing to compare the performance of other parts of the army in similar circumstances and also to compare performance across time, the beginnings of a system of management accounting (Young, 1906, pp. 1282–1283). "Surely", concludes Young (1906, p. 1283), publication of this information "would effect more real economy than any number of rules and regulations". Accounts which exposed and reported the costs of activities, he insisted, were to be regarded as important for their contribution to military efficiency and ultimate victory, not as ends in themselves which was the nature of the army accounting required by the politically motivated financial regulations under which the army labored (Young, 1906, p. 1284). In this way the cost accounts advocated by Young and Harris would also serve to reassure the Nation, from which the army gained its financial sustenance, that its taxes were not being recklessly squandered. This had concerned also Charles Fox (1749–1806) who, much earlier in the late 18th century, warned Parliament that "to pledge a man's honor is not the most honorable mode of accounting. . . . I have no intention of disputing the point of honor, but I want to know what you have done with the money" (quoted in Constitutionalist, 1901, p. 59).

Although both Harris and Young may have been justified in their appreciation of the potential benefits of cost accounting, or accounting based upon an object basis, Harris was well aware that the new system that he enthusiastically advocated could not be superimposed upon the existing structure of the army's administration (Harris, 1911). This, as established earlier, was entirely derived from the need to provide constitutional protections against the military. The obsession with the centralization of financial administration in civilian hands that this demanded would have to be replaced by a devolved system of financial administration if cost accounting was both able to be implemented and able to deliver the benefits professed in its favor. When the opportunity was provided for the army to implement a limited form of cost accounting after World War I, the essential fundamental reform required for the organizing principles and motives of military accounting, away from those which were derived from constitutional needs to the principles of business efficiency, were ultimately too much to expect of the government and the Treasury (see Chapter 4). This was despite the traumatic failures of military administration in World War I.

The inability of army accounts to provide information about the cost of specific aspects of its operations, such as the cost of running training maneuvers, not only betrayed long-standing constitutional concerns but also the tension between the positive rationalities of accounting and those of a military culture based upon qualitative characteristics in which matters of finance traditionally had little significance. Honor, duty, tradition and valor defined the priorities of military men and upon these traits their behavior would ultimately be judged by superiors and peers. Rarely was their ability as good accountants and financial managers deemed to be significant under the system of civilian financial control pertaining at the onset of war in South Africa in 1899. It seemed a contradiction to expect the military in the heat of battle to act as good managers and consider the financial consequences of their actions, for victory above all else was the expectation irrespective of the financial cost (Ormsby, 1908a, p. 841; Amery, 1903, pp. 159–160). "On active service", reminded Amery (1909, p. 407), "economy is not the supreme test; the supply officer must feed the troops in the face of every difficulty, irrespective of cost". Unavoidable cost arising from efficiently administering to the needs of the army in extremis, however, was something very different from financial burdens arising from the incompetence, ignorance and poor organization which were shown to have dominated and imperiled British forces in the South African War. Military success, reminded Captain Ormsby (1908a, p. 841), lay "in the inculcation of the principles of economy and finance in the combatant officer".

THE SOUTH AFRICAN WAR (1899–1902)

The South African War, also known as the Boer War, was the culmination of over two centuries of expansion in the south of Africa by Afrikaners, the Dutch settlers who arrived with the Dutch East India Company in 1652 at the Cape of Good Hope. In 1806, during the Napoleonic Wars, Britain took the opportunity to take possession of Dutch coastal settlements at the Cape and imposed its will on a large and resentful Boer population. When Britain outlawed slavery in 1834 the Boers took their black servants and began their "Great Trek" inland across the Orange and Vaal rivers, establishing the Transvaal and Orange Free State which were subsequently recognized by the British between 1852–1854 (de Wet, 1902; Iwan-Muller, 1902). However, over the next two decades the British became increasingly unsettled by the growing political stridency of the Boer states, culminating in 1877 with the peremptory annexation of the Transvaal by the British, which was meant to be the prelude to the creation of a federated British South Africa. After a Boer revolt in 1881, the independence of the Transvaal was reinstated (Elgin Commission, 1904, p. 12; Kruger, 1959, p. 7), but the apparent political calm was soon to be disturbed by the discovery of gold in the Transvaal in 1886.

Gold attracted large numbers of British citizens, known as Uitlanders, whom Boer authorities, fearing that they would be politically overwhelmed, refused to give equal political rights (Pakenham, 1979, pp. xxi–xxii, 66). Not surprisingly, British dignity and its mission to civilize the world[3] demanded that the Uitlanders not be abandoned (Porter, 1980, p. 58). Lord Milner[4], the British governor of South Africa, believed that the only way that the British were going to induce the Boers to capitulate to the demands of the Uitlanders was with the threat of force (Pakenham, 1979, p. 64). When agreement could not be reached at a meeting in May 1899 between Milner and President Kruger of the Transvaal, the outbreak of war followed in October (Amery, 1902, Vol. I, p. 1; Spiers, 1992, p. 312). Pakenham (1979, p. xv) has described the resulting South African War as the longest, costliest and, with 22,000 British and 25,000 Boer dead, the bloodiest war for Britain between 1815–1914.

Contrary to British displays of confidence in their ability to defeat what they saw as a disorganized rabble, at the declaration of war the small British force in South Africa found itself at the mercy of an adversary which was well prepared, effectively organized and determined to achieve an early victory. By the Boers striking early, swiftly and decisively between 10–15 December 1899, the British experienced major defeats under General Buller's command at Stormberg, Magersfontein and Colenso during what was later described as "black week" (Spiers, 1992, p. 309). With the arrival in early 1900 of British troops from India, Britain and the colonies, the Boers suffered major reversals between April and June at Bloemfontein, Mafeking and Praetoria, leading to a third phase of prolonged and bitter guerilla warfare for which the Boers were well suited. Despite the many warnings of impending hostilities during the long lead-up to the outbreak of war, the government had not informed the army of its intentions nor had the army been allowed to prepare for the eventuality of war (Elgin Commission, 1904, p. 34). Britain's expectations of the war had been dulled by half a century of limited colonial wars which required only small expeditionary forces to fight against poorly armed natives (Esher Committee, 1904, p. 10).

Although the British army was ultimately victorious, the humiliations that it suffered in the early stages of the war at the hands of ill-disciplined farmers before a "gloating world" (Spiers, 1992, p. 309) awoke a complacent

Nation (Barnett, 2000, p. 353; Searle, 1971, p. 34). The inability of the British to defeat decisively and quickly a non-professional army created a public outrage (Barnett, 2000, p. 353; Searle, 1971, p. 34), finally provoking the British Government to convene the Elgin Commission in 1904, the Esher Committee in 1904 and the War Stores Commission in 1906. As a result of the findings of the latter Commission, the public, informed Richard Haldane, the new Secretary of State for War in 1906 was "quivering with excitement over the spectacle of a great mass of very important work badly done to the detriment of the national purse" (*Tribune*, October 26, 1906).

"Improvisation, afterthought and strategical blundering . . . characterised the conduct of the war" (Amery, 1902, Vol. I, p. 1, and 1903, p. 162, 164). The British army, as had been the case in the Crimean War, was forced to confront the Boers with shortages in almost all forms of warlike stores (see the Elgin Commission, 1904, Appendix 33, pp. 218–240 for details of supply preparations). In addition, although the War Office in the late 19th century planned to have 100,000 fully equipped troops for overseas service, the best that they could manage by the close of 1899 was 50,000 (Pakenham, 1979, p. 251). This would eventually swell to more than 400,000 troops by the cessation of hostilities on June 1, 1902. However, in the meantime, the army's predicament was also aggravated by the rivalry that existed between the soldiers at the War Office who had served in India, represented by Lord Roberts, and those who had mainly served in Africa, led by General Wolseley (Pakenham, 1979, p. 71; Searle, 1971, p. 43). Milner, whose jingoistic opposition to the Boers precipitated a declaration of war, was scathing in his appreciation of the British army: "The central machinery and the chosen leaders . . .—was there ever such a series of misselection?" (Milner to Lord Selbourne, January 31, 1900, quoted in Headlam, 1933, p. 61).

For the politicians the fault was all the army's. Even before war had been declared Chamberlain believed that his government would be let down badly by the War Office. In a letter to Milner a month before the Boer ultimatum, Chamberlain decried the way in which the War Office had assured him that "they were ready 'to the last button'—now they talk of four months before they can put an army corps to the front" (Chamberlain to Milner, August 2, 1899, in Headlam, 1931, p. 525; Wilson, 1973, p. 164). Chamberlain's scathing denunciation of army administration was to be confirmed by the strident criticisms of the Esher Committee in 1904 (p. 10) and, in almost exact terms at the cessation of hostilities, by the then Secretary of State for War, for whom the South African War

> made it abundantly clear that the Army in its present form is not suited . . . [to] war. . . . The Army, such as it is, is not fully and scientifically organized for war; whereas the sole object of an army . . . is to be able to engage in war at the shortest notice . . . we have been

maintaining an army in peace time a large portion of which was totally
unfit for war. . . .

(Elgin Commission, 1904, p. 311; Esher
Committee, 1904, p. 10; see also
comments by Hamer, 1970, p. 174)

Early deficiencies in preparedness were compounded by the absence of
any forethought by the Finance Department at the War Office to assist officers in the field with the financial complexities now forced upon them and for
which they had been allowed little preparation (Hinchliffe, 1983, p. 45). This
left the army vulnerable to criticisms of incompetent management and irre-
sponsible stewardship of public monies which had not only led to needless
extravagance but also had permitted numerous frauds to occur at significant
cost to the public purse (see, for example, Haldane, 1929, pp. 137, 185).

THE ROLE OF ACCOUNTING IN THE MICROMANAGEMENT OF WAR

Accounting in the Field and the Accountant-General's Department

Whereas during peace the paternalistic, stultifying and relentless presence
of the War Office was obvious in most administrative decisions, throughout the South African War senior commanders were cast adrift by the War
Office to manage as best they could, despite the unparalleled financial and
organizational complexities that were "thrust" upon them on the frontline
of war (Elgin Commission, 1904, Minutes of Evidence, Question 5847,
p. 130). Notably, the Accountant-General had made no special arrangements
prior to the war to ensure that generals in the field had access to financial
advice and that the accounting systems in place in peace would be appropriate for the conditions of a major military conflagration. Accountant-
General Sir Frank Marzials, who admitted to the War Stores Commission
that the South African War was unlike anything experienced for 50 years
(1906, Minutes of Evidence, Question 580, p. 31), had not realized the difficulties that his office would face in a protracted war thousands of miles
from Britain. Not surprisingly, the Dawkins Committee (1901, p. 189)
was highly critical of the Accountant-General's inaction, lamenting the lost
opportunities for improved financial management that the appointment
of representatives of the Accountant-General to military divisions would
have provided. Although the former Secretary of State for War, St. John
Brodrick, assured the War Stores Commission (1906, Minutes of Evidence,
Question 11, p. 2) that he had been dissatisfied with the financial advice
available to officers in the field of battle, little if anything was done to
improve the situation.

The strength of the Commission's criticisms of Marzial and his office and the unambiguous directedness of the criticisms towards Marzial as Accountant-General and other senior officers, both military and civilian, indicates that the inquiries were not cynical political exercises which sought to deflect blame from senior administrators. Each of the senior civilian and military administrative officers were brought before the various inquiries after the war and made to give an account of their behavior. Reading the minutes of evidence one is struck by the relentless way in which the commissioners pursued those before them, irrespective of rank. The insistent questioning of senior army and War Office personnel indicates that the sympathy of the War Stores Commission lay with the ranks and junior officers of the Army Service Corps and the Army Pay Corps who had been left in a vulnerable position by the neglect of the Accountant-General and other senior officers. The recommendations of the inquiries reflected this with their concern for systems rather than individuals except where, as in the case of Marzials, the individual was in a position to know better and to take their responsibilities seriously.

According to the War Stores Commission, the absence of representatives of the Accountant-General's office had jeopardized the prospect of a decisive victory, contributed unnecessarily to the pressures under which the generals operated and to the "unreasonable" cost of the war, estimated by the Accountant-General to be in excess of £201 million (Elgin Commission, 1904, Appendix 50, pp. 336–339; Spiers, 1992, p. 312). The Esher Committee (1904, p. 139) also saved its most scathing comments about the army's financial preparedness and accounting systems for the Accountant-General's incompetence and that of his staff. The Committee criticized the clerks in the Accountant-General's office, few if any of whom were trained accountants, for being too prone to interfere from London in the military actions of officers commanding troops in the field as checks were made that all army expenditure had been made according to War Office and Treasury regulations. So overbearing were these intrusions, most of which were matters of pettifogging clarifications about spending authorizations for amounts recorded in the accounts, that they were "intolerable, and they fully account for the administrative inefficiency of the War Office" (Esher Committee, 1904, p. 139). According to the Esher Committee (1904, p. 137) the civilians in the Accountant-General's Department (formed in 1855) at the War Office were "promiscuous" in their auditing, accounting and contract making, for the War Office's financial system was

> based upon the assumption that all military officers are necessarily spendthrifts and that their actions must be controlled in gross and in detail by civilians. . . . This theory is largely responsible for the unreadiness for war which has been exhibited, as well as for reckless and wasteful expenditure. . . . The department of the Accountant-General has become a huge and costly machine which is supposed to control

expenditure by the aid of involved regulations which serve to aggran-
dize its power over the military branches.

As a result of the oppressive way in which the Accountant-General's
office mechanically enforced "cumbrous" financial safeguards on behalf of
Parliament, "the whole army", lamented Amery (1902, Vol. I, p. 141),

> spent the greater part of its existence in checking its accounts. . . .
> [E]very item of daily accounts was checked and rechecked and copied
> out in duplicate and triplicate. . . . It was accountancy run mad. The
> object of it all was to prevent defalcations. The object was obtained but
> at a ruinous cost.
>
> (see also the War Office Cost Accounting
Committee, 1918, p. 2)

In defense of his department, the Secretary of State for War claimed that
any problems with the performance of the Accountant-General's office did
not arise from want of conscientious application. Rather, the clerks in the
Accountant-General's office were so overworked in superintending regulations
that some of them had died from their exertions and others had lost their
reason (War Stores Commission, 1906, Minutes of Evidence, Question 13,
p. 3). Irrespective of the apparent zeal of the Accountant-General's office,
the Esher Committee, however, came to the conclusion that "no branch of the
War Office more urgently needs radical reform than that of the Accountant-
General" (Esher Committee, 1904, p. 138).

In light of the level of operational ignorance and inactivity displayed
by the Accountant-General, the War Stores Commission was intrigued
by General Kitchener's decision to appoint a financial adviser to his staff.
Kitchener, who had a notorious reputation for economy and a concern
for the taxpayer (Magnus, 1958, p. 217), had realized very early after
his arrival in South Africa in January 1900 that he would need the assistance of a skilled finance officer located in South Africa who would take
responsibility for managing the complexities of the military's finances.
Most importantly, Kitchener needed someone to oversee the contracting arrangements with firms in South Africa, which supplied the army
with most of its consumables. When the Army Pay Corps was unable to
provide someone suitably qualified for this new position, Kitchener was
offered the services of Guy Fleetwood Wilson, the Assistant Under Secretary of State for War (Ormsby, 1908a, p. 846; Hinchliffe, 1983, p. 45).
Fleetwood Wilson had entered the civil service in 1870, thereafter serving
as private secretary to four cabinet ministers. He then held the position
of Director of the Royal Army Clothing Department, moving to the War
Office as Assistant Under Secretary of State in March 1898 from which
he was appointed to Kitchener's staff in October 1900 (War Stores Commission, 1906, Minutes of Evidence, Question 382, p. 22). Fleetwood
Wilson's appointment was the first time that a general commanding in

the field had been able to have expert financial advice readily available. It was to set a precedent for World War I. Fleetwood Wilson (1922, p. 114) saw his duty to "insist on a shilling being sufficient when it could be made to produce the same result as half-a-crown. . . . I was constantly employed in pricking bubbles and pointing out weak spots in military 'adventures'. . . ." Towards the end of his time in South Africa Fleetwood Wilson assured Kitchener that if

> a Financial Adviser had been appointed at the beginning . . . he could have prevented excessive charges from arising, instead of merely curtailing them when large. . . . He could have established a system of watching and controlling expenditure. . . . He could probably have arranged that supply accounting was conducted along defensible lines.
>
> (Elgin Commission, 1904, p. 128; see similar comments by Amery, 1909, p. 621)

Fleetwood Wilson left South Africa soon after Kitchener in June 1902, to be replaced by Major Armstrong from the War Office, who found himself in a very different position to that enjoyed by Fleetwood Wilson. Whereas Fleetwood Wilson was given a senior appointment on Kitchener's staff with attendant authority, Armstrong and the financial assistance that he was able to provide were no longer acceptable to Kitchener's successors, who forced Armstrong's repatriation to England on the grounds that his rank exceeded the requirements of the position. Armstrong was eventually replaced by a more junior officer "who had absolutely no knowledge of markets or of the difficult work of dealing with South African contractors" (War Stores Commission, 1906, p. 9). The presence of a financial adviser in their headquarters, even one with a military rank, was alien to the generals in South Africa. Neither their training nor the War Office had allowed them to appreciate the military contributions of a resident financial officer. To expect that they, unlike Kitchener, would change the habits of a lifetime of soldiering was unrealistic in the ferment of war. The inaction of the Finance Department at the War Office in stopping Armstrong's removal also reflected the "absence of inter-communication, of common action or of common interest between the various departments of the War Office" (War Stores Commission, 1906, p. 8). This, criticized the War Stores Commission, exposed the British Government to very significant costs in the months immediately following the war as the army sought to dispose of large stocks of supplies. The commissioners believed that if a specialist financial adviser and his staff had been present much of the fraudulent activity discovered subsequently could have been avoided. Military commanders who were fully occupied with the pressing demands of engaging with the enemy would be unlikely to be also finance and business experts (Ormsby, 1908a, p. 841 and 1908b, p. 1534). They needed financial advisors so that they would be in a position to judge the extent to which financial considerations might affect the prospect of victory.

The Army Pay Corps

Normally the day-to-day interpretation and application of War Office financial and accounting regulations during war would be referred to the Army Pay Corps, created in 1882 as the Quartermaster-General's representative in the field (Elgin Commission, 1904, p. 131). As part of the Cardwell army reforms, in 1878 all army officers who were Army Paymasters became part of the Army Pay Department while their non-commissioned officers were formed into the Army Pay Corps four years later (Hinchliffe, 1983, p. 1). The scale and complexity of the operations which confronted Kitchener when he arrived in Cape Town on January 11, 1900, however, required sophisticated financial and accounting abilities well beyond the routinized, regulation-obsessed expertise of the Army Pay Corps. The Army Pay Corps, upon whom the Accountant-General as the army's accounting officer[5] was dependent but over whose military personnel he had no control,[6] had no financial advisory responsibilities nor the necessary experience in peace which would have allowed them to provide these services to the General Officer Commanding (GOC) in times of war. Their function was to complete in a mechanical fashion on behalf of the army any accounting returns prescribed by the Treasury, most of which involved accounting for soldiers' pay and stoppages and the safekeeping of cash (for details see Redway, 1902; Ormsby, 1908b, p. 1538). Often these duties meant that paymasters were responsible for large sums of money but without the responsibility of superintending the way in which the money was used. From his dealings with the Army Pay Corps, General Kitchener believed that their "purely clerical and mechanical" labors meant that they carried out their duties "without any idea either of improvement or economy . . . [ignoring] financial considerations of any kind" (Elgin Commission, 1904, Minutes of Evidence, Question 218, pp. 130–131). So circumscribed were their duties that they had "really no accounting to do at all, except a purely cash account; [they] pay out money, . . . [and] get a voucher for it" (Public Accounts Committee, 1924–1925a, Minutes of Evidence, Question 6716; Churchill, 1895, p. 37).

Army accounting systems in South Africa, but most importantly those needed for the crucial task of accounting for stores, could not cope with the turmoil and unpredictability of war, resulting in accounting information which was so incomplete as to be unreliable for any decision making purposes. Amery (1909, pp. 461–462) described accounting in the field "resolving itself into utter chaos . . . , ludicrous . . . [and] hopelessly inadequate in war". It was not that there was a shortage of accounting going on but rather that there were too many meaningless accounting regulations which overwhelmed combatant officers (see Ellison, 1918, p. 4). James, in 1901 (p. 711), referred to the British Officer as "a return-making animal" and as "an overworked accountant" which, according to Sir Garnet Wolsey, prevented officers from carrying out their military duties (Hinchliffe, 1983, p. 38).

The "nonsense" which masqueraded as accurate accounts, urged the Public Accounts Committee, could only be remedied with the appointment to all wartime forces of a body of expert officials who understood how to keep military accounts (Public Accounts Committee, 1902, Fourth Report, pp. 21, 22, 26). Unfortunately, confirmed the Public Accounts Committee, "no such supply of officers now exists, and . . . their absence has been the main cause of the imperfect control of expenditure in South Africa" (Public Accounts Committee, 1902, Fourth Report, p. 21). As a consequence of dissatisfaction with the performance of the Army Pay Corps in the South African War, both it and the Accountant-General's Department were replaced in 1905 with the Army Accounts Department, which was finally disbanded in 1910 (Ormsby, 1908a, p. 843; Hinchliffe, 1983, p. 49).

COMMERCIAL NAIVETY, COST ACCOUNTING AND THE WAR STORES SCANDAL

Army Service Corps officers in South Africa were put in the invidious position of being forced to make decisions on matters about which they had no training in peace. In particular, in peace they were excluded from, and kept ignorant of, most aspects of contracting and the disposal of excess stores. During times of peace prior to the South African War, all army contracts were arranged by the office of the civilian Director of Army Contracts at the War Office in London. Immediately at the outbreak of war, however, contracting with local suppliers in the first instance was to become the responsibility of the Army Service Corps, with the approval of the local commanding officer. In peace, ordnance officers were not authorized to spend more than £25 without receiving prior approval from the Director of Army Contracts, neither was there any training in purchasing large quantities of stores on commercial markets. Similarly, an officer of the Army Pay Department stationed in England during peace was required to send for approval all claims for amounts over £100 to the War Office. On an overseas posting, however, there was no need to seek War Office approval, irrespective of the amount. While serving in the South African War, Lieut. Col. Churchill was able to pay out, on his own initiative on a regular basis, amounts as large as £160,000, "showing how on active service all the ridiculous instructions of the War Office have to be set on one side" (Churchill, 1903, p. 281).

Despite the vast array of new responsibilities imposed on the Army Pay Corps and the Army Service Corps during war and the state of commercial ignorance in which they were kept in times of peace, during the South African War there were no representatives of the Director of Army Contracts in the field. Consequently, the Elgin Commission (1904, p. 129) was not surprised to learn that throughout the war there was "serious mismanagement of ordnance business and a waste of public money". Yet it was not to be unexpected, warned the Esher Committee (1904, p. 138), that a financial system in which officers in peace were not given any financial responsibility would be anything other than "futile in peace . . . [and] ruinous in war". The anomalous, contradictory expectations of supply officers in peace and war, suggested the Dawkins Committee (1901, p. 193), was symptomatic of the general state of commercial innocence and confusion in which the office of the Director of Army Contracts carried out its duties. This confusion was to be a major preoccupation of the War Stores Commission (1906, p. 54) which, amongst its strident criticisms of the Accountant-General and the Director of Army Contracts, reflected upon how the Director and his assistants were ignorant of even the basics of commercial contracting; so much so that they fell short of the knowledge which could be expected of even the "average layman". After the declaration of peace, when it came time to dispose of surplus stores, the contractual inexperience of the Army Service Corps, the absence of any system of cost accounting for stores and their isolation from the Director of Army Contracts left them especially vulnerable and exposed to the commercial chicanery of local contractors in South Africa.

Prompted by the evidence disclosed during the audit of army accounts by the Comptroller and Auditor General, the War Stores Commission uncovered a litany of errors, ignorance and mismanagement in dealing with army stores. These had permitted repeated and sustained instances of fraudulent activities, the cost to the Nation of which, in the absence of any systematic cost accounting records, the Commission was only able to make the roughest estimate. Without too much difficulty, the War Stores Commission "established a degree of neglect of the public interest well-nigh incredible . . .", widely referred to at the time as the "war stores scandal" (Amery, 1909, p. 616; 'B', 1907, p. 665; Searle, 1971, p. 38). Thus, according to the Commissioners, the Army Service Corps had failed miserably in its first test since its formation in 1888 (Young 2000, p. 5; Fortescue, 1930, pp. 229–265). The public, informed Lord Haldane, the new Secretary of State for War in 1906, was

> quivering with excitement over the spectacle of a great mass of very important work badly done to the detriment of the national purse. . . . [There] has been the revelation in South Africa of an altogether inadequate organisation and training to cope with the business of supply in time of war, and the disorganized period which follows upon war. Supply is one of the most difficult things anyone can tackle. . . . [It] is a science in itself which requires high training.
>
> (*Tribune*, October 29, 1906)

While very few Army Service Corps officers were found to have engaged directly in fraudulent activities, professional ignorance of even the most basic aspects of commercial accounting and business practices was found by the War Stores Commission to be endemic to the Army Service Corps. This, believed the Commissioners, was due both to the personal failings of individual Army Service Corps officers and to their training, which gave them little knowledge of business principles and cost accounting, thereby leaving them at the mercy of sharp businessmen who knew only too well the deceptive ways of business ('B', 1907, p. 667). Their peacetime training had prepared them to act as "a mere accountant, an intermediary between the troops and various contractors, coming but rarely into contact with business men . . ." ('B', 1907, p. 668). Most of the peacetime training of the Army Service Corps was heavily military. It was devoted to military dressage, shooting and riding with only the most minimal attention given to the commercial and technical skills upon which the success of the Army Service Corps depended in war ('B', 1907, p. 668). So widespread, unnecessary and obvious were the failures of the Army Service Corps to detect supply malversations that the War Stores Commission characterized the Army Service Corps as conducting its business

> with inexcusable carelessness and extraordinary ineptitude, and that of the Pay Department with a want of intelligence that is deplorable. . . . We consider that . . . [they] have not properly appreciated that it was their duty to protect the public and to act as trustees of the money which they were dispensing. . . . [T]he faults of their administration . . . spring mainly from . . . irresponsibility, indifference, and want of intelligence. . . .
>
> (War Stores Commission, 1906, p. 58)

According to one knowledgeable critic, the Army Service Corps was composed of men who were devoid of all business abilities and who brought with them neither business nor trade experience ('B', 1907, p. 666). The Army Service Corps was alleged to be the home of the undesirable, the indolent and the craven, with the result that its activities were widely regarded by its members with "contempt" and as a sideshow to the real activity of fighting. They had exchanged a career in military regiments which had an honorable standing for one "which appealed neither to their zeal nor to their pride" ('B', 1907, p. 666; Young, 2000, p. 3).

The problems exposed by the War Stores Commission were dramatically exacerbated by the absence of any cost accounts, either in the field or at the War Office. The War Store Commissioners were dismayed to find that throughout all the store accounts kept by the Army Service Corps and those kept by the Accountant-General at the War Office nowhere was there to be found together a record of the prices paid and the quantities of stores to allow the Army Service Corps to calculate the cost of the stores consumed by the army from Army Service Corps warehouses (War Stores Commission, 1906, pp. 3, 64, and Minutes of Evidence Vol. I, Question 504, p. 27; War Office Cost Accounting Committee, 1918, p. 3). Lists of prices were to be found only at the War Office. Not only were Army Service Corps officers unaware of the cost of the items in their charge but, possibly more worrying still for the War Stores Commission, their training was such that they were not even aware that they should have this information before committing their government when contracting with local suppliers. This deficiency, suggested the War Stores Commission, should have been obvious, if at no other time, when prices were finalized for the disposal of surplus army stores. If a system of cost accounting had been maintained at the War Office on behalf of combatant officers and supply officers, the War Stores Commission believed "knowledge of that fact would have proved a very valuable deterrent on both improvidence and peculation in South Africa" (War Stores Commission, 1906, p. 64).

The disarray found in the Army Service Corps accounts compelled the War Stores Commission to employ the services of chartered accounting firms to assist them in untangling the confusion. Deloitte, Dever, Griffiths, Annan and Coy were engaged in Johannesburg, and Annan, Kirby, Dexter and Coy in London. Despite the large establishment of staff employed by the Accountant-General at the War Office and by the Army Pay Corps and the Army Service Corps in South Africa, the Commissioners could not rely upon the accounting knowledge of these officers nor had they any confidence of their appreciation of commercial accounting practices. According to Deloitte, Dever, Griffiths, Annan and Coy, whose experiences of army accounting were eerily similar to those of the Royal Commission Appointed to Inquire into the Supplies of the British Army in the Crimea in 1856 (McNeil and Tulloch Commission), the Army Service Corps store accounts provided little if any useful information and precluded the possibility of conducting an audit that would produce anything of value, especially when belatedly conducted two years after the end of the war. So confused were the store accounts that there was no means "by which the Secretary of State could ascertain, even approximately, how the supplies had been disposed of, or the quantities or costs of what had been lost from deficiencies . . . and the condition of purchases and sales" (War Stores Commission, 1906, p. 3).

Fundamental structural deficiencies in the accounts were compounded by the business naivety of the Army Service Corps, who were no match for the business sagacity of experienced, wily businessmen able to manipulate to their own considerable advantage the inexperience and docility of the Army Service Corps. The War Stores Commissioners were astonished at how the Army Service Corps had entered into contracts with local merchants which committed the army to selling stores at low prices to local contractors and, on many occasions, at the same time buying back at extravagantly higher prices precisely the same items, which may not have left the army's storehouses, from the same contractors to whom they had been sold (War Stores Commission, 1906, p. 59). In one instance, examined in some detail on behalf of the War Stores Commission by Deloitte,

Dever, Griffiths, Annan and Coy, one contractor, Meyer and Co., purchased 22,557,916lbs. of surplus oats in December 1902 at a price of 11s per 100lbs. The same oats, without being removed from the Army Service Corps storehouses, were then purchased from Meyer at 17s 10d per 100lbs. (War Stores Commission, 1906, Minutes of Evidence Vol. I, Question 102, p. 11 and page 6 of the report). The chartered accountants employed by the War Stores Commission estimated that on one such similar transaction alone Meyer had made a profit of £69,264 (War Stores Commission, 1906, Appendix, p. 81).

CONCLUSION

The findings of the War Stores Commission and its admiration for the achievements and methods of the private sector, recognized by its reliance upon the investigations of chartered accountants and the opinions frequently solicited from successful businesses, proved instrumental in convincing Lord Haldane, then Secretary of State for War, to expose military administrators more fully to the methods of business (see Haldane in the *Tribune*, October 29, 1906). Indeed, the South African War and the attendant report of the Esher Committee marked the point at which the business side of army administration assumed considerably more importance (see, for example, McGuire, 1918, p. 27). However, attempts at systemic reform of military accounting by the introduction of cost accounting would have to wait until after World War I. With the extensive evidence before him, Haldane was only too aware that without knowledge of the customs of private contractors with whom the army spent many millions of pounds, and in the absence of expertise with sophisticated cost accounting systems in the field with which to manage, the Army Service Corps would never be a match for astute and often unscrupulous businessmen (Amery, 1909, p. 407; Airey, 1913, p. 466). Appreciation of the benefits of cost accounts by military administrators anticipated both demands by the British Ministry of Munitions during World War I that munitions contractors maintain accurate cost accounts and the use of cost accounts by many if not most British manufacturers.

It was convincingly demonstrated to the British Government during the South African War that the goals of economy and military efficiency were incompatible with a very rigid, centralised and civilian-controlled finance function, the concern of which was subjects of expenditure instead of objects or purposes of expenditures. Although this had been appreciated well before the South African War by senior civilian officials in the Finance Department in the War Office, most notably Sir Charles Harris and Accountant-General Sir Ralph Knox, cost accounts were entirely absent in military and administrative branches of the army at the time of the war. Indeed, in the departments at the War Office which administered the largest business in Britain, that is, the army (Watt, 1988, p. 160; Mackinder, 1907, p. 2), it was rare at the end of the 19th century to find an appreciation of the relevance and the benefits which might be obtained in the field of battle from the most basic cost accounting practices. This reluctance by government departments to adopt cost accounting was entirely political and institutional, unlike the slow progress of cost accounting in business throughout the late 19th century, which has been attributed to economic imperatives, a tendency to treat cost accounting procedures as trade secrets or because cost accounting did not appear to provide any commercial advantages (Armstrong, 1987, p. 419).

While economic motivations were not entirely absent in the decision to experiment with the introduction of cost accounting in the early 20th century in government departments, these were always secondary in the initial stages to motives of national interest and constitutional proprieties. The potential contribution of cost accounting to improved economy in the army was certainly recognized as a benefit to commend cost accounting. However, this had never been sufficient of itself to convince the British Government that cost accounting was either necessary or constitutionally appropriate. Instead, the potency of economic arguments for the adoption of cost accounting by the British Government in the decades spanning the close of the 19th century was entirely dependent upon circumstances providing sufficient political justification, in the form of military crises, and also the necessary assurance that there would be no threat to the constitutional protections provided by appropriation accounting. Neither the Executive nor Parliament was convinced that cost accounting systems would not dilute the constitutional protections of the existing system of appropriation accounting.

The dictates of a rigid interpretation of the constitutional function of government accounting would continue to preclude serious consideration of cost accounting for the army and other government departments until after World War I, and even then the engagement would be only fleeting (War Office Cost Accounting Committee, 1918). Even after the findings of the War Stores Commission and the Royal Commission Appointed to Inquire into the Military Preparations and Other Matters Connected with the War in South Africa (Elgin Commission) had convinced many in government of the financial and military benefits of management-orientated control systems, constitutional imperatives still prevailed. However, mounting threats to Britain's imperial supremacy in the first decades of the 20th century were to prompt a concerted effort to allow the military a major role in the management of their finances.

The humiliations suffered by Britain in the South African War provoked the British Government finally to reform the administration and organization of the army after over half a century of ineffectual, feigned reforms (Barnett, 2000, p. 353; Searle, 1971, p. 34; Churchill, 1959, pp. 56, 70, 72). While reform of army administration was most obviously prompted by the political crisis of the South African War, this was but the final catalyst by which persistent demands for the reform of military administration and prevailing social and political anxieties were finally able to gain expression.

This chapter is based on the paper, "Accounting on the Frontline: Military Efficiency and the South African War", which originally appeared in *Accounting and Business Research*, 35, No. 4 (2005), pp. 307–326. The author would like to thank the publisher, Taylor & Francis, for permission to use this material.

NOTES

1. "Administration" refers to those aspects of the army that are concerned with meeting the material and warlike needs of the army. These are sometimes referred to as the business or financial side of the army (see 'Colonel', 1914, p. 71).
2. The journal of the Corps of Military Accountants 1923–1925.
3. George Curzon, later the Marquis Curzon of Kedleston, believed that Great Britain "was the greatest Instrument for good the world had seen" (quoted in Pearl, 1967, p. v).
4. Milner had been appointed by Lord Lansdowne, the Secretary of State for War between June 1895 and November 1900. Richard Haldane (1929, p. 136) described Milner as "a man of most attractive qualities but was difficult to work with".
5. The "accounting officer" was usually the head of a government department who was responsible for providing to Parliament the annual appropriation accounts, through the Comptroller and Auditor-General.
6. The Accountant-General was required to conduct an audit of the Army Pay Corps accounts to establish that they were carrying out their duties according to regulations. Army Pay Corps personnel were responsible to the Accountant-General for their accounts but were under the ultimate command of the military.

4 Military Accounting and the Business of War

INTRODUCTION

In the closing decades of the 19th century Britain was suffused by an aura of pessimism which arose from its uncertain standing and future as an imperial power in a world in which Germany and the United States had emerged as formidable competitors. The prescience of these anxieties seemed to be confirmed by the alarming deficiencies of the British army that were exposed during the South African War. The consequence of Britain's perceived vulnerability in the early 20th century, note Miller and O'Leary (1987, pp. 243–245), was a "discourse of national efficiency". The movement for national efficiency led by the former Prime Minister Lord Rosebery, other prominent Liberals and the Fabians Sidney and Beatrice Webb, proved to be especially effective for a short period in early Edwardian Britain in cohering discontent and in exploiting the opportunity for reform generated by the Nation's outrage at the army's failings in South Africa. Through networks of influence established at the highest levels of government, society and business, the movement for national efficiency was able successfully to promote its goals.

Lord Rosebery's supporters called for all areas of British life to be reinvigorated with new purpose, energy and commitment to restore British prestige and prosperity. Nothing, according to the imperialist creed of Rosebery's national efficiency movement, was more important to restoring national efficiency, and British prestige, than the efficiency of the army as the guarantor of the Empire. According to Lord Rosebery and his followers, with war in the 20th century no longer the habitation of the gifted amateur, military prowess could only be restored to the British army if army administrators adopted the character and practices of business and became "soldier businessmen" (Mackinder, 1907, p. 5). This, urged the War Stores Commission in 1906, was dependent upon the diffusion of business accounting practices, but especially cost accounting, throughout all administrative branches of the army. The modern army could no longer afford to deny its administrative officers an education in the ways and principles of business: accounting would serve the interests of British imperialism through its contributions to military efficiency. The Army Class established at the London School of Economics (LSE) at various times between 1907 to 1932 by two members of Rosebery's national efficiency movement, Halford Mackinder and Richard Haldane, was to be the means by which the army administrator would be inculcated with the ways of business.

The army cost accounting experiment introduced in 1919, in which the LSE again played a prominent role, was another response to the political crisis of war. The cost accounting experiment confirms the ideological or political imperative of military accounting. Unlike the Army Class, which worked within existing accounting systems and did not question constitutional fundamentals, the success of the cost accounting experiment was wholly dependent upon the introduction of a new accounting system which challenged entrenched positions of influence in the major departments of state, especially that of the Treasury. However, as shown earlier, the constitutional nature of accounting by government departments had also been a persistent impediment to organic change in government accounting. Thus, even after the experience of the South African War, constitutional requirements still conspired to thwart the introduction of cost accounting throughout departments of state. Nor could the financial and human exhaustion of World War I dislodge the constitutional imperative of departmental accounting in favor of the contributions of cost accounting to efficient government.

ARMY EFFICIENCY AND THE VIRTUES OF BUSINESS

After the scathing condemnation of military administration and operational efficiency by the official inquiries after the South African War, public pressure ensured that successive governments prior to World War I would not be able conveniently to set aside the hard-won lessons of the war which called for a fundamental reform of military administration, especially the way in which military finances were managed (Semmel, 1960, p. 74; Watt, 1988, p. 156). Indeed, the administrative reforms demanded were to provide Britain with the modern army that it needed at the outset of World War I. No longer, believed the Esher and Elgin inquiries, could the British army be kept in the state of financial ignorance which had jeopardized military success in South Africa. Consideration of economy and military efficiency were only possible in the presence of a high degree of financial autonomy for the military.

Even before findings of administrative failings were available after the South African War, the *Daily Telegraph*, on January 6, 1902, suggested that the South African War had brought about a "profound transformation" in the political tenor of the Nation which was manifested in a determination to ensure that the army in the future would be better prepared for war and not be forsaken in the manner that it had been prior to, and during, every major and minor war in the 19th century (Searle, 1971, p. 41; Airey, 1913,

p. 466; Trevelyan, 1856, p. A2). The South African War and the official inquiries that it spawned belatedly confirmed what had become tragically obvious during the calamitous Crimean War; that qualities of individual heroism and military brilliance upon which the military had traditionally prided itself and which defined military culture would be no longer sufficient as a guarantee of victory. The modern "scientific" war, which had ceased to be the sport it had been once for gentlemen amateurs, allowed nothing to be left to chance or to personal eccentricities (Turner, 1956).

Bismarck's easy success against the largest armies of Europe in the wars of German unification in the 1860s had accelerated Britain's insecurity by conclusively demonstrating the benefits of an efficient army organized and modelled on scientific principles (see Wells, 1934, p. 763; Searle, 1971, p. 6; Emy, 1973, p. 125). War now required a very different set of qualities and capacities; those which relied upon technical knowledge and scientific organization to facilitate the "manipulation of material resources" (Anderson, 1967, pp. 101, 104; Haldane in the *Tribune,* October 29, 1906). War had become a "commercial enterprise" (Gladstone in the *Quarterly Review,* Vol. CVI, 1859, p. 10) which required the manners of the gentleman soldier to be replaced by the expertise of the "soldier businessman" (Mackinder, 1907, p. 5).

As a result of Leopold Amery's appointment during the South African War as *The Times*'s war correspondent, the experience of which filled him with a deep disgust for military expertise and the personal qualities of the typical British senior officer who was exclusively drawn from the titled and landed classes, Amery demanded nothing less than a "revolution" in army organization and administration. Britain needed "an expert army", one in which "the whole caste system, the whole idea of the Army as a sort of puppet show where smartness, gilt braid . . . must vanish and give place to something real, something business like" (Amery, January 9, 1900, in Barnes and Nicholson, 1980, p. 33). The old amateurish military elite had become a dangerous anachronism which threatened not only Britain's pre-eminent imperial position but also its very existence in the presence of a militarily and industrially ascendant Germany.

As the South African War entered its second year, the *Nineteenth Century* magazine (July 1900, p. 1) emphasized, in terms that were later to characterize criticisms of the work of the Ministry of Munitions in World War I (Marriner, 1994), the "need for conducting the business of the country, as administered by the various Departments of State, upon ordinary business principles and methods". Army administration needed "to be as nearly as possible on all fours with the business arrangements which are understood in civil life" (Secretary of State for War Richard Haldane, quoted in Watt, 1988, p. 158). Indeed, suggested Captain Young (1906, p. 1284), if the army's administrative departments in particular were to be operated in the best interests of military efficiency they must be led and administered by men who were trained as businessmen and had the values of businessmen. In an age of modern warfare it was necessary to recognize the very different responsibilities, qualities and training of officers who were appointed to administrative posts. The "misfortune which has come to our Army of late", noted Haldane, "has been the revelation in South Africa of an altogether inadequate organization and training to cope with the great business of supply in time of war, and the disorganized period which follows upon war. Supply is one of the most difficult things anyone can tackle. . . . [It] is a science in itself which requires high training" (*Tribune*, October 29, 1906; War Stores Commission, 1906). Army administrators needed to be trained in the ways of business so that they

> should know how to have everything on the spot when wanted. . . . [Supply officers] should know how to organize the great masses of stuff and organize their lines of communication in a fashion that will make the military machine work without friction and difficulty.
> (Haldane in *The Tribune*, October 29, 1906;
> see also Mitrany, 1918, p. 5)

According to the Director of the LSE, Halford Mackinder, the War Office and the Lords of the Admiralty were in reality boards of directors which sought to produce "power" rather than profits (Mackinder, 1907, p. 2). The War Office was a "vast business organization—a huge factory, whose output should be a number of efficient fighting units . . . and whose managers are responsible to a nation of shareholders that these units are produced at the lowest possible cost" (Young, 1906, p. 1282; Searle, 1971, p. 87). The Dawkins Committee in 1901 was also convinced that

> a general, if not a precise analogy, can be established between the conduct of large business undertakings and that of the War Office. There are certain well-defined principles of management in all well-conducted business corporations and the more closely that the War Office can be brought into conformity with such principles, the more successful will be the administration.
>   The vast extent and the great diversity of the work centred in the War Office differentiates it from that of a larger business undertaking only in degree, and there is no reason to doubt that the methods adopted in the latter for securing efficiency and economy could be employed in the former. . . . [The] present methods of the War Office are out of harmony with the best business practice.
> (Dawkins Committee, 1901, pp. 182–183, 200)

Although there were fundamental differences in aims between government and business, after the failures of the army in the South African War these were deemed insufficient to refuse the army the opportunity to benefit from the methods of business, given the coincidence of intent of these organizations (Wilson, 1973, p. 53). If the army was to be successful at the business of war, the aim of the army

> must be to produce the necessary amount of power at the least possible cost, and one of the main elements in a city business tending to produce profits is the saving of working expense. . . . If you are to spend and yet be economical, you must spend with knowledge, and in accordance with policy, in other words your expenditure must be efficient.
>
> (Mackinder, 1907, p. 3)

The enthusiastic commendation by the Dawkins Committee (1901, p. 691) of the principles and practices upon which businesses relied, and the government's decision to appoint only businessmen to this committee chaired by Clinton Dawkins, a partner in the American banking firm J.P. Morgan, demonstrated how for some it was no longer necessary to regard the ways of business as alien to the public services (Giffen, 1901, p. 1). This was soon to be confirmed by the findings of the War Stores Commission (1906) and later by the Select Committee on National Expenditure in 1918 and the Lawrence Committee in 1924. All sought control of the military's spending not through detailed financial regulations emanating from the War Office and the Treasury but through accounting reports which, as in business, would facilitate the most efficient use of available resources. It was upon this that victory increasingly depended. The Dawkins Committee (1901, p. 204, also see p. 196), for example, wanted to reduce Treasury control to a minimum. Included in the Terms of Reference of the Dawkins Committee (1901, p. 180) was the requirement to consider whether "existing checks at the War Office hinder the efficient transaction of business". Control of military operations through negation and the denial of responsibility, the seeking of approval for virtually every action, either by reference to printed instructions or to a higher authority, needed to be replaced by a managerial form of accountability permitted by accounting systems which could monitor performance and apportion responsibility. The existing system, which assumed that "military officers of all ranks are, by the fact of wearing uniform, shorn of all business instincts" had resulted in the very deficiencies that it was meant to prevent (Esher Committee, 1904, p. 138). Indeed, government accounting systems had never been designed with the intention to promote military efficiency.

When pressed by the Select Committee on National Expenditure in 1918, Sir John Bradbury, Joint Permanent Secretary to the Treasury, agreed that only with great difficulty could the then present systems of appropriation accounting provide information to enhance military efficiency. He recognized that "the control of expenditure, in the sense of securing that various public services are efficiently administered at a reasonable cost, was no part of the object which the framers of the system [of accounting and accountability] . . . had in view" (Report of the Select Committee on National

Expenditure, 1918, p. 157, para. 16). The Comptroller and Auditor General, alluding to the tensions in military finance between military needs and constitutional proprieties, reminded the Public Accounts Committee that this was only to be expected for

> the answer to many of the questions which may be raised by the accounts must depend not on considerations which can be measured in terms of money or of financial units but on general considerations of military necessity, to which accounting must be subordinate. . . . There is this fundamental difference between Army expenditure and commercial expenditure; the first has as its main object the production of an efficient Army—and the factor of military efficiency is an abstract idea not susceptible to appraisement in terms of cash. . . .
>
> (Public Accounts Committee, 1924–1925b,
p. 825; Clode, 1869)

Irrespective of the criticisms of constitutional anachronisms, consideration of the contributions of business methods to military efficiency by army administrators and commanders was unlikely to gain any prominence while ever the middle classes, but especially the sons of businessmen, continued to be excluded from army commissions. Prior to the 20th century resistance to the adoption of business methods and a business mentality in army administration, sustained by government suspicion that an efficient army might also be a potential rival in the exercise of power, had been perpetuated by officer recruitment in the combatant forces almost exclusively from the upper and landed classes for whom the bourgeois ethic of business was anathema. Despite the rapid rise of middle-class professionals and many new professions in the second half of the 19th century, there continued a lingering admiration for the "gentleman amateur" rather than trained professionals who were considered to be mere "players" (Wilson, 1995, p. 116; Otley, 1970, p. 215; Turner, 1956).

From the Restoration of the Stuarts in 1660, Parliament ensured that the army would be officered only by men of high social position who had the most to lose should the army threaten Parliament. Through tightly guarded selection procedures throughout the 18th and 19th centuries and the prospect of low pay, the army elite sought to deny the middle classes the representation that their influence in the wider society justified. The Crimean War may have marked the ascendancy of the professional values and working habits of the middle classes by exposing the aristocratic leaders of the army as incompetent bunglers "who should make way for the efficient, self-reliant men of the age", but this had had little lasting effect on army command and administration (Anderson, 1967, p. 109). Whatever change might occur in creating a highly efficient, well-managed military could only ever be gradual in the absence of officers in large numbers from the middle classes who would bring with them the skills and attitudes of their class.

Research by Haye (in Otley, 1970, p. 229) suggests that prior to 1870 only one businessman's son had passed through the officer training college at Sandhurst with a steady, though minimal, rise in business representation thereafter. In 1912 the landed classes still accounted for 64% of new officers while the elite levels of command remained predominantly aristocratic. Competitive civil service examinations introduced progressively since the *Report on the Organization of the Permanent Civil Service* in 1854 had made little difference to opportunities to gain a commission in the army, for to be admitted to Sandhurst all applicants still had to be nominated by the Commander-in-Chief on the advice of his senior officers. They, of course, tended to nominate only sons of men of their own class. This tight control of the gateway into Sandhurst generally ensured that wealthy business families, for whom the low officer pay was no impediment, would not obtain the social status that an infantry commission would bring to their sons (Otley, 1970, p. 214). Apart from protecting the purity of their class and the privileges that attended their class, the exclusion of middle and lower classes from the officer class was also sometimes seen as an important accounting control. One officer who had attended the LSE Army Class

> learned the organizational value of that dual control of money, where the accountant and the cashier are of a different social status, of which we have such an admirable example in the Army—the captain and the colour-sergeant. The chance of fraudulent collusion between these two is extremely remote.
>
> (Airey, 1913, p. 467)

The South African War forced a reappraisal of the wisdom of institutionalizing professional ignorance and arrogance in a haughty, proud and socially isolated military elite. The almost immediate effect that this had on officer recruitment was sufficiently noticeable for Richard Haldane, upon assuming office as Secretary of State for War in late 1905, to be impressed by the way in which a "a new school of officers has arisen since the South African War, a thinking school of officers who desire to see the full efficiency which comes from new organization and no surplus energy running to waste" (quoted in Barnett, 2000, p. 362).

NATIONAL EFFICIENCY AND THE BUSINESS OF WAR

By itself the South African War did not bring about the unprecedented appreciation of business practices, rather the problems experienced in the South African War crystallized a pervasive anxiety and pessimism in the early 20th century about Britain's declining industrial and political competitiveness in a movement calling for the promotion of national efficiency in all areas of government and business (Read, 1972, p. 13; White, 1901). Miller and O'Leary (1987, p. 245) refer to a national mood that at times "shifted to hysteria" while Scally (1975, p. 92) describes calls for national efficiency during the Edwardian period as a "fashionable attitude" which defined the political tenor of government (see also Rose, 1986, p. 117). The *Spectator* in 1902 (August 16) suggested that "at the present time and perhaps it is the most notable social fact of its age . . . there is a universal outcry for efficiency in all departments of society, in all the aspects of life". The economist J.A. Hobson, for example, provided economic justifications for an approach to economics which sought to enhance human efficiency (Emy, 1973, p. 107). Soon the catholic appeal of national efficiency became a demand in the first decade of the 20th century for the establishment of a government of "business men" to allow government to take advantage of the superior practical abilities and efficiencies which were perceived to be associated with private businesses (Searle, 1971, p. 43; Anderson, 1967, pp. 104–105).

Accordingly, efforts to "commercialize" the training of army administrators were not merely isolated responses by reformist zealots to the practical difficulties and humiliating failures experienced in the field in South Africa. Instead, they were symptoms of the far more serious malaise of inefficiency, which was declared by both Liberals and Conservatives to be endemic to British society but especially to government. Given the perilous state of Britain, where "there was now not an inch of ground in any one of the international markets for which we were not fighting with all our available strength" (Lord Rosebery, 1901, in Matthew, 1973, p. 224), Lord Rosebery warned Sidney Webb in 1901 that "if we have not learned in this war that we have lagged behind in efficiency we have learned nothing" (quoted in Scally, 1975, p. 56). The ruling class, judged H.G. Wells (1934, p. 764), was "profoundly lazy. The Edwardian monarchy, Court and society were amiable and slack". Thus, efforts to inculcate in the army the values and practices of business, in which accounting was to be accorded a prominent place, cannot be understood in isolation from an appreciation of the wider social and political frustrations which were intensified by the national soul-searching induced by the military and political failures of the South African War and the responses that these elicited. In particular, for a short, but crucial, period around the turn of the 20th century, the movement of national efficiency, although ultimately politically moribund and surviving as a political movement under the leadership of Lord Rosebery only until late 1903 (Emy, 1973, p. 129), provided a locus for the formation of more enduring efficacious relationships and networks of influence among prominent social and political activists from both the Liberal and Conservative Parties.

Lord Rosebery (1847–1929) and the Fabians Sidney and Beatrice Webb became synonymous with efforts in the pursuit of national efficiency to prize the British out of their self-satisfied, slothful acceptance of mediocrity and amateurism into which they were said to have fallen (Mackenzie and Mackenzie, 1977, pp. 286, 287; James, 1963; Bentley, 1984, p. 317). According to Sidney Webb, the Edwardian Englishman was preoccupied with a burning feeling of shame at the 'failure' of England—. . . shame for the pompous inefficiency of every branch of our public administration, shame for the slackness of our merchants and traders that transfers our commercial supremacy to the United States, shame for the supineness of our race by drunkenness and gambling. . . .

(Webb, 1903, p. 7; Read, 1972, p. 95)

From the late 1880s Rosebery had been advocating the urgent need for governments to put all of Britain and its empire on a "business footing". Rosebery, who had been Foreign Secretary in Gladstone's Government in 1886, had learnt from Gladstone the importance to the successful politician of concentrating the public's attention on "a single great question" rather than the plethora of small issues which "dazed and blunted" the nation's intelligence (Rosebery in Hamer, 1972, pp. 247, 248; Bentley, 1984, p. 318). In Gladstone's case the single issue had been at various times the Irish Church, Home Rule for Ireland and British imperialism. For Rosebery, after the defeat of the Liberals in 1895, the great issue for "concentration" was national efficiency, a policy which he believed would appeal "to the silent but supreme tribunal which shapes and controls in the long run the destinies of our people, the tribunal of public opinion and common sense" (Rosebery quoted in James, 1963, p. 431). Efficiency, according to Rosebery and his acolytes, offered the only way in which the ills which now afflicted British society, politics and industry could be addressed. Unfortunately for Rosebery and his political career he was unable to convert his one big issue into a clear political program capable of gaining the support of the public (Webb, 1975, p. 223).

The efficiency movement which Rosebery led was a political movement which had no direct, formal association with the efficiency movement in America arising from Frederick Taylor's school of scientific management. Rosebery was less concerned with the specifics of how to improve efficiency than with the need to generate the political will to recognize and remedy British ills. Rosebery defined the national efficiency which he sought as "a condition of national fitness equal to the demands of our Empire—administrative, parliamentary, commercial, educational, physical, moral, naval and military fitness . . ." (Rosebery quoted in Semmel, 1960, p. 63; Rosebery in the *Nineteenth Century,* July, August, November 1900). This national efficiency was not about the sanctimonious parsimony of the Victorians in which retrenchment in government spending was valued of and by itself, but rather about the operational benefits it might provide (Funnell, 2004). National efficiency was not to be about cheapness but instead the methodical, cool-headed weighing of the long-term costs and benefits of government policies which were in the nation's best interests (Rose, 1986, p. 117). Coincidently, the Fabians also believed that efficiency, not equality, was the means by which socially responsible government should seek to raise living standards. Soon after the end to Britain's ignoble war in South Africa, Sidney Webb indicated his belief that Britain was "ripe for a domestic programme, which shall breathe new life into the administrative dry bones of our public offices . . . [with] a policy of National Efficiency" (*Nineteenth Century,* September 1901, as reproduced in Webb, 1903, p. 7). With the publication of George Bernard Shaw's Fabian tract *Fabianism and Empire* in 1900, the Fabians had made the achievement of national efficiency dependent upon a secure empire and social reform which would guarantee, according to Sidney Webb's description, a "national minimum" in all areas of social activity (Mackenzie and Mackenzie, 1977, pp. 277–278).

The goal of national efficiency required "as the starting-point of industrial competition" the eradication of disease, the replacement of slums with good housing and the end to working-class ignorance through educational reform (Webb, 1903, p. 8; Scally, 1975, p. 51). "What is the use of talking about an empire", demanded the Liberal Prime Minister Herbert Asquith (1908–1916), "if here . . . there is always to be found a mass of people, stunted in education, a prey to intemperance, huddled and congested . . . ?" (quoted in Webb, 1975, p. 223; see also Mackinder in Parker, 1982, pp. 62, 64). Haldane (quoted in Matthew, 1973, p. 238) believed that temperance needed to be the first step to achieving national efficiency. Belying their earlier championing of the rights of the individual and their condemnation of the evils of state interference, Rosebery's Liberal Imperialists now saw that the national interest demanded that the poor and the ignorant be raised from their impoverishment through government programs to a position where they could enhance national efficiency. Both Liberals and Fabians accepted that social and imperial efficiency were entirely dependent upon extensive and sustained domestic reform (Asquith in the Matthew, 1973, pp. 71–72). This was best achieved, suggested the Webbs in their book *Constitution for a Socialist Commonwealth of Great Britain,* by the creation of an elite corps of social engineers; a civil bureaucracy, whose aim was efficiency and who would be independent of politics (Scally, 1975, p. 83; Rose, 1986, pp. 122–123).

At times some members of the movement for national efficiency, notably the Fabians and Lord Rosebery, were so dismayed at the poor quality and, therefore, the inefficiency of the British working man and woman that they were tempted to stray into Social Darwinism by offering eugenic solutions to resurrect national efficiency. Rosebery criticized the "physical degeneracy of our race" (quoted in Matthew, 1973, p. 80), while Beatrice Webb referred at one point during the South African War to "breeding the right sort of man" (Mackenzie and Mackenzie, 1977, p. 291). Hence, the Webbs were easily attracted to their fellow Fabian George Bernard Shaw's prescriptions for society's ills in *Man and Superman* and those of Herbert Spencer (Spencer, 1960). Arnold White's (1901) book *Efficiency and Empire,* with its extreme eugenic prescriptions for raising national efficiency, was especially popular amongst the liberal imperialists who were attracted to Lord Rosebery and the Webbs.

Not surprisingly, given the importance of a large, secure and productive empire to Britain's well-being, Rosebery's and the Webbs' conception of national efficiency as the source of the resurrection of British imperial prestige and power was dependent upon a strong and efficient army (Semmel, 1960, p. 72; Matthew, 1973, pp. 80, 215, 225). According to Sidney Webb and the Liberals, *the* essential requirement for an "efficient army" which would allow "scientific fighting to replace soldiering" (Webb quoted in Scally, 1975, p. 52) was improvements to general education, technical education and military education. "Nothing", assured Webb (1903, p. 15), "is more calculated to promote National Efficiency, than a large policy of Government aid to the highest technical colleges and the universities". Not only was the great majority of young men who had offered themselves for service during the South African War in poor health and of stunted physique, they were also invariably illiterate (Mackenzie, 1978, p. 169). Little was to change in the physical and educational quality of army recruits at the time of World War I, when the government was shocked at the high rejection rate in the early days of the war. Thus, immediately after the war major reforms were instituted in the education of army recruits with a heavy emphasis on basic reading, writing and arithmetic skills, so great was the educational need of the army ("Report on Educational Training in the British Army", 1920). Under these circumstances, Britain was at a considerable disadvantage in modern warfare when compared to the higher quality, better educated recruits available to the French and German armies. Thus, after the South African War, the German obsession for rigor, detail, efficiency and excellence became the model upon which Richard Haldane (1856–1928) based his vision for a modern British army (Editor, 1907, p. 304; Haldane, 1929). As Secretary of State for War between 1905–1912, Haldane had a singular influence on the reform of the British army prior to World War I. Some historians have referred to Haldane as the greatest army reformer in British history, surpassing even the attainments of Lord Cardwell in the early 1870s (Watt, 1988, p. 157; Koss, 1969).

Well before he entered politics, Haldane had established a formidable reputation as a lawyer, an educational reformer, an implacable defender of the empire and as an expert in German philosophy (*Dictionary of National Biography*, Vol. 1922–30, pp. 380–386; Webb, 1975, pp. 95, 98, 217). H.G. Wells (1934, p. 766), who came to hold opposing views to Haldane on imperialism, described Haldane as

> a self-indulgent man, with a large white face and an urbane voice that carried his words as it were on a salver, so that they seemed good even when they were not so. . . . I think he floated on strange compensatory clouds of his own exhalation. He rejoiced visibly in the smooth movements of his mind.

Before entering politics, Haldane's interest in educational reform and his work in helping the Webbs establish the LSE in 1895, and later in 1901 the reorganization of the University of London, provided the basis for a long-standing and close friendship with Sidney and Beatrice Webb (see correspondence by Beatrice Webb in September 1892 in Mackenzie, 1978, pp. 2–3, and Sidney to Beatrice Webb April 22, 1899, p. 99). Thus, it was not surprising that he was also an early member recruited for the small dining club called the "Co-Efficients", formed by Leopold Amery and Beatrice Webb in November 1902 to promote, as the name selected for the group suggested, the coincident social aims of the Fabians and those of the national efficiency movement. Amongst the first beneficiaries of their strivings for efficiency were the administrative departments of the British army.

The Co-Efficients was notable, if not for its immediate political accomplishments, for the opportunities that were provided for its members to develop personal and professional associations which could be carried into other spheres of their lives. Most important for the British army, the association that developed between Mackinder (1861–1947) and Haldane, who were recognized by the other Co-Efficients as the main intellectual forces behind their discussions (Amery, 1953, p. 228; Semmel, 1960, p. 61), provided the means by which the business education of army administrators could begin. Their friendship owed much to a shared and passionate commitment to educational reform, to their Liberal loyalties and to the close friendship that both enjoyed with the Webbs (Gilbert, 1961, pp. 19, 21). Mackinder, who had achieved fame as the founder of the modern discipline of geography and the creator of the new field of historical geography, was also a well-known economic theorist (Semmel, 1960, p. 166). While a member of the Co-Efficients and a member of the Liberal Party, Mackinder was appointed Director of the LSE in 1903, succeeding W.A.S. Hewins, who had also been a member of the Co-Efficients, holding the post until June 1908. This appointment, soon to converge with Haldane's own appointment as Secretary of State for War, proved fortuitous for the introduction of business education to the administrators of the British army.

During Mackinder's term as Director of the LSE, Haldane took advantage of his friendship with the Webbs and the momentum for reform created by the damning report of the Elgin Commission in 1904 on army administration to approve the commencement in 1907 of formal business training for army administrators with a "Course for the training of Officers for the Higher Appointments in the Administrative Staff of the Army" at the LSE, most often referred to as the "Army Class" (see the entry in Beatrice Webb's diary for November 21, 1906 in Mackenzie and Mackenzie, 1984). Haldane's political assistant, Sir Edward Ward, referred to the "practical experience in recent campaigns . . ." which had demonstrated the need for specialized administrative officers whose training should include "financial, commercial and legal qualifications" (Ward quoted in Watt, 1988, p. 157). Ward believed that other government departments would soon follow the army's example and adopt instruction in business administration as the preferred means to train their senior staff (Watt, 1988, p. 159). Haldane seized the opportunity, for which he, Rosebery and the Webbs had been preparing, to create the efficient army upon which the proselytizers of national efficiency believed that Britain's future as an imperial power depended. The Army Class allowed Haldane to give further effect to his intention to "put education first . . . , other interests second" and to apply business methods to domestic and imperial policies (Haldane quoted in Matthew, 1973, pp. 94, 149).

THE LSE AND THE "SOLDIER BUSINESS MAN"

Ever since the foundation of the LSE in 1895, through the Webbs and Haldane it had enjoyed a strategic association with Lord Rosebery and the movement for national efficiency (Matthew, 1973, p. 68). Indeed, Rosebery had used his influence with his brother-in-law, Lord Rothschild, to secure the necessary funding for the foundation of the LSE. In addition, from his time in power during Gladstone's last ministry, Haldane also had enjoyed close personal and political connections with Lord Rosebery (Matthew, 1973, pp. 17, 19). Thus, in effect, post-Gladstonian Liberalism and the decade-long preparations of the advocates of national efficiency converged in 1907 on the LSE in the form of the Army Class. Prior to the Army Class, the LSE had provided business training to many industries, including eight of the largest railway companies in Britain and several water authorities (Mackinder, 1907, p. 4; Searle, 1971, pp. 90, 124; Rose, 1986, p. 125). According to Napier (1996, p. 454), the close association with industry upon which the LSE developed its reputation was not unusual amongst British universities. The directors of the LSE believed that administration, whether in business or government, required dedicated professional training: "the old way of blundering into the position of a responsible administrator will no longer do" (Mackinder, 1907, p. 4). Accordingly, it was Beatrice Webb's aim to make sure that "no young man or woman who is anxious to study or to work in public affairs can fail to come under our influence" (quoted in Webb, 1975, p. xxx), starting with the army whose officers at the opening of the South African War had managed to keep at bay the training and educational requirements of modern war.

Consistent with the determination of senior military officers to ensure that commissions in the army remained the domain of the landed classes, throughout the 19th century the education of army officers had changed little. The Duke of Wellington's belief that "the best education for an officer is whatever may be considered the fittest education for a gentleman" (quoted in Slessor, 1901, p. 516) remained the touchstone for the training and the qualities sought of officers, the majority of whom were still drawn from the propertied classes (Bond, 1972, p. 20). The result was a body of officers whose education was perceived at the close of the 19th century to be significantly deficient when compared to that of leaders in the professions and business. It was particularly unsatisfactory and found wanting in comparison to German military education, against which the British appeared amateurish and dissolute (Searle, 1971, pp. 14–15). At the time of the South African War, instruction for British officers had deviated little from military law, basic mathematics necessary for surveying, military history and fortifications which had been favored in Wellington's time. Nor was there any incentive to change during long periods of peace after the Crimean War when the deadening routine of military life demanded by unchanging regulations denied officers the opportunity or encouragement to improve their skills and to use their initiative to do so (Slessor, 1901, pp. 516–517). The plight of administrative officers, but especially those engaged in supplying the army with its material needs, when compared to the training of their brother officers in command positions, was even more parlous. Secretary of State for War Haldane, when introducing the new Army Class at the LSE, reminded his audience how

> up to now no step has been taken to give a higher training to certain officers who may be experts in connection with the administrative side of war. You want those experts in the whole mechanism of modern business, in accounts, in supply, organization, and transport. . . . [W]e have never trained our officers designated for that work . . . [but] we have already decided that we will train a school of administrative officers on the same high level that we try to train our staff officers. . . . [T]rained business experts; soldiers but soldiers trained in the highest civilian principles so far as is administrative business is concerned, who would be fixed with the responsibility for what they did, and made accountable for the highest service.
>
> (Haldane in the *Tribune,* October 29, 1906)

Haldane regarded the Army Class at the LSE as the means, if only experimental at first, of getting the army on "a sound business footing" (quoted in Watt, 1988, p. 159; Mackinder, 1907, p. 5). At the opening ceremony of the new class in January 1907, Mackinder (1907, pp. 5, 7, 10) emphasized the importance of understanding the ways of

> civilian business and . . . working the people according to their habits. . . . What we require as business men is such working knowledge as will enable us to do our business safely and in order. . . . We wish to obtain for you the experience of practical business men.

With the benefit of the recent findings of the War Stores Commission, Haldane (quoted in Watt, 1988, p. 159) expected instruction at the LSE to ensure that

> never again shall a state of things occur in which officers placed in charge of the business of dealing with local contractors are unable to

make or even to understand the nature of the contracts involved—never again shall we have officers unable to keep their company accounts and ignorant of questions of currency, or familiar with the general processes governing the management of markets. . . .

The creation of an Advisory Board for Haldane's new Army Class at the LSE, on which sat some of the most senior officers of the various army departments, was a clear indication of the importance with which the army, the War Office and the government regarded the new Army Class (see Advisory Board, 1912). The success of this essentially revolutionary innovation in the education of British army officers and in the approach of the War Office to army administration depended upon a visible commitment at the very top levels in each of the army's departments. Each year the Advisory Board provided a detailed report to the government and to the War Office in which the Board outlined the accomplishments of the Army Class and gave its recommendation that the class be allowed to continue. In its 1911 Report, for example, the Advisory Board commended the way in which the class provided "the general working knowledge which enables an officer to conduct business matters in safety and in order . . ." (Advisory Board, 1911, p. 3). Indeed, there was no shortage of graduates who believed that the course appreciably enhanced the value of army administrators (Airey, 1913, p. 457).

Each year 30 students in the latter part of their careers were selected to begin their 20-week course in October, finishing in the following March. The students, who were affectionately referred to as the "Mackindergarten" after the Director of the LSE, were most often officers of the rank of captain and above, selected from line commands and most of the administrative departments, with the Army Service Corps providing each year the largest number of students; 10 out of 30 in 1911 and 8 in 1912 (Gilbert, 1961, p. 21). Other departments which were eligible to provide students included the Royal Artillery, Royal Engineers, Infantry, Medical Corps, Ordnance Corps and the Indian Army (Badcock, 1926, p. 104). The students were instructed by eminent experts in their fields who were drawn from business, the universities and government. Haldane was a frequent lecturer, and Sir Charles Harris and Colonel Grimwood of the Finance Department at the War Office, who, as the previous chapter has shown, had been implacable critics of army accounting systems (Harris, 1911, pp. 65, 67; Harris, 1931, p. 314; Brodrick Committee, 1898, Questions 484–487, p. 21), took an active interest in the success of the Army Class, with Harris appearing often as a guest lecturer (Letter from Lawrence Dicksee to LSE, June 14, 1919, LSE Archives, File 232/C and 232/D; Grimwood, 1919). Indeed, the army class signified the beginnings of the convergence of Harris's perennial agitation for business enhancements to the army's accounting systems, but especially the introduction of cost accounts, and the national efficiency movement which would finally come to full, if temporary, fruition with the cost accounting experiment in 1919. Haldane's (1929, p. 186) high regard for Harris, leading him to describe Harris as a "very remarkable man", was borne out of a close professional association between them at the War Office. Thus, from the first, Haldane as Secretary of State for War had at the War Office an unwavering champion for his reform plans. For Harris, the Army Class was but a preliminary step in the importation of cost accounting from business to provide Britain with a highly efficient and cost-effective army.

Lectures were given on 14 subjects with numerous "observation visits" to complement the material delivered at the LSE. These visits included the offices of The Times newspaper, the Great Western Railway Works, the London Docks, the London Omnibus Works, the Railway Clearing House, the Royal Arsenal at Woolwich, the House of Parliament and Lloyds (Badcock, 1925, 1926, p. 106). Typically the curriculum was weighted heavily towards commercial law and accounting, the latter delivered by the well-known Lawrence Dicksee three mornings a week (Badcock, 1926, pp. 104–105; Advisory Board, 1912, p. 5). These two subjects were recognized by Mackinder (1907, p. 6) as constituting the core of the new course, providing many of the basic essentials of business upon which the other subjects would need to draw. Indeed, accounting was allotted more than three times the number of lectures allowed most of the other subjects (Badcock, 1926, pp. 104–105). The full curriculum for the army course was: Public Administration; the British Constitution; Economic Problems of War; Accounting and Business Methods; Inland Transport; Sea Transport; Transport in War; Commercial Law; Economic Geography; Banking and Currency; International Institutions; Social Institutions; and Army Control. Haldane appeared often to deliver guest lectures on "Organisation for War" (Badcock, 1926, pp. 104–105). The accounting course sought to provide

> a thorough explanation of the principles upon which business systems of Accounting are founded, with a view to enabling officers to understand any accounts that may be presented to them. . . . The manner in which these principles are applied to meet the varying requirements of businesses will be fully considered, together with the organisation of systems of control. Attention will also be directed to the various uses made of accounting records by business men.
>
> (Advisory Board, 1912, p. 5)

Captain Airey of the Army Service Corps, who had completed the Army Class in 1912, recommended Accounting as the subject of the most practical value for the Army Service Corps officer (Airey, 1913, pp. 465, 466), while Lieutenant Colonel Badcock (1925, p. 140), another graduate, praised the way in which students were taught how to keep accounts and to understand how these accounts might be used to ascertain whether money had been wisely spent. Captain Airey (1913, p. 466) was particularly impressed with the way in which knowledge of balance sheets would allow officers to choose contractors more wisely and to be better informed in any fights with the War Office's Finance Department. Most of this praise was for the teaching of Lawrence Dicksee, whose books were in constant use as the sole accounting texts for the entire history of the Army Class. Dicksee's accounting texts included: *Bookkeeping for Accounting Students; Fraud in Accounts; The ABC of Bookkeeping; Depreciation, Office Organisation and Management; Advanced Accounting* (LSE Archives, File 232/A). After Dicksee's classes students found that "every account becomes an interesting statement of fact rather than an irritating collection of figures, so much despised because so little understood" (Airey, 1913, p. 466).

The Army Class continued to operate until 1914 when the need for war economies induced the War Office to refuse further funding, by which time nearly 300 officers had passed through the class. The success of the Army Class in improving military efficiency, suggested Dicksee (1915b, p. 2), was clearly evident in the early part of World War I by the "wonderful success" of transport and supply. When the LSE sought to resurrect the Army Class in 1919 it also sought to support its case with the boast that "its value has been testified to be very satisfactory, in the War just ended, by the work done by many officers who had gone through the course" (LSE Archives, File 232/C). The Army Class was eventually resurrected in 1924 after much lobbying by the LSE, continuing until 1934 when the need for economies during the Great Depression again saw the War Office and the Treasury withdraw financial support (see Dahrendorf, 1995, p. 89). On October 11, 1934, in reply to inquiries from the LSE about the future of the Army Class, the government's Emergency Committee wrote on behalf of the Secretary of State for War, Lord Hailsham, informing the LSE that the Army Class would not receive any further funding (LSE Archives, LSE History Collection, Box 1). However, between the end of World War I and the resumption of the Army Class, the LSE was able to take advantage of the considerable experience it had acquired in teaching accounting to army officers in the Army Class by providing the formal accounting training to the soldiers recruited to implement the army cost accounting experiment between 1919 and 1925, the second and ultimate stage in early attempts at army accounting reform.

POLITICAL LIMITS TO ADMINISTRATIVE REFORM AND THE ARMY COST ACCOUNTING EXPERIMENT (1919–1925)

Initiating the Experiment

Although like its predecessor, the Army Class, the cost accounting experiment sought to raise the business efficiency of army administrators and commanders, this would not be achieved without political cost. The Army Class involved no changes to the army's accounting systems and, therefore, presented no threat to the organizational basis of existing networks of power and influence or to the role performed by the "subject-based" form of accounting constitutionally required by appropriation accounting. The cost accounting experiment, with its perceived challenge to a system of accounting from which political power and influence derived much of its nourishment, was a very different proposition. Accordingly, whereas the Army Class was widely praised and supported, the cost accounting experiment was the progeny of a few visionary financial administrators who were opposed, either out of ignorance or self-interest, by numerous powerful adversaries determined to ensure the demise of the experiment.

Prior to World War I cost accounting was unknown in government departments. Cost accounting systems had been introduced in all War Office factories in 1890, but not the War Office itself, mainly for the purpose of justifying the prices charged by contractors (Public Accounts Committee, 1917–1918, p. 246). Apart from the Finance Department at the War Office, in the departments at the War Office, which administered the largest business in Britain, that is, the army (Watt, 1988, p. 160; Mackinder, 1907, p. 2), it was rare at the end of the 19th century to find an appreciation of the relevance and the benefits which might be obtained in the field of battle from the most basic cost accounting practices. The army was a business in the sense that in order to achieve its purposes it entered a large number of different markets to buy, and sometimes sell, vast quantities of goods and services both in Britain and in many other locations throughout the world. Indeed, it was not uncommon in many cities in Britain for the army to be the single most important contributor to the local economy.

The army cost accounting experiment, which commenced in April 1919, at a time when there was a surge in cost accounting interest in private industry, was the ultimate manifestation of the army's flirtation with business methods and commercial culture and another example of the nexus between government accounting reform and political crisis. It arose most immediately out of the financial extravagance of World War I, the extent of which was revealed in the First Report of the Select Committee on National Expenditure in 1918. According to the Select Committee, during the war the national debt had been increasing by £1000m every six months and by the close of fighting war expenditure had accounted for 72% of all government expenditures (Hinchliffe, 1983, p. 70). Most immediately, the idea for the experiment had emerged from conversations between Sir Charles Harris at the War Office, members of Parliament and Sir Henry Gibson, then Comptroller and Auditor General, who had been "impressed by the uncontrolled extravagance proceeding in all directions and in the absence of any machinery whatever for seeing that financial considerations received attention . . ." (Sir Charles Harris, Public Accounts Committee 1924–1925c, Appendix 33, p. 826). Those advocating the introduction of cost accounting also had on their side the very persuasive recommendations in favor of cost accounting by the Royal Commission on War Stores in South Africa (1906).

During the short few years in which the cost accounting experiment struggled for survival, the LSE, mainly through Lawrence Dicksee, became an important ally through the provision of the necessary courses in cost accounting to hundreds of army personnel who had been entrusted with the success of the experiment. Dicksee referred to these courses as the "Army Accountants' Course", the first of which had 82 students enrolled (Dicksee in a letter to the War Office July 8, 1919, LSE Archives, File 232/C). Dicksee, who had been approached to provide these accounting courses by Colonel Grimwood, representing the War Office, urged the LSE governors to "make every effort to provide what he wants . . ." (Dicksee to the Secretary of the LSE, March 5, 1919, LSE Archives, File 232/C). The LSE took his advice, securing responsibility for the course at £11 per student, based upon a minimum of 60 students for each class. Dicksee, who was at the same time a partner in Sellars, Dicksee and Co. in London, was then contracted to teach the new course for a fee of £300. The salient difference between the Army Class and the cost accounting experiment was that the Army Class was outward looking to the army's dealings with contractors, in the commercial world. The cost accounting experiment, in contrast, was primarily, although not exclusively, for the purpose of providing information which would be useful for internal decision making, for example, the running of a military unit in a cost-effective manner (War Office Cost Accounting Committee, 1918, p. 3).

According to Sir Charles Harris, the most vigorous and influential advocate of the cost accounting experiment, cost accounts were to "become the main channel of administration and the main channel of parliamentary control" (Select Committee on National Expenditure, 1918, Minutes of Evidence, Question 220 and 248, pp. 334–336). In his evidence before the Select Committee on National Expenditure in 1918, Harris told the Committee (Evidence, p. 391), how "thirty years' experience of the actual working of the present system of external control of War Office expenditure, in peace and war, has convinced me that it fails to produce real economy". In the last days of the experiment, when Harris appeared before the Public Accounts Committee in 1924, he referred to the way in which army cost accounting, if allowed to persist, would be the means of achieving impressive economy in military spending by providing information on the costs of operating army units and allowing officers greater opportunity to make decisions to enhance economy. After the experiment had been approved in 1918, the War Office Cost Accounting Committee (1918, p. 2; Ellison, 1918; Black, 2001), which had been established by the Army Council to superintend the experiment, had also praised cost accounts for the way in which they would "fix responsibility . . . and secure economy . . . while increasing efficiency" (War Office Cost Accounting Committee, 1918 pp. 2, 4; Ellison, 1918). In his last appearance before the Public Accounts Committee, Harris again emphasized the way in which a cost accounting system would allow officers to manage expenditure properly. . . . [I]t is the difference between a system of account which is designed to control expenditures and a system of account that has nothing to do . . . with seeing whether the Public Services are being carried on efficiently and administered with reasonable care for economy. The present system has nothing to do with that question at all. . . . This new system is intended, in particular, to take into account the psychological factor and produce economy . . . by showing people the results of their actions and appealing to their reason.

(Public Accounts Committee, 1924–1925a,
Minutes of Evidence, Question 7206)

Recruitment of students who might be suitable for the Army Accountants' Course at the LSE began with the issue of *Army Council Instruction No.113 of 1919* which, in "connection with the introduction into the Army of a new system of accounts of a costing type", sought expressions of interest from officers, warrant officers and N.C.O.s who in civilian life had practiced as a chartered or incorporated accountant. The army was interested also in soldiers of any rank who in civilian life had been audit clerks for at least two years and any soldiers with a good education and with some knowledge of accounts. Once they had completed their training at the LSE they would be then assigned to units within army establishments where, apart from matters which affected their technical competence and duties, they would be under the usual authority of the officer commanding. The *Army Council Instruction* also referred to the possibility of the formation of a special Corps of Army Accountants. This Corps was eventually formed in November 1919 as part of the Army Service Corps under the Quartermaster-General while Sir Charles Harris was Assistant Financial Secretary and Accounting Officer in the War Office (Black, 2001).

Implacable Opposition

At the outset of the experiment, it was readily appreciated that the success of such a massive and profound undertaking depended upon the goodwill and enthusiastic cooperation of all departments concerned. Unfortunately, the dictates of a rigid interpretation of the constitutional function of government accounting and thinly disguised Treasury self-interest denied the cost accounting experiment the opportunity to become anything other than a tenuous expression of hope on the part of its most committed advocates, thereby precluding the adoption of cost accounting throughout departments of state as a decision making tool, effectively until the latter decades of the 20th century. From the inception of the experiment in 1919 and the confinement of its application to just 14 sites distributed throughout the army, the Treasury had no intention of allowing it to be successful. The Treasury, realizing at the close of hostilities the strength of the desire for culprits to blame for the profligacy, both human and material, measured its response to the demands for accounting reform and gave the appearance of a willing, yet cautious, participant. Its true intentions, however, were clear by its insistence that the introduction of cost accounting be conducted as an experiment alongside the existing system of appropriation accounting. The Treasury made sure that the new system of cost accounting would be adopted as a trial, an experiment with all the connotations of impermanence that this implied. The new system of cost accounting would be given six years to prove itself but would have to do so alongside the existing system of accounting.

The government, with the support of Parliament, which was yet to be convinced of the need for cost accounting throughout all government departments, had no intention of relinquishing the existing system of accounting and the revered political purposes it served without convincing, cumulative evidence of the advantages of the new system. The political stakes were too high should the new, relatively untested system fail. Thus, constitutional suspicions of Executive ambition were enshrined in appropriation accounting; cost accounting and the operational imperative that it was to serve as portrayed by the Treasury could not hope to provide a similar level of constitutional assurance. While Sir Charles Harris and a small circle of like-minded finance officials from the War Office were convinced of the financial and operational benefits of cost accounting, the unsatisfactory results during the trial of the new system seemed to prove the opposite and made the case against cost accounting even more convincing. It had not proved either its constitutional credentials or its financial credentials.

These institutionalized impediments to the assumption of cost accounting by government departments which thwarted Sir Charles Harris were compounded and perpetuated by the education, class prejudices and social insularity of senior civil servants. At a time when, as a body, members of the accounting profession remained mostly oblivious to the benefits of cost accounting, deeming it to be irrelevant to the professional concerns of chartered and incorporated accountants[1] (see Fells, 1900 in Locke, 1979, p. 6), there was even less opportunity for senior civil servants recruited with a classics education from Oxford and Cambridge to be acquainted with the existence, developments in, and the possibilities of cost accounting (Finer, 1937; Skidelsky, 1983). Besides, ignorance of commercial practices was still a cherished characteristic of the British civil service (Marriner, 1994, p. 454). Even if this knowledge had been available to civil servants, evidence before the Public Accounts Committee as late as 1924 made it clear that cost accounting practices developed in the private sector for private purposes, and therefore tainted by the "base" motives of commerce, were not deemed appropriate by many in government and in the senior departments of state, especially the Treasury, for the different roles and accountabilities of government.

Like any experiment, the cost accounting experiment would have to satisfy conditions of success far more onerous than those expected of well-tried incumbent systems. Not only did it have to prove that it was at least as good as the existing system but that it was superior to the existing system according to a number of criteria. These included the cost of implementing the experiment, enhancements to the economy and the financial and operational efficiency of the army and, most crucially, the ability of Parliament to continue to exercise its constitutional powers of accountability over the army with the cash-based system of appropriation accounting. The Secretary of State for War, Sir Herbert Creedy, when expressing his opposition to the continuance of the experiment before the Public Accounts Committee in 1924, gave some idea of the prejudices that from the beginning had ensured its demise and which had exaggerated the requirements of what were in reality complementary additions, rather than replacements, to the existing cash-based appropriation system. He firstly expressed concern to the Public Accounts Committee that to move to the new system of cost accounting in preference to existing systems of accounting would require the entire reorganization of all levels of army administration, from the War Office down, which were presently organized on a "subject basis", and the attendant costs and dislocations that this would involve. Such an undertaking "could only be carried out if there were very, very great and assured advantages, both in efficiency and cost, and I was not satisfied that either of those advantages was inevitable" (Public Accounts Committee, 1924–1925a, Minutes of Evidence, Questions 6839, 6884, 6887).

Prior to the hearings of the Public Accounts Committee in 1924, the Lawrence Committee appointed in 1922 by the Secretary of State for War, under General Herbert Lawrence, recommended: that the new system of cost accounting be fully implemented across the army and not just the 14 sites that had been chosen for the experiment; that cost accounting was essential to securing an efficient army; and, most controversially, that a complete reorganization in army administration was needed to allow administrative responsibility and accounting to be decentralized as far as possible (Public Accounts Committee, 1924–1925b, Appendix 32, p. 822). This report was considered by the Army Council, which had then established the Crosland Committee to examine detailed implementation of the Lawrence recommendations. Soon after the Army Council changed its mind.

More fundamentally, Creedy's opposition suggested that retaining the new system in the army and extending it to all government departments represented a dramatic innovation in constitutional practices, the merits of which had yet to be proved. Even if savings were to be obtained, and the performance of the trials in this regard had been far from convincing, this should not come at the expense of constitutional protections as embodied in the system of appropriation accounting. Thus, the *possibility* of improvements to military efficiency was again insufficient to counter latent, and misplaced, political apprehensions. It wasn't enough just to save money. The contribution of cost accounting to improved economy in the army, the first department of state allowed to experiment with cost accounting, while certainly recognized as a benefit to commend cost accounting, was never sufficient of itself to convince the British Government that cost accounting was either necessary or constitutionally appropriate. Instead, the potency of economic arguments for the adoption of cost accounting by the British Government in the decades spanning the close of the 19th century was entirely dependent upon the necessary assurance that there would be no threat to the constitutional protections provided by the existing form of appropriation accounting (see, for example, the Public Accounts Committee, 1924–1925a, Minutes of Evidence, Questions 6839, 6884, 6887).

Unfortunately for Sir Charles Harris and the supporters of the cost accounting experiment, the Comptroller and Auditor General was also not convinced of the wisdom of continuing the experiment. He was concerned about the vast number of errors that his office was finding year after year in the new cost accounts, which had rendered the accounts virtually worthless. More importantly, he believed that any attempt to widen the experiment to other departments, irrespective of whether the accuracy of the cost accounts improved, would fatally interfere with the system of Treasury control on which the government and Parliament relied for the administration of policy. He also criticized the new accounts required for the experiment for being too complicated for Parliament, thereby confusing most members and inhibiting effective parliamentary criticism (Public Accounts Committee, 1924–1925b, Appendix 32, pp. 823–824).

Thus, the Treasury's strategy to undermine the experiment by sowing seeds of doubt about its constitutional credentials had worked. It implanted the erroneous presumption, which angered Harris and others associated with the cost accounting experiment, that should cost accounting ultimately be allowed to spread from the army to all government departments it would replace the cash accounts upon which appropriation accounting was dependent and the simplicity which was understandable to parliamentarians (Ormsby, 1908b, p. 1533; Marriner, 1994, p. 467; Black, 2001). Opponents of the experiment were successful in creating confusion, apparently even with the Comptroller and Auditor General, between cost accounting for management purposes *within* government departments and the cash accounting systems used by departments of state to acquit themselves of their constitutional accountability obligations to Parliament. Thus, not surprisingly, Harris believed that the experiment had not been given a fair chance and that its future was prejudiced from the start by constant Treasury sniping and innuendo (Public Accounts Committee, 1924–1925a, Minutes of Evidence, Question 6708). Indeed, he complained, after being drawn from retirement to appear before the Public Accounts Committee, that calling the new system of accounting "cost accounting" was a mistake for it played into the hands of the Treasury and the unease that they were able to foment about possible threats to Parliament's constitutional supremacy. Political pressures had both ushered in the experiment and ensured its demise, irrespective of economy considerations or potential enhancements for military performance in peace and war.

In contrast to beliefs which were actively encouraged by the Treasury, none of the major inquiries into army organization in the early 20th century saw any contradiction between providing constitutional protections and the aims and practices of a system of army cost accounting (see Young in Wright, 1956, p. 465; Mackinder, 1907, p. 5). Instead, the Treasury, as the major financial adviser to Parliament, was accused of perpetuating the existing politically motivated structure of financial control largely because of motives of self-interest. The then present structure, which was entirely based upon the format of the appropriation accounts, suited the Treasury because of the considerable power and influence it afforded. The process of categorizing expenditures according to "votes" or subjects of spending, such as soldiers' pay and forage, had to commence at the earliest recording of expenditure (Grimwood, 1919, p. 114; Harris, 1911, p. 64).

Until World War I, vouchers pertaining to accounting entries would be bundled according to their respective vote numbers in the parliamentary-approved estimates and then forwarded to that section of the War Office to which the relevant expenditures related. Certification of spending by the War Office according to parliamentary votes was the responsibility of the Accountant-General who headed the finance section of the War Office. His close association with the Treasury, to which he was ultimately accountable, further ensured a constant, insistent and all-pervading presence for the Treasury in all matters of military finance and accounting. A system of accounting of which the concern was the cost of delivering specific functions would require officers in the field to be able to manage their finances without constantly seeking approval for every expenditure and require a different form of appropriation accounting and estimates which could only operate successfully by giving military officers greater decision making autonomy.

The Treasury feared that extension of the cost accounting experiment to all government departments, and the resulting substitution of subject-based accounts by object-based accounts, would greatly diminish the Treasury's importance by allowing the devolution of authority and responsibility for spending away from the center, that is, the War Office (Select Committee on National Expenditure, 1918, Minutes of Evidence, Sir Charles Harris, also Seventh Report, pp. 157, 163). Surrender of its pivotal position in military finance was not something the Treasury sought to promote or abet (Wright, 1956, p. 465). Keenly aware of Treasury self-interested deceptions, witnesses before the Public Accounts Committee in 1924 attempted to reassure the Committee that when the conventional accounting system which had been running parallel to the cost accounting experiment was removed there would be no diminution of Treasury control and, therefore, no threat to Parliament's constitutional oversight of army expenditure (Public Accounts Committee, 1924–1925a, Minutes of Evidence, Question 6748, also Appendix 33, p. 826). Unfortunately, these and Harris's arguments were not sufficient to neutralize Treasury opposition and, thereby, to convince the Public Accounts Committee to find in favor of the experiment's continuance. Harris's retirement in 1924 signaled the loss of the experiment's most influential champion who had fought for many years against the unrelenting opposition of the Treasury (see reference to this opposition by the Public Accounts Committee, 1924–1925a, Minutes of Evidence, Question 6878). Once the regrets and recriminations, which tend to follow the cessation of war, had died away, institutional realities again asserted themselves when the cost accounting experiment, eventually deprived of its main benefactors, was allowed to wither.

CONCLUSION

At times of political crisis, of which war is the most extreme form, the ideological possibilities and intent of government accounting become more obvious and contested. Indeed, the first tentative steps to modernize British military accounting in the early decades of the 20th century have been shown to have owed much to the crises of war. At the end of the 19th century accounting for most British departments of state presented few problems and even less reason to ferment change. Departmental performance was evaluated according to the ability to respect spending limits contained in the annual appropriations and for the purposes approved by Parliament. The British army, however, operated under a very different set of circumstances from most government departments. Not only as the largest spending department would its activities attract attention but also its responsibilities to defend the liberty, rights and dignity of Britain meant that its performance in times of extreme crisis would be of paramount interest to all British citizens.

While the army was expected to be always victorious, the Nation also required the army to achieve its victories in the most financially efficient manner. This was only possible if the army was well led and expertly administered. Deficiencies in command and administration could remain hidden, as in other government departments, for many years in times of peace. However, in the panic of war any weaknesses were soon mercilessly exposed. Thus, when the British army experienced great difficulty in defeating an ill-disciplined, yet highly effective, group of farmers in South Africa, and was forced to endure a prolonged and debilitating war against Germany, both its command and administrative arrangements became the targets of intense scrutiny. From these inquiries the British people learnt of the commercial ineptitude of War Office administrators responsible for the supply of the army. This determined the government that amateurism and ignorance in those services with the ability to spend very large amounts of money with few controls in times of war could be no longer tolerated. Amongst other things, military administrators would have to become proficient in business accounting.

The problems of the army in South Africa were also further confirmation for the supporters of Lord Rosebery's movement of national efficiency that British inefficiency had placed Britain in a vulnerable state, which needed to be urgently addressed by measures designed to elevate the efficiency of all aspects of British life, which depended upon preserving the empire. The Army Class at the LSE immediately after World War I provided the means by which the army could begin this transformation, while the cost accounting experiment between 1919–1924 promised that the innovations in cost accounting in the army might be extended to all departments. However, the reactionary impediment of Britain's "ancient" constitution proved far stronger than any professed financial or military advantages from a system of cost accounting.

Although the adoption of business accounting practices promised economic gains, the ultimate purpose of military accounting was to provide constitutional protections. While economic motivations were not entirely absent in the decision to experiment with the introduction of cost accounting in the early 20th century in the British army, these were always secondary in the initial stages to motives of national interest and constitutional proprieties. Thus, the contribution of cost accounting to improved economy in the army, the first department of state allowed to experiment with cost accounting, was certainly recognized as a benefit to commend cost accounting. However, this had never been sufficient of itself to convince the British Government that cost accounting was either necessary or constitutionally appropriate. Instead, the potency of economic arguments for the adoption of cost accounting by the British Government in the decades spanning the close of the 19th century was entirely dependent upon circumstances providing sufficient political justification, in the form of military crises, and also the necessary assurance that there would be no threat to the constitutional protections provided by appropriation accounting.

This chapter is based on the paper, "National Efficiency, Military Accounting and the Business of War", which originally appeared in *Critical Perspectives on Accounting*, 17 (2006), pp. 719–751. The author would like to thank the publisher, Elsevier, for permission to use this material.

NOTE

1. The first British professional association of accountants skilled in cost accounting, the Institute of Cost and Works Accountants, was not founded until 1919.

5   Taming the Untamable
The Normalization of Nuclear War

INTRODUCTION

The previous chapter examined how the British political elite used cost accounting as a tool to manage the perception that Britain was still a great empire, despite the inroads the U.S. and Germany were making into this domain. This chapter also demonstrates how accounting can be used to manage political crises. Accounting helped to normalize nuclear war by transforming it from a horrific potentiality to a series of problems to be solved. Echoing the British experience discussed in Chapter 2, accounting was intentionally deployed by civilians to shift the balance of power in the U.S. Department of Defense (hereafter DOD) away from the armed services to the Office of the Secretary of Defense with the introduction of Planning, Programming and Budgeting (hereafter PPB) into the DOD by Robert S. McNamara, Secretary of Defense from 1961 to 1968.

McNamara used PPB to redefine the normative and cognitive facets of the defense political process in such a way that military expertise (something McNamara lacked) was discredited while quantitative rationality (a trait McNamara excelled at) was elevated to the status of authority and legitimacy. This allowed McNamara to gain control of the defense acquisition process by first stifling the Armed Forces' ability to use asymmetric information gained through military experience as a source of power and, second, by forcing the Armed Forces to substantiate their requirements using his technically rational articulation of how to best meet defense needs. PPB assisted with transforming war from a horrendous occurrence to a series of problems to be solved by subjecting weapon system choices to rigorous cost-benefit analysis. This caused the economics of defense to be elevated to a position of supremacy, transforming the planning for war into a routine resource allocation exercise, rather than an insane preparation for genocide.

REPRESENTATION AS A POLITICAL ACT

Accounting is a form of representation. Representation is, itself, a political act in that descriptions determine our collective social understanding of a situation and, thus, what behaviors are deemed appropriate and which are not (Eagleton, 1990; Edwards, 1996; Hall, 1982). For example, at present, efficiency is one of the primary means by which actions are evaluated in a corporation. This form of assessment validates certain acts, such as expending extra energy on the job, while discouraging others, which could include socializing during working hours. However, business entities have not always been spaces where efficiency reigned supreme. According to Miller and O'Leary (1987), the introduction of standard costing and budgeting in the early 1900s as a method for describing and evaluating the performance of inputs was integral for normalizing corporate efficiency as a socially desirable goal and directing workers' behavior towards acts that sustained this normalcy. Thus, accounting representations can transform the world we live in by creating new ways of seeing and norms for social behavior.

If the meanings humans attribute to events are socially and historically determined, then these meanings will reflect the value system necessary to reproduce the distribution of power in society for, as Eagleton (1990, p. 37) notes, "Power succeeds by persuading us to desire and collude with it. . . ." Further, Hall (1982, p. 81) illustrates how the description of a problem frequently contains the resolution preferred by the dominant race, class or sex through reference to the debate concerning black immigrants to Britain as a problem "about numbers". He notes how entering the debate on these terms was tantamount to giving credibility to the white position that racial tension was the result of having too many black people in the country, not the result of white racialism. Hence, it is around the representation of a problem that the fiercest debates should occur, because the possible outcomes will be severely restricted by the way in which the situation is described (Chomsky, 1987; Edwards, 1996; Hall, 1982; Latour, 1987).

In order for a particular representation of a phenomenon to gain dominance, alternatives must be downgraded and marginalized. Once a particular representation becomes dominant and issues are debated within the acceptable terms, the underlying assumptions become instilled as sacred truths, rather than human constructs (Chomsky, 1987; Edwards, 1996; Hall, 1982; Latour, 1987). Accordingly, quantified representations, such as budgets and cost-benefit analysis, presuppose an unequal distribution of wealth in society. Hence, the more issues of resource allocations, equity and other related matters are addressed through these quantitative techniques, the more existing power relations are rationalized by making the unequal distribution of wealth which sustains them appear to be inevitable and, hence, beyond the realm of possible change.

However, rationalizing existing power relations is only one consequence of quantified representations. Budgets and cost-benefit analysis have also succeeded in transforming the political into a technical zone of control and calculation by forcing many issues to be discussed in an abstract, scientific discourse ostensibly devoid of subjective content. This has benefited the politician, in particular the bureaucrat, by making the decision making process appear to be an objective mechanism beyond the influence of individual human beings (Covaleski and Dirsmith, 1988; Porter, 1995; Rose, 1991). Porter (1995, p. 8) notes that

> the appeal of numbers is especially compelling to bureaucratic officials who lack the mandate of a popular election or divine right. Arbitrariness and bias are the most usual grounds upon which such officials are criticized. A decision made by numbers (or by explicit rules of some other sort) has at least the appearance of being fair and impersonal. . . . Quantification is a way of making decisions without seeming to decide. Objectivity lends authority to officials who have very little of their own.

In addition, by representing a phenomenon through numbers, knowledge can be lifted up and separated from its local context, equating diverse occurrences of similar events and, thus, minimizing the need for intimate knowledge of each situation (Porter, 1995). As a result, commodities can be bought and sold by traders who have no knowledge of agriculture, production processes can be managed by people who have never physically engaged in the activity, and weapon decisions can be made by people with minimal knowledge of war. However, not only do numbers allow administrators, bureaucrats, traders and others to equate and manage disparate events from great distance, they also simultaneously create new things (Porter, 1994a, 1995). Quantitative techniques work best if the world they aim to describe can be remade in their image (Porter, 1995). Thus, statistics can describe our social reality, in part, because statistics help to create it (Porter, 1994b).

Discourses help shape behavior by limiting visibilities and, therefore, the range of possible actions. Hence, a transformation in how a phenomenon is represented can drastically alter the phenomenon itself. This was clearly demonstrated with the way in which McNamara was able to enact profound political changes in the defense arena and normalize the preparation for nuclear war by enforcing PPB as the only acceptable means for discussing the acquisition process.

MCNAMARA APPOINTED AS SECRETARY OF DEFENSE

When John F. Kennedy was elected President of the United States in 1960 there was strong political clamor for a Secretary of Defense who would be able to realize the unity amongst the Armed Forces that the creation of the DOD in 1947 was supposed, but failed, to achieve. Kennedy believed that he found such a person in Robert S. McNamara (Stubbing, 1986). McNamara, the first non-family member to become president of the Ford Motor Company, came from a new breed of corporate executives that rose to power during the 1950s. These were men who had not grown up in the business, who were not part of the family but who were modern, well-educated technicians who prided themselves that they were not tied to the past but brought the most progressive analytical devices to modern business, who used computers to understand the customers and statistics to break down costs and production. Men who had mastered the art of isolating the end oriented actions of business from (by definition) irrational norms, such as tradition or family loyalty, by assessing business performance through the use of quantifiable measures. This masked the impact of their decisions on others and, thus, increased their efficacy by preventing them from confronting the ethical implications of their acts (Bauman, 1989).

There were several reasons why the position of Secretary of Defense needed to be filled by a technocrat at this point in time. First, the Eisenhower Administration had relied exclusively upon the doctrine of "massive retaliation" to ostensibly deter communist aggression. In order to make the threat of massive retaliation viable, the Eisenhower Administration engaged in a huge build-up of nuclear weapons (Bottome, 1986; Kaplan, 1983; Raskin, 1970, 1979). Second, while Eisenhower imposed limits on how much the Armed Forces could spend by establishing budget ceilings, once the funds were allocated the Armed Forces were virtually free to spend the money in any way they chose (Kaufmann, 1964; Raskin, 1979). The combination of an exclusive reliance on nuclear weapons for defense and a laissez-faire management style resulted in the Armed Forces vigorously competing with one another to get a larger portion of the strategic mission (Kaufmann, 1964; Murdock, 1974). This arms race amongst the Armed Forces in the U.S. produced a proliferation of weapon systems and a dramatic shift of all the services to high tech weaponry (Armacost, 1969; Canan, 1975; Markusen and Yudken, 1992). However, the human beings who were supposedly in charge of the technological transformations taking place in weaponry during this time period could not keep pace with the rapid rate of change. Reasons, rationales and strategies were lagging behind technological innovations (Canan, 1975). According to Dr. Wiesner, Special Assistant to the President for Science and Technology from 1961 to 1964:

> The dizzying pace of change (during the 1950s) was very disorienting both for the professional strategists and for the civilian leadership in the Executive Branch of the government and the Congress. Even the academic panelists who studied strategic problems and journalists interested in national security affairs could not keep up with the rapidly evolving situation.
>
> (quoted in Canan, 1975, pp. 221–222)

Thus, by the end of the 1950s, technological innovations in nuclear warfare were outstripping human control and creating an extremely dangerous and volatile situation. Further, by 1959, 64% of Americans considered nuclear war to be the nation's most urgent problem (Boyer, 1985, p. 355). This fear of nuclear war was fuelled by a series of historical events. In September 1949, the Soviet Union exploded their first atomic bomb, destroying the U.S.'s atomic monopoly. This was followed by the Executive decision to develop and produce the hydrogen bomb, making the potential to destroy the world an actuality. In addition, intercontinental ballistic missiles and the digital computer became operational realities during the 1950s, creating the conditions that made it possible to kill millions by simply pushing a button. Feeding the nuclear anxieties was a heavy governmental emphasis on civil defense, while the atmospheric testing of nuclear weapons created a fallout scare (Boyer, 1984, 1985; Canan, 1975; Tyler May, 1989). Boyer (1984, p. 842) notes that

> the cultural ethos of the 1950s and early 1960s, held that the nuclear arms race was a fundamentally irrational, unstable, and highly danger-ous process that might at any time escape from control through human error, technical malfunction (the *Fail-Safe* syndrome), or a fateful esca-lation by a nuclear power facing defeat in a non-nuclear conflict.

Hence, the extreme dangers associated with fallible human beings possess-ing an infallible weapon were the primary emphasis in cultural and social representations of nuclear weapons during the 1950s. Given the deadliness of nuclear weapons and the population's profound fear of them, a situation in which technological innovations were outstripping human control could not be tolerated for long. If the Cold War was to maintain a sense of legitimacy, an administrative structure that lent an air of rationality and logic to the weapons acquisition process and, hence, gave the appearance that the arms race could be managed, and in so doing made less dangerous and more sane, was essen-tial. Thus, when Kennedy looked for a Secretary of Defense he did not seek an individual who managed by instincts, but rather one who could impose organizational rationality on "nuclear weapons, thermonuclear weapons, napalm, millions of men, rifles, chemical weapons, pencils, missiles, promo-tions, counterforce, aircraft carriers, anthrax virus and counter-insurgency" (Raskin, 1970, p. 66). In other words, he sought "a supreme accountant" and found one in Robert S. McNamara (Halberstam, 1992, p. 227).

MCNAMARA AND THE RAND CORPORATION

One of the preconditions McNamara set before accepting the offer from Kennedy was that he could choose his own subordinates (McNamara, 1996). In his search for someone to fulfil the position of Pentagon Comptrol-ler, several people mentioned Charles Hitch, the director of the economics division at RAND. RAND, a private think tank composed predominantly of civilian military strategists, was created shortly after World War II to help the Armed Forces incorporate nuclear weapons into their tactical plans (Kaplan, 1983).

Nuclear weapons not only changed the destructiveness of war but the very nature of war itself. Previous inventions were limited enough in scope to allow for timely adaptations by opponents. However, if atom bombs were used in a war the destruction would be so immediate that there would be no time to adjust (Herkin, 1987; Kaplan, 1983). Thus, nuclear weapons minimized the value of combat experience for planning future war fighting scenarios and for the first time in U.S. history the field of military strategy was opened to non-soldiers (Trachtenberg, 1991). As a result, a new breed of military planners, civilian strategists who were better versed in economics and mathematics than military expertise, engaged in inventing a new type of warfare, an intellectual, paper war (Kaufmann, 1964). Given that nuclear war was unencumbered by empirics, these strategists did not have to conform their thinking with reality but could instead help shape the new reality of living with the bomb (Sherwin, 1982).

It was two RAND scientists, Merrill Flood and Melvin Dresher, who, with the aid of Von Neumann and Morgentern's theory of games, devised a game entitled the Prisoner's Dilemma, which became the primary vehicle by which the nuclear arms race between the United States and the Soviet Union was rationalized (Kaplan, 1983; Poundstone, 1992). The Prisoner's Dilemma showed that both the U.S. and the U.S.S.R. would be better off if they agreed to a treaty to stop building nuclear armaments. However, this move required trust, and because the enemy might cheat by building more weapons and go onto win, continuing to compete was the only solution (Kaplan, 1983).

Thus, game theory helped to rationalize and normalize the Cold War by elevating distrust and the fostering of international tensions to truisms, making the arms race appear to be an inevitable consequence of human nature. Further, game theory assisted with providing the abstract discourse by which "thinking about the unthinkable" became possible. Game theory accomplished this by transforming nuclear war into a problem of arithmetic, calculus and probability, which made the danger seem so theoretical and abstruse as to become almost non-existent (Boyer, 1984; Kaplan, 1983). Plus, in game theory, the weapons themselves are the primary referent point (Cohn, 1987; Schell, 1982). This is illustrated below in Congressional testimony by RAND analyst Dr. Albert Wohlstetter regarding the Anti-Ballistic Missile System (ABM), in which his only concern was whether or not the ABM would protect the primary land-based ballistic missile at the time, the MINUTEMAN.

> My remarks, however, center, so far as the second strike function of ABM is concerned, on the problem of protecting MINUTEMAN. . . .
>
> I have tried with some effort to reconstruct various numerical proofs recently presented or distributed to the Congress that purport to show our MINUTEMAN will be quite safe without extra protection. . . .
>
> This seems to me a sound way to supplement the protection of the MINUTEMAN in a period when we can expect it to be endangered. . . .
>
> (Wohlstetter, 1969, pp. 668–670)

Hence, "strategic theory seems to have taken on a weird life of its own, in which the weapons are pictured as having their own quarrel to settle, irrespective of mere human purposes" (Schell, 1982, p. 32). By making the weapons the focus of attention, the war planners were able to elevate themselves to a position of user and actor, not victim, enhancing their ability to think about the unthinkable (Cohn, 1987; Nash, 1980). Thus, during the 1950s, as a result of the success of game theory, the RAND strategists gained considerable credibility as experts on strategic issues.

In order to decide whether or not to offer Hitch the position of Pentagon Controller, McNamara read Hitch and McKean's book, *The Economics of Defense in the Nuclear Age,* and became immediately enamored with Hitch's ideas (Kaplan, 1983). According to Kaplan (1983, p. 252):

> Here was someone who was doing the same sort of thing that McNamara had done during the war—applying principles of microeconomics, operations research and statistical analysis to defense issues— but doing it on a much broader scale, covering the whole gamut of national security, including comparing and choosing weapons systems, restructuring the defense budget, formulating military strategy.

RAND had been employing the techniques of systems analysis for nearly a decade in its efforts to relate the Air Force's military needs to budget constraints (Hitch, 1969; Novick, 1969; Sanders, 1973).[1] As early as 1949, the analysts at RAND recognized the economic implications of the Cold War and as a result believed that the traditional military characteristics for measuring a weapon system's effectiveness—for example, for aircraft, higher, faster and more payload capacity—were no longer adequate. Rather, the drain a weapon system placed on the U.S. economy as well as the enemy's reaction to it had to be considered when assessing the desirability of additional armament (Novick, 1969). Thus, systems analysis elevated the economics of defense to a position of primacy in the weapon acquisition process and, as a result, was a method for redefining the defense problem in such a way that the criteria of rational economic choice, rather than professional military judgement, applied.

After accepting the job of Pentagon Comptroller, Hitch brought with him to the Pentagon several RAND analysts including Alain Enthoven, who would become the first Assistant Secretary of Defense for Systems Analysis in 1964, and Henry Rowan, who became Deputy Assistant Secretary of Defense for International Affairs (Digby, 1989). The marriage of the RAND Corporation to the Office of the Secretary of Defense (OSD) insured that a "rational organizational discourse" would prevail over decision making in the civilian sector of the DOD (Murdock, 1974). The problem faced by McNamara was how to thrust this discourse on the Armed Forces; budgeting became the strategic tool by which he would accomplish this.

PLANNING, PROGRAMMING AND BUDGETING

McNamara believed that there were two styles to management; a passive method in which the chief administrator played a judiciary role, and an active approach in which the chief administrator provided effective leadership (Kaufmann, 1964; Stubbing, 1986). McNamara concluded that in order to achieve the goal set for him by President Kennedy, "security for the nation at the lowest possible cost", he would have to employ the latter strategy in managing the DOD (McNamara, 1996, p. 23). Upon assuming his responsibilities as Secretary of Defense, McNamara immediately recognized the power inherent in dominating the budget process and quickly moved to establish himself as "czar" in this arena by operationalizing PPB (Sanders, 1973; Schelling, 1971; Stubbing, 1986). Schelling (1971, p. 386) notes that

> some people have more instinct than others, or better training than others, for using the purse strings as a technique of management and a source of authority; but almost anyone concerned with administration sooner or later discovers that control of budgetary requests and disbursements is a powerful source of more general control.

Prior to McNamara, the military planning and budgeting processes were performed separately with plans expressed in terms of outputs, namely missions, weapon systems and forces, and budgets expressed in terms of inputs, including personnel, operations, maintenance and construction (Enthoven, 1963; Murdock, 1974). With the budgeting and planning processes being separated, management did not have the information needed to determine the financial consequences of alternative plans and, hence, could not conclude which weapon systems and forces would provide the most efficient means of carrying out a particular mission (Testimony of Hitch, U.S. Senate, 1961). PPB overcame this problem by restating the budget in terms of outputs and, therefore, allowed the costs of alternative methods of accomplishing various tasks to be compared, for example, different combinations of weapons systems and forces (Testimony of Hitch, U.S. Senate, 1961). According to Enthoven (1963, pp. 416–417):

> The key to the Programming System is decision making by program elements and major programs; this is, by the outputs of the Department rather than by the inputs. A program element is an integrated activity combining men, equipment, and installations whose effectiveness can be related to our national security policy objectives. The list included B-52 wings, infantry battalions, and combatant ships, taken together with all the equipment, men, installations, and supplies required to make them an effective military force. The program elements are assembled into major programs which contain inter-related elements which closely complement each other or are close substitutes for each other

and which must therefore be considered together in arriving at top-level decisions.

For example, on June 1, 1961, the program package for the Central War Offensive Forces, whose mission was to deter Soviet aggression through the threat of nuclear war, contained the following program elements: Aircraft forces, such as B-52 and B-58; Missile forces, land-based, prominent examples of which were ATLAS and MINUTEMAN; Missiles, sea-based, the Polaris Submarines and FBM submarines; Command, control and communication; Headquarters and command support (Testimony of Hitch, U.S. Senate, 1961, p. 1039). The alternative missile basing systems, to a certain degree, are substitutes for one another. Thus, according to the logic of PPB, the number of B-52s acquired should depend upon the number of Polaris submarines purchased, as well as the number of MINUTE-MAN procured, with the greatest emphasis placed on the weapon system which accomplished the strategic mission in the most cost-effective manner (Testimony of McNamara, U.S. Senate, 1961). Hence, PPB rationalized the weapons acquisition process by articulating missions for the DOD, proposing alternative force structures for these missions, and choosing among the alternatives based on a specified objective: cost-effectiveness. The Armed Services were required to prepare their budget requests using PPB beginning with the 1963 fiscal year defense budget and each year thereafter.

ANALYSIS VERSUS MILITARY EXPERTISE

As stated previously, all knowledge is socially and historically determined. Hence, in order for one representation of an event to be regularly used, other significations must be marginalized and downgraded. PPB privileged rationality and analysis over military expertise as a means for knowing defense and, in so doing, made a radical break from the past.

> Under the postwar organization of the military establishment the Secretary of Defense presumably had the authority to establish a strategic concept and require agreement on force size and composition. But he labored under several severe handicaps. He lacked any independent basis on which to assess what the Services were demanding. And, in the American tradition, he tended to assume that it was impossible for him to understand, much less learn, the art of military planning. That was a mystery that could only be performed by the military staffs themselves. To argue with veteran commanders in these circumstances seemed presumptuous and dangerous. Military judgement was sacrosanct.
>
> (Kaufmann, 1964)

In order for McNamara to privilege his way of knowing defense over the military's, that is, using PPB, the system analysts had to discredit the pre-conceived notion that military experience alone provided the background for understanding security matters. In order to do so, the systems analysts argued that because the Cold War required the threatened use of a weapon for which there was no combat experience, Cold War preparedness problems could only be addressed by employing abstract, analytical models, and it was the systems analysts, not the military, that maintained the expertise in this realm (Enthoven and Smith, 1980; Kaplan, 1983). Further, given that the purpose of innovations in military technologies was to deter wars by rendering the opponent's weaponry obsolete, war was increasingly becoming a process of managing technological change. The system analysts argued that technological change could be more effectively managed by the careful analysis inherent in PPB rather than the heuristic judgement of the military commanders (Enthoven and Smith, 1980; Palmer, 1978).

In addition, the system analysts elevated rationality and analysis over military expertise by arguing that decisions based on authority, experience or simple intuition lacked rigour and precision because the precepts underlying the choice were unexamined and the process by which the data was linked to the decision was not explicated (Palmer, 1978). Thus, governmental actions predicated on authority and intuition were classified by the systems analysts as "uninformed, arbitrary, and based on unenlightened opinion" (Rowen, 1969, p. 613). The systems analysts, however, used the scientific method to arrive at conclusions. The benefits of the scientific method were explicated by Enthoven (1969, p. 567) while testifying before the U.S. Senate as follows:

> First, the method of science is an open, explicit, verifiable, self-correcting process. It combines logic and empirical evidence. The method and tradition of science require that scientific results be openly arrived at in such a way that any other scientist can retrace the same steps and get the same result. Applying this to weapon systems and to strategy would require that all calculations, assumptions, empirical data, and judgements be described in the analysis in such a way that they can be subject to checking, testing, criticism, debate, discussion, and possible refutation. . . . Second, scientific method is objective. Although personalities doubtless play an important part in the life of the Physics profession, the science itself does not depend upon personalities or vested interest.

The systems analysts further discredited military expertise by arguing that the Armed Forces were incapable of creating an efficient defense establishment because their decisions were biased by parochialism. Given that the systems analysts were not bound by a particular service tradition, they perceived themselves as possessing the objectivity needed to perform the analysis that would lead to a cost-effective defense (Enthoven and Smith, 1980; Hitch and McKean, 1963).

The system analysts, having come from RAND, were aware of how a new class of civilian strategists had been empowered by creating a new type of warfare based on abstract, analytical games. The system analysts attempted to reproduce this power within the DOD itself by elevating their way of knowing defense, for example, abstract analysis, to a position of privilege. By changing the discourse, the system analysts changed visibilities in defense in such a way that their approach appeared to be unquestionably reasonable and sound. Thus, initially Congress overwhelmingly approved of PPB, bestowing compliments on McNamara as in the following exchanges:

THE CHAIRMAN: Mr. Secretary, I want to complement you again for your splendid statement. You have made such an outstanding statement, so logical, so clear . . . (House of Representatives, 1962a, p. 3185).

MR. PHILBIN: First, I would like to complement you very much on that fine statement that you made. . . . I think it is really unprecedented. I have never seen one quite like it. Both in scope and quality it was really superb (House of Representatives, 1962a, pp. 3190–3191).

MR. PRICE: Mr. Secretary, I not only want to join my colleagues in complimenting you on your fine presentation made here, but I also want to compliment you and commend you for the forthright and commendable manner in which you have answered your questions this morning, indicating an amazing grasp of this Defense Establishment setup, in just the period of 1 year. In my opinion, you must be some kind of a human IBM machine. I don't know how you do it (House of Representatives, 1962a, p. 3195).

However, once the political ramifications of PPB, as discussed in the following section, became apparent, Congress's praise was converted into apprehension. For example, during the Senate hearings on PPB in 1967, Senator Jackson debunked the ostensible objectivity of systems analysis by stating, "Cost-utility analysis can be used as easily to justify a decision as to make a sensible choice. It can be employed as a weapon to try to overwhelm and beat down other viewpoints" (U.S. Senate, 1967b, p. 220). Further, the fact that the data and analysis used by McNamara to make decisions was considered proprietary information, and therefore not accessible to

Congress, became an issue of concern. The Initial Memorandum for the Senate hearings on PPB stated that

> Congress, too, may not welcome all the implications of PPBS. The experience to date does not suggest that the Department of Defense is likely to place before Congressional committees the analyses of costs and benefits of competing policies and programs on which the Department based its own choices. Without such comparisons, however, Congress will be in the dark about the reasons for selecting this policy over that.
>
> (U.S. Senate, 1967a, pp. 15–16)

Given that Congress did not have access to the data used by McNamara to make decisions, it was difficult for members to argue with the immanently rational results of PPB. As illustrated by the following dialogue, which took place between Representative Sikes and McNamara, regarding the MINUTEMAN versus the POLARIS, the logical forcefulness of PPB lent an air of scientific certainty to McNamara's choices, making it problematic for others to challenge him:

> MR. SIKES: You recommend substantially more MINUTEMAN and comparatively fewer POLARIS submarines. . . . What were the guidelines that caused you to use this level?
>
> SECRETARY MCNAMARA: The factors determining the mix of POLARIS and MINUTEMAN were: (a) the requirements for an invulnerable force and the quantity of such a force required to achieve certain units of target destruction; and (b) the relative costs of achieving that force.
>
> Now POLARIS is a bit more expensive than the MINUTEMAN.
>
> MR. SIKES: Is cost the basic difference? . . . Is that the principal reason for selecting the MINUTEMAN?
>
> SECRETARY MCNAMARA: No. If there were no cost differential then I think we would probably select more POLARIS because it is probably at least in the short run more invulnerable than MINUTEMAN. But there is a cost difference and therefore it seems wise to select as many MINUTEMAN as possible in relation to the requirement for invulnerability and for a force of a given size, and that was the sequence of logic through which we went and it eventually resulted in these conclusions (U.S. House of Representatives, 1962b, pp. 24–25).

In addition, the Armed Forces greatly resented the intrusion of systems analysts into military planning (Kaplan, 1983; Murdock, 1974; Sanders, 1973).

In one case, in the U.S. Naval Institute Proceedings of 1964, an active duty naval officer felt compelled to express his concerns regarding the systems analysts' rise to power:

> Young civilian intellectuals, with little or no experience in war or lead-ing men, with no significant non-academic accomplishments in any area, with no first-hand knowledge of what ships, aircraft and armies (along with their associated weapons and support) are like, with no real appreciation of the operational environment, are largely replacing pro-fessional military officers as the primary source of advice on the great defense decisions.
>
> (quoted in Sanders, 1973, p. 150)

Hence, even though the Kennedy Administration greatly increased the defense budget, this did little to appease the military's resentment at being stripped of the power to allocate their own funds. Thus, the service's evasion of OSD policy remained a distinct possibility throughout the 1960s and was taken into consideration by the systems analysts when making recommen-dations (Murdock, 1974; Schlesinger, 1974).[2]

PPB AND THE CENTRALIZATION OF POWER

Prior to McNamara, the military planning and budgeting processes were performed separately. As a result, the information needed to determine the financial consequences of alternative plans was not available. PPB overcame this problem by combining planning with budgeting. While the integration of planning and budgeting was immanently reasonable, it moved the conflict between military need and budgetary constraint from Congressional com-mittee to the DOD itself (Joseph, 1981; Palmer, 1978). This exacerbated the trend that had started with the establishment of the National Security State in 1947 towards centralizing power within the Executive branch of the government and led one scholar to express the fear that PPB contained a "contempt for democratic values and processes" (Mosher, 1969, p. 590).[3]

However, shifting power away from Congress towards the Executive branch of the government was not the only political ramification of PPB; it also influenced the balance of power in the DOD itself (Joseph, 1981; Mosher, 1969; Murdock, 1974; Palmer, 1978; Sanders, 1973; Schelling, 1971). Under PPB, military requests were evaluated in terms of function, rather than the Armed Service putting forth the appeal, allowing similar purpose weapon sys-tems to be compared (Congress and the Nation, 1969). Hitch explained that

> a new program, like the POLARIS in the strategic offensive area, would be submitted by the service in the strategic offensive package. In the review it would tend to be competing directly not with other Navy

programs, but with the other means of carrying out the strategic offensive mission.

It would not be compared with the antisubmarine warfare activities of the Navy; rather it would be compared with other strategic systems such as Air Force bombers and land-based missiles.

(U.S. Senate, 1961, p. 1013)

With decision making under PPB based on comparisons which spanned traditional service lines, the final budget could only be put together by the Secretary of Defense (Kaufmann, 1964; Wildavsky, 1967). Thus, as Wildavsky (1967, p. 390) notes in relation to PPB, "A more useful tool for increasing [a chief executive's] power to control decisions vis-a-vis his subordinates would be hard to find". Given that PPB shifted power over resource allocations to the highest level in the organization, it allowed McNamara to gain control over the Armed Forces through funding decisions.

However, while centralization of power was endemic to the techniques of PPB, PPB also changed the balance of power between the Armed Services and the OSD by influencing the organizational discourse. McNamara insisted that the Armed Services base their force structure planning on systematic analysis. Not only did he withhold the ultimate yes or no decision from the military but, in addition, he dictated to the Armed Services the type of information that would serve as the basis for his decision (Murdock, 1974). Thus, McNamara forced the military to argue their case on his terms, with his language and his style of decision making (Sanders, 1973). As a result, throughout the 1960s, defense debates increasingly became clothed in the language and style of system analysis (Business Week, 1969; Gross, 1971; Sanders, 1973; Wildavsky, 1967). Art (1968, pp. 161–162) notes that

> the revolutionary manner in which McNamara made his decisions (revolutionary, that is for the Defense Department), transformed the "expert" career bureaucrat into the "novice" and the "inexperienced" political appointee into the "professional." By demanding that decisions be made through a cost-effectiveness analysis, McNamara freed himself from the secretary's usual dependence on the experience and knowledge of the military officer and the career civil servant. By demanding something that only he and his small personal staff possessed the experience and competence to do, McNamara declared insufficient or invalid, or both, the customary criteria for making decisions and the traditional grounds for justifying them.

Outcomes will be restricted by the way in which the situation is described. By forcing the services to defend their budget requests through cost-benefit analysis, McNamara ensured that his preferred solution, the most analytically cost-effective, would prevail. Thus, through introducing PPB, McNamara was able to prescribe the acceptable discourse for defense decision making and in so doing dictate the decisions. The centralizing tendency of PPB was one of the major concerns voiced by Congress during the PPB hearings in 1967. For example, the Initial Memorandum for the hearings stated:

> A major goal of PPB, according to Charles Hitch, was to enable the Secretary of Defense to run his Department on a unified basis, and PPB has meant a greater centralization of decision-making and control. A consequence, whether intended or not, is that it may be more difficult for voices of doubt and dissent at lower levels to make themselves heard at high levels. It means, among other things, less bargaining between OSD and the service departments and the services. This in turn makes it easier for OSD to ignore or simply not to hear things it would rather not hear—other beliefs about technological change, different estimates of costs and gains, conflicting views of the contingencies and uncertainties. Defense programs may therefore be more nearly tailored to one estimate of the future and to one cost-benefit calculus than in a period when decision making was less centralized.
>
> (U.S. Senate, 1967a, p. 12)

The way in which PPB did stifle dissent and ignore conflicting points of view was evident, for example, in McNamara's decision to forego a nuclear powered aircraft carrier in favor of an oil-fuelled one. McNamara rationalized his decision by arguing that a nuclear powered carrier would cost one third to one half more to construct and operate than a conventionally powered carrier and that the operational benefits derived from nuclear power did not justify the higher costs (House of Representatives, 1962b, p. 67). However, the systems analysis upon which McNamara based his decision relied only upon variables that could be quantified. As the following Congressional testimony by Vice Admiral H.G. Rickover illustrates, it is frequently the non-quantifiable variables that are the most important:

> In the cost-effectiveness studies performed by the analysts, they compute numerical values for the effectiveness of nuclear power. However, before they make the calculation, they make certain simplifying assumptions in order to be able to do the arithmetic. These assumptions just happen to eliminate from consideration the principal military reasons for wanting nuclear power in the first place. The analysts generally start their calculations with the assumptions that oil for the conventional ships is readily available whenever and where-ever it is needed, and that the logistic support forces will not be subject to attack.
>
> Now, if the Navy could be assured that they would not be asked to perform missions where it would be difficult to get oil to our ships, there would be less need for nuclear propulsion. However, the Navy cannot afford to count on such a euphoric situation, since the history of war is replete with examples of major military defeats that were brought

about by the inability of military forces to maintain a supply of propulsion fuel to the forces in combat.

(Rickover, 1969, p. 601)

PPB radically changed the discourse of defense acquisition and in so doing changed the process itself. Prior to McNamara, defense acquisitions were justified based on military necessity. PPB completely disabled this rationalization and, thus, stifled the Armed Forces' ability to use their asymmetric information gained through experience as a source of power. By forcing the services to justify their requests using a technique which only McNamara and his staff of systems analysts possessed the expertise to employ, McNamara was able to define what was relevant and important in such a way that he gained the information advantage and, hence, control of the process.

TAMING THE UNTAMABLE

By the end of the 1950s technological developments in nuclear weapons, which were outstripping human control, meant that the innovative process needed to be slowed down if the arms race with the Soviet Union was to retain its legitimacy. PPB provided a mechanism by which this could be accomplished in that its ostensible purpose was to rationalize defense expenditures by aligning technological developments with stated military needs. Hence, only advancements in weaponry that sensibly fitted into the missions of the DOD would be pursued. However, rejecting weapon systems that did not logically fit into a mission was not the only way PPB slowed down nuclear developments. According to Hitch (1969, p. 578), "The function of systems analysis is to get dollars into the calculations at an earlier stage—into the planning process, into the evaluation of alternative ways of achieving a military objective". Getting costs into the analysis at an early stage was a powerful tool for decelerating the arms race, for once the need, cost and effectiveness of each proposed weapon system were carefully examined and compared with alternatives, certain technologies would not make it through (Murdock, 1974; Sanders, 1973).

Forcing dollars to be considered at an early point in the decision making process not only decelerated the arms race, it also elevated the economics of defense to a position of superiority. This was a radical change for the DOD because prior to McNamara military officers had succeeded in arguing that dollars did not matter when the survival of the Nation was at stake. Their appeals to Congress for funding were primarily emotive with their justifications relying purely on military necessity (Fitzgerald, 1972; Kaufmann, 1964; Sanders, 1973; Sapolsky, 1972). However, an acquisition process guided by conflict and bargaining showed the extent to which interested human beings participated in decision making. According to the logic of game theory, the arms race was not controlled by fallible human beings but by technical, non-partisan forces inherent in nature. The acquisition process had to be made to appear to be guided by these same impartial forces in order for the physical preparation for Armageddon to be sustained by the game theoretic justification.

By elevating the economics of defense to a position of superiority, PPB ensured that the acquisition process would be discussed within the rhetoric of rational economic choice. In rational economic choice models, the structural features of an economy, notably supply and demand, are endowed with life. Thus, within this perspective, it is the characteristics of an economy, not humans, that determine what will be produced and what will not. Hence, PPB made humans appear to be superfluous to the weapons acquisition process by fetishizing policy objectives, for example Mutually Assured Destruction or MAD, making it seem as if weapon systems were chosen by national goals, not interested human beings. The extent to which PPB fetishized policy objectives and made the arms race appear to be free from human interest is illustrated in the following Congressional testimony by Enthoven in which he laid out the "objective" criteria by which U.S. strategic forces were established:

> Our basic policy objectives and Soviet strategic nuclear capabilities are the main factors that determine the size and kind of forces we should have. Many criteria are available for measuring the ability of our forces to meet the need established by these two factors. We could use megatonnage, payload, or simply numbers of delivery systems. However, these are input measures which tell us what we have, not what we can do.
>
> We prefer to concentrate on outputs to measure effectiveness. To determine how well our strategic offensive forces will achieve their objectives, we must know their ability to destroy particular kinds of targets. We then relate this target destruction capability to our basic objectives in order to measure the adequacy of our forces.
>
> (U.S. Senate, 1968a, p. 120)

Thus, PPB made it appear as if defense questions could be subsumed under an all-purpose military science in which the choice variables were given by nature and the effects of alternatives could be stated with certainty. Thus, choosing the appropriate nuclear weapons became a matter of routine calculation. This allowed McNamara to discuss nuclear weapons in a discourse that was free of emotions or human concerns. Just as game theory converted nuclear war into a problem of arithmetic, calculus and probability, PPB converted the choice of nuclear weapons into the same. This is illustrated by McNamara's cool and calculated description of how strategic retaliatory forces were chosen:

> In contrast to most other military requirements, the requirement for strategic retaliatory forces lends itself rather well to reasonably precise

calculation. A major mission of these forces is to deter war by their capability to destroy the enemy's war making capabilities. With the kinds of weapons available to us, this task presents a problem of reasonably finite dimensions, which are measurable in terms of the number and type of targets or aiming points which must be destroyed and the number and types of weapon delivery systems required to do the job under various sets of conditions.

The first step in such a calculation is to determine the number, types and locations of the aiming points in the target system.

The second step is to determine the numbers and explosive yields of weapons which must be delivered on the aiming points to insure the destruction or substantial destruction of the target system.

The third step involves a determination of the size and character of the forces best suited to deliver these weapons. . . .

Clearly, each of these crucial factors involves various degrees of uncertainty. But these uncertainties are not completely unmanageable. By postulating various sets of assumptions, ranging from optimistic to pessimistic, it is possible to introduce into our calculations reasonable allowances for these uncertainties.

(House of Representatives, 1962a,
pp. 3171–3172)

In the U.S., the fear of nuclear weapons culminated during the Cuban Missile Crisis of 1962 and started ebbing thereafter, remaining fairly dormant until the 1980s. Several reasons have been suggested as to why this occurred, including the Limited Test Ban Treaty of 1963, which literally took nuclear weapons underground and out of sight, the promotion and acceptance of the "peaceful atom", and the eruption of a hot war in Vietnam. However, the ebbing of fear has also been attributed to the gradual adaptation of the world to nuclear weapons, as well as the sense that the matter was being taken care of by reliable experts (Boyer, 1984; Lifton and Markusen, 1990). The abstract, technically rational discourse of PPB contributed to the latter.

THE DECEPTIONS OF PPB

While PPB contributed to normalizing nuclear war by converting the arms race into a routine and mundane resource allocation problem, such a frame of reference distorted visibilities and this created even more internal inconsistencies in the logic of national defense. PPB presupposed and, therefore, eliminated from critical appraisal the assumption that security could be achieved by perfecting the art of killing. However, this occurred at exactly the same time that the Cuban Missile Crisis and the Bay of Pigs demonstrated that military might was not a successful means for achieving geopolitical goals (Barnet, 1972; Lifton and Falk, 1982). Thus, PPB assisted with lending militarism credibility at a point in time when its ineffectiveness was becoming apparent and, hence, should have been deeply questioned.

Further, PPB assumed that the inefficient allocation of resources was the primary problem plaguing the defense establishment. However, given the fact that by 1961 the U.S. possessed enough nuclear weapons to destroy the world several times over, it is questionable how improving efficiency would benefit humankind. Frederick Scherer (1964, p. ix), one of the first academicians to do an analysis of weapons acquisition process, gave particular emphasis to the goal of efficiency:

> I am troubled by a basic policy premise . . . that efficiency is a desirable objective in the conduct of advanced weapons development and production programs. It is by no means certain that this is true. The weapons acquisition process may be too efficient already. To be sure, there are gross inefficiencies. But despite them, the process has given mankind all too much power for its own annihilation. One might justify efficiency measures in the hope that freed resources could be devoted to education, exploration of the universe, technical aid to emerging nations, urban redevelopment, etc. Given the pervasive pressures for added arms spending, however, it seems likely that efficiency gains would lead more to increases in our already formidable arsenal than to the reallocation of resources into applications yielding greater social benefit.

In addition, PPB's emphasis on efficiency distracted attention away from other possible goals for the DOD (Knorr, 1969; Murdock, 1974; Schlesinger, 1974). As one concerned scholar would ask, could not the minimization of military conflict or the loss of human life in the event of conflict be as important objectives as efficiency for defense (Knorr, 1969, p. 582)? Further, given that cost-effectiveness studies required all variables to be quantified when performing the analysis, stress was placed on the tangible characteristics of a weapon system, including firepower, vulnerability and survivability (Knorr, 1969; Murdock, 1974; Palmer, 1978; Schlesinger, 1974). As a result, intangible factors, such as the way human beings are impacted by or impact the system, were ignored. Unfortunately, in the case of the M-16 rifle used in the Vietnam War, PPB's narrow focus on efficiency and quantification actually led to an increase in the loss of human life (Gibson, 1986). In attempting to explain the disaster of the M-16, Senator Mundt referred to how

> the flap [about the M-16] developed from the fact that after we got the new rifle and found we had a lot of cartridges that wouldn't fit into the rifle, and we had a lot of powder that hadn't been used from another war, we would put the powder in these bullets, and save a lot of money, which was a perfect example of how a cost analysis system would save

a lot of money. There was only one thing, that something in the powder was too sticky and it clogged up the rifle, until they got a new rifle cleaning system. Many lives were lost, of course.

But here is a case where a cost analysis could go wrong, whereas, perhaps, cranking in a lot more human elements, we should have said, 'Perhaps these rifles would be all right, but let's try them on the firing range at home with this old powder and see how they work.'

(U.S. Senate, 1968b, p. 353)

Further, in order to employ systems analysis to determine the most cost-effective defense, a particular conflict situation, whether guerrilla war, conventional war or nuclear war, had to be assumed. Yet, as Schlesinger (1974, p. 65) notes, "The typical fare of the present world struggle is not the expected wars, but rather the crises that erupt at times and in places where they are not anticipated. In Vietnam, U.S. forces have been deployed to deal with conflict situations other than those for which they were optimized". For instance, when selecting aircraft for the Air Force the systems analysts presupposed the use of nuclear weapons in a major conflict. This meant that the bombers in inventory during the 1960s were designed for nuclear delivery and, therefore, very expensive. Given that nuclear war would require few sorties, the anticipated losses due to attrition were bearable in terms of the cost of the bombers and the drain on the aircraft inventory. Hence, when the U.S. engaged itself in Vietnam, it needed to rely on expensive and vulnerable aircraft to fly repeated sorties against heavy ground fire. Attrition was higher than planned, resulting in greater costs and inventory drainage (Schlesinger, 1974). In other words, the most cost-effective weapons for the planned war were the least cost-effective for the actual war. Thus, in many situations, PPB failed to provide the best defense for the least cost.

Lastly, the instrumental rationality of systems analysis and PPB made Enthoven's equation of the economics of nuclear war with that of a multi-product firm appear reasonable. Using the thesis of diminishing marginal returns, Enthoven devised a cost-effective way to destroy the Soviet Union with nuclear weapons (Enthoven, 1963). His analysis for a cost-effective nuclear war proceeded as follows. First, it was determined that the Soviet Union would be sufficiently devastated if 30% of the population was killed and half of the industrial capacity demolished. Second, it was ascertained that this could be accomplished by destroying all the major cities in the U.S.S.R. Lastly, the precise amount of megatons necessary to accomplish this task was calculated as 400 megatons. Because the remaining cities and economic sites in the U.S.S.R. were dispersed, to kill an additional 25% of the population would require ten times as many bombs. In other words, if the megatons were doubled to 800, Soviet fatalities would only rise by ten percentage points and industrial capacity destroyed would only increase by three percentage points (Fallows, 1981; Kaplan, 1983; Testimony of

Enthoven, U.S. Senate, 1968a). Clearly, there were diminishing marginal returns to nuclear war and a cost-effective method for fighting them.

What was vastly ignored in this formulation was that once nuclear war began no one would be concerned about efficiency and it is highly unlikely that the dictates of rational economic choice models would be guiding human behavior. Rather, in the advent of nuclear war, chaos and insanity would most likely reign supreme. Schell (1982, p. 32) notes that

> the outbreak of nuclear hostilities in itself assumes the collapse of every usual restraint of reason and humanity. Once the mass killing of a nuclear holocaust had begun, the scruples, and even the reckonings of self-interest, that normally keep the actions of nations within certain bounds would by definition have been trampled down, and would probably offer little further protection for anybody. In the unimaginable mental and spiritual climate of the world at that point it is hard to imagine what force could be counted on to hold the world back from all-out destruction.

Further, the problem with nuclear weapons is that they keep throwing up surprises. One well-known example was how it took scientists more than a decade to realize why electrical equipment at atomic bomb test sites failed: nuclear weapons create an electromagnetic pulse which damages solid state circuitry (Schell, 1982). The implications of such a finding for the ability to command and control a nuclear war are devastating. As few as one to five high-altitude nuclear explosions could trigger an electromagnetic pulse strong enough to ruin the circuitry underlying the command and control system in the U.S., destroying the country's capacity to launch a counterattack. This command vulnerability has been one of the most significant problems to plague strategic thought, yet because it is not quantifiable it does not fit neatly into standard measures of the strategic balance and therefore has been ignored (Lifton and Falk, 1982; Ravetz, 1990; Steinbruner, 1981–1982).

It was not until the beginning of the 1980s that scientists started recognizing the possibility of a nuclear winter following nuclear war. Nuclear explosions would create fires which would release enormous amounts of smoke particles into the earth's atmosphere. These smoke particles would prevent the sun's rays from reaching the earth, cooling a large fraction of the northern hemisphere's land surfaces by more than ten degrees centigrade if nuclear war occurred in summer. In addition, it was estimated that 100 megatons might be sufficient to produce severe climatic effects, if the 100 megatons consisted of 1,000 individual 100-kiloton (about eight times the size of the Hiroshima bomb) bombs aimed at the 1,000 largest cities in the Northern Hemisphere. However, nuclear winter could be caused by even less than 100 megatons if the bombs were predominantly aimed at oil refineries, because of the huge amount of sooty smoke this would produce (Birks and Ehrlich, 1990). Hence, by the 1980s, scientific evidence demonstrated that Enthoven's cost-effective 400-megaton nuclear war, if conducted properly, could have destroyed the whole world, not just the Soviet Union.

CONCLUSION

In 1965 President Johnson ordered all departments within the Executive branch of the government to adopt PPB by fiscal year 1968 (Johnson, 1969). However, within a brief period of time PPB proved to be a complete failure (Jablonsky and Dirsmith, 1978; Wildavsky, 1978). In a paper examining the reasons for PPB rejection, Jablonsky and Dirsmith (1978) concluded that what was noticeably absent from their research was a discussion as to why a system so bound for failure was introduced to begin with. Calling PPB a toxic agent, they queried, "Maybe there is a valid reason why this type of toxic agent was found in the corpse in the first place" (Jablonsky and Dirsmith, 1978, p. 224).

This chapter has demonstrated that the political ramifications from an accounting technique can far exceed any ostensible gains in efficiency from the implementation. First, it has been demonstrated that McNamara used PPB to gain control of the Armed Forces by centralizing decision making in the OSD and by forcing the services to justify their budget requests using cost-benefit analysis. By prescribing the acceptable discourse for defense decision making, McNamara ensured that his preferred solution, the most analytically cost-effective, would prevail. It has also been shown that PPB assisted with rationalizing and normalizing the arms race by converting it into a series of problems to be solved. This contributed to masking the horrendous death and destruction that a nuclear war would create and thus made the preparations appear to be "the normal motions of normal men, not the mass compulsions of people bent on total death" (Mumford, 1946, p. 5). Further, the scientific discourse of PPB gave the impression that the acquisition process was under the control of experts and this helped to alleviate the U.S. population's fear of nuclear war. Hence, while the accounting technique of PPB did disappear, the economically rational discourse it introduced to defense continued to be a useful tool for later politicians. On one occasion in March 1983, when President Reagan sought support for his $290 billion defense budget, he stated in a televised address:

> What seems to have been lost in all this debate is the simple truth of how a defense budget is arrived at. It isn't done by deciding to spend a certain number of dollars. Those loud voices that are occasionally heard charging that the Government is trying to solve a security problem by throwing money at it are nothing more than noise based on ignorance.

We start by considering what must be done to maintain peace and review all the possible threats against our security. Then a strategy for strengthening peace must be agreed upon. And finally our defense establishment must be evaluated to see what is necessary to protect against any and all of the potential threats. The cost of achieving these ends is totalled up and the result is the budget for national defense.

(quoted in Stubbing, 1986, p. 55)

Thus, even though PPB failed, it did introduce a rhetoric which lent rational support to a highly irrational act. By masking the human and social costs of war, PPB turned the preparation for violence into a process free from emotions and moral judgements and hence contributed to masking the increasing barbarity of the 20th century (Bauman, 1989; Hobsbawm, 1994).

This chapter is based on the paper, "Taming the Untamable: Planning, Programming and Budgeting and the Normalization of War", which originally appeared in *Accounting, Organizations and Society*, 26 (2001), pp. 501–519. The author would like to thank the publisher, Elsevier, for permission to use this material.

NOTES

1. According to Murdock (1974), systems analysis is a five-step process which includes defining objectives, describing alternative ways of achieving the objectives, determining the costs associated with each alternative, creating a mathematical model of the decision situation with the assumptions clearly stated, and clarifying the criterion by which the preferred alternative will be chosen.
2. Murdock (1974) relates how Enthoven could have intellectually defended a "thin" anti-ballistic missile defense system (ABM). However, he did not believe that the OSD could prevent the services from expanding it if approved and thus recommended that no ABM be built.
3. The National Security State, composed of the National Security Council, the Central Intelligence Agency, the Atomic Energy Commission and the Department of Defense, was established to manage the Cold War and was given discretion to function above the laws of the U.S. and protected from democratic control by being accountable to no one but the Executive branch of the government (Raskin, 1991; Udall, 1994).

6 The Vietnam War, Performance Measures and Representations of Reality

INTRODUCTION

Allowing civilians who were divorced from the field of battle to make decisions about military needs during a time of war led to debilitating unintended consequences for the military, such as in the Crimean War. This chapter demonstrates how during the Vietnam War, accounting created a representation of the conflict for the civilian managers that was divorced from the reality experienced by the foot soldiers, and that this contradiction contributed to the downfall of the U.S. command in Vietnam.

During the 1960s and early 1970s reports such as the following permeated the evening news programs in the United States:

> *CBS, April 12, 1967, Mike Wallace.* One high-ranking official who reflects the feeling in top circles in Saigon says he sees no possibility of a negotiated settlement until after the U.S. presidential election, not before January 1969 at the earliest. The official said he thought the enemy was willing to take a million casualties, which at the current ratio would mean 200,000 U.S. casualties, with at least 25,000 killed, and that figure may be conservative.
>
> (quoted in Hallin, 1986, pp. 160–161)

> *CBS, October 31, 1967, Walter Cronkite.* In the war, U.S. and South Vietnamese troops smashed the second Communist attempt in three days to capture the district capital of Loc Ninh, some 72 miles north of Saigon. The allies killed more than 110 VC, boosting the enemy death toll since Sunday to 365. American losses were reported at 4 dead and 11 wounded.
>
> (quoted in Hallin, 1986, p. 141)

This presentation of the Vietnam War through the lens of statistics became so pervasive that by the end of the war the "body count" would be infamous. Although Vietnam was the most elaborately measured war in U.S. history, it was, however, also the least successful (Gibson, 1986; Gross, 1971;

Ross, 1968; Schlesinger, 1974). This chapter explores the role accounting, in particular Planning, Programming and Budgeting (PPB), played in this debacle. Chapter 5 showed how, with McNamara's introduction of PPB into the DOD, an economically rational discourse that equated truth with that which could be counted and instrumentally related to an objective came to dominate the defense decision making process. PPB mirrored McNamara's management style, which he (1996, p. 24) described as:

> Put very simply, it was to define a clear objective for whatever organiza-tion I was associated with, develop a plan to achieve that objective, and systematically monitor progress against the plan. . . . The objective of the Defense Department was clear to me from the start: to defend the nation at minimal risk and minimal cost, and, whenever we got into combat, with minimal loss of life.

Objective, plan, monitor, minimal, cost, risk—these are concepts that underlie a bureaucratic model of reality in which problems can be stated, resources mobilized to resolve them, and results compared against the plan. PPB's ostensible purpose was to rationalize defense expenditures by artic-ulating missions for the DOD, proposing alternative force structures for these missions, and choosing among the alternatives based on their cost-effectiveness. Thus, PPB related the inputs of defense to the outputs in an economically rational manner, creating the impression that there were objective, scientific solutions to every defense problem.

PPB dominated the discourse in the DOD and caused the U.S. leaders to perceive the inputs of the Vietnam War, such as number of troops, sorties and bombs, as instrumentally related to the outputs, most especially deaths, hamlets secured and reduction in enemy resources, leading to the belief that the war could be won by the proper management of resources. This instru-mentally rational representation of the war disagreed with the foot soldier's experience of combat, and frequently contributed to the breakdown of the U.S. command in Vietnam.

DISCOURSES SHAPE ACTION

Language is the symbolic medium through which we represent and simul-taneously create the world in which we live (McLaren and Giroux, 1997; Potter, 1996). Representations are a political act in that they produce par-ticular understandings that limit our available subject positions, points of view and potential actions (Eagleton, 1990; Edwards, 1996; Hall, 1982; McLaren and Giroux, 1997; Sarup, 1993; Shapiro, 1989). Representations do this in part by highlighting certain aspects of a situation and silenc-ing others (Shapiro, 1988). For instance, Weedon (1987) illustrates how language was used by the *Daily Telegraph* to marginalize the activities of the Greenham women's peace campaign during the 1980s. *The Daily*

Telegraph, which was eager to sustain status quo patriarchal relationships, described the "peace women" as engaging in ritual dances, feminist and lesbian rites reminiscent of ancient witchcraft cults, worshiping the Great Earth Mother, entangling themselves in great webs of colored wool, and hanging symbolic objects on the camp wire (Weedon, 1987, pp. 91–92). Characterizing the "peace women" in this way made their actions appear anti-rational and radically feminist and, as such, served to alienate rank and file women from the cause. Hence, descriptions actively shape the world in which we live by legitimating some acts and discouraging others (Hall, 1982; McLaren and Giroux, 1997). As a result, it is around the representation of an event that the fiercest debate should occur, for once the discourse is set, outcomes will be biased towards those that the representation validates as reasonable and preferred (Chomsky, 1987; Edwards, 1996; Hall, 1982; Latour, 1987).

Discourses succeed in guiding actions to particular results by making those acts appear natural and necessary (Potter, 1996; Shapiro, 1988). Naturalizing occurs, in part, by removing human actors from the discourse and making it appear as if the structural features of a problem, economy and society are responsible for the outcomes. For example, in one of the discourses that validate the behaviors required for the maintenance of capitalism, that is, neoclassical economics, market imperfections and not human beings create the need for regulations. In addition, discourses mask the interests that they serve by making the basic principles that sustain an unequal distribution of power the framework for thinkable thought, rather than an object of rational consideration (Chomsky, 1987; Eagleton, 1991). Again, this is illustrated in neoclassical economics where it is assumed that an economy consists of owners of capital (principals) and workers (agents). Alternative productive relations are dismissed ex ante.

Accepted discourses close debate by imposing constraints on the issues that can be raised and what can be said about them (Porter, 1994b). Cohn (1987) cogently illustrates how the instrumentally rational discourse used by defense intellectuals who plan nuclear war, which relies heavily on game theory, makes certain concepts like peace unspeakable. The closest one can get to peace is "strategic stability", a term that refers to the number and types of weapons systems, not the emotional and social conditions implied by peace. Thus, discourses are effective at limiting change by constraining what can be said and done about an issue, while simultaneously masking the interests that are served.

Quantified representations, such as accounting and cost-benefit analysis, are particularly successful at restricting political change in that they remove an issue from the realm of personal and political debate and transfer it to the domain of objective, scientific solution by making it appear as if the numbers, not the people, are responsible for decisions (Covaleski and Dirsmith, 1988; Mies, 1990; Porter, 1994a, 1994b, 1995; Rose, 1991). Porter (1995, p. 8) notes that "quantification is a way of making decisions without seeming to decide". As such, numbers have served to depoliticize politics (Rose,

1991). Further, in order for numbers to be perceived as an adequate representation of a phenomenon, characteristics that are not amenable to addition, subtraction, multiplication and division must be abstracted away. This frequently implies that important meanings, as well as a moral vocabulary, must be sacrificed. That which quantification ignores, however, may from a different perspective be considered most essential (Porter, 1994a, 1994b, 1995; Ross, 1968).

This chapter argues that PPB introduced a new discourse into the DOD that equated truth with that which could be counted and could be instrumentally related to an objective. In so doing, it made visible those aspects of defense problems that could be measured and logically related to a goal, while rendering invisible less tangible aspects. By elevating instrumental rationality over alternative ways of knowing, PPB dismissed as irrational any judgment based on heuristics or intuition and also made it difficult to evoke a moral vocabulary. As such, essential meanings were lost and important social and political issues were disregarded. In addition, PPB enlivened the structural features of defense problems rather than the human actors, leading to the belief that every problem could be managed and that technical solutions were available. All these features impacted the U.S. leadership's perception of the Vietnam War and consequently the way in which it conducted it.

By introducing PPB and ensuring that defense debates were dominated by an instrumentally rational discourse, McNamara not only gained control of the DOD, he also changed what was viewed as important and essential. PPB made visible the technical and instrumental aspects of defense decisions, while masking the more ephemeral political and social. Thus, PPB lifted up those qualities that could supposedly be planned, controlled and monitored, giving the impression that any defense problem could be administered into producing desired results. This mindset led the U.S. leadership to believe that the Vietnam War could be won if the inputs were properly managed.

THE BUREAUCRATIC MODEL OF REALITY AND THE VIETNAM WAR

PPB reduced the world to the ordinary and manageable by restructuring everything into a problem to be solved and in so doing war, starvation and intrigue simply became potential solutions (Barnet, 1972; Brighton and Uhl, 1995). In reducing these strategies to their instrumental value, PPB made them a more viable option in that the ethical and moral questions that could have interfered with their practical use were removed (Barnet, 1972; Weizenbaum, 1976). This was to be dramatically confirmed during the Vietnam War. The Vietnamese nationalist revolution became a problem to be solved for the Kennedy Administration in that it threatened the stability of the world order the U.S. leadership hoped to create after World War II (Barnet,

1972; Blum, 1995). Thus, as Weizenbaum (1976, p. 251) notes, "When every problem on the international scene is seen by the 'best and the brightest' problem solvers as being a mere technical problem, wars like the Viet Nam war become truly inevitable".

McNamara's reduction of the Vietnamese nationalist revolution to a problem to be solved, with violence as one potential solution, is evident from his memoir on the war, entitled *In Retrospect*. Published more than 35 years after his involvement, McNamara still perceived the U.S. defeat as caused by a failure to analyze alternatives thoroughly. McNamara (1996, p. 101) believed that

> Johnson was left with a national security team that, although it remained intact, was deeply split over Vietnam. Its senior members had failed to face up to the basic questions that confronted first Eisenhower and then Kennedy: Would the loss of South Vietnam pose a threat to U.S. security serious enough to warrant extreme action to prevent it? If so, what kind of action should we take? . . . What would be the ultimate cost of such a program in economic, military, political, and human terms? Could it succeed? If the chances of success were low and the costs high, were there other courses of action. . . .

The attempt at vindication by McNamara does not question the United States' right to intervene in Vietnam. Nor does his statement contain any reflection on the ethics of doing so. His continued reliance on the problem-solving motif he had concretized through PPB limited his vision to the effect alternative courses of action would have on U.S. security and economy alone. PPB's reduction of the world to abstract goals, strategies, costs and results removed the human lives his decisions impacted, making it very difficult for him to engage in the ethical and moral reasoning that may have prevented this tragedy.

THE ATTRITION STRATEGY

The Vietnam War began in earnest for the United States when Kennedy established the U.S. Military Assistance Command, Vietnam (MACV) in February 1962. During that year the number of U.S. military personnel in the South increased from 3,200 to 11,300 (Sheehan, 1988, p. 37). By 1969, when President Nixon initiated the "Vietnamization" of the war, there would be 541,000 U.S. troops in South Vietnam (Gibson, 1986, p. 95). In the end, the Vietnam War would be the longest, most cost-ineffective and appalling war ever fought by the U.S. (Gross, 1971; Schlesinger, 1974). This was due, in part, to the U.S. leaders perceiving all defense problems, including the war, through the instrumentally rational discourse introduced by PPB.

As noted previously, PPB equated truth with that which could be counted. This impacted the way in which the U.S. leadership measured progress in

Vietnam in that the options most reducible to quantification were the ones that received the most attention. Given that death could be counted, an attrition strategy in which the goal was to kill the Viet Cong (VC) (the term used by the U.S. for communist Vietnamese) faster than they could be reproduced became the primary means of evaluating the war's progress (Edwards, 1996; Gibson, 1986; McNamara, 1996; Sheehan, 1988; Van Creveld, 1985). Given that the Vietnam War was a guerilla war with no fronts, progression was difficult to determine in anyway except the number of VC killed (McNamara, 1996; Sheehan, 1988). Thus, the logic of PPB not only directed the U.S. leadership's gaze towards those aspects of the war that could be counted, it also reinforced the legitimacy of such a strategy by equating improvement in any concrete metric with advancement (Edwards, 1996; Van Creveld, 1985).

PPB's limiting discourse also impacted the way in which the U.S. measured progress in the war to win the hearts and minds of the Vietnamese people, referred to as pacification. The political loyalties of the Vietnamese people were assumed to increase with the number of classrooms the U.S. built, the number of roads the U.S. constructed and the number of toothbrushes the U.S. distributed (Appy, 1993, Gibson, 1986). The equation of political loyalties with commodities distributed by the U.S. created a false sense of control in that this measurement system masked fundamental political tensions that could not be resolved instrumentally.

Thus, PPB impacted the Vietnam War by directing attention to those aspects that could be counted and instrumentally related to a particular goal while simultaneously providing a discourse that rationalized the U.S. leadership's choices by masking fundamental political issues. The resulting institutionalization of a falsehood is captured by Halberstam's (1992, p. 248) description of McNamara during the Vietnam War years:

> Thus the portrait of McNamara in those years at his desk, on planes, in Saigon, poring over page after page of data, each platoon, each squad, studying all those statistics. . . . He scurried around Vietnam, looking for what he wanted to see; and he never saw nor smelled nor felt what was really there, right in front of him. He was so much a prisoner of his own background, so unable, as indeed was the country which sponsored him to adapt his values and his terms to Vietnamese realities. Since any real indices and truly factual estimates of the war would immediately have shown its bankruptcy, the McNamara trips became part of a vast unwitting and elaborate charade, the institutionalizing and legitimizing of a hopeless lie.

THE CAUSE–EFFECT WAR

According to the world view articulated by PPB, there was an instrumental relationship between the inputs and outputs of any defense strategy. This notion led to the belief that the outcome of the war could be predicted by the level of U.S. troops. This is illustrated by Assistant Secretary of Defense John McNaughton's 1965 proposal to send 44 battalions to Vietnam. In this proposal he expressed his expectations in terms of probabilities with respect to U.S. success/inconclusive/collapse:

For the year 1966: .2/.7/.1
For the year 1967: .4/.45/.15
For the year 1968: .5/.3/.2

(The Pentagon Papers, Vol. III, p. 484)

This analysis not only implied that the outcome of the war would be determined by the number of U.S. troops, but that this relationship was so predictable that concrete probabilities could be stated. The belief in a cause–effect relationship between the number of U.S. soldiers and the conclusion of the war is further illustrated in *The Pentagon Papers'* discussion of a meeting that took place on April 27, 1967, between General Westmoreland, President Johnson and General Wheeler. At this meeting, Westmoreland predicted that if the U.S. presence in Vietnam was limited to the 470,000 U.S. soldiers present at the time, then

unless the will of the enemy is broken or unless there was an unravelling of the VC infrastructure the war could go on for 5 years. If our forces were increased that period could be reduced although not necessarily in proportion to increases in strength, since factors other than increase in strength had to be considered. . . .

(The Pentagon Papers, Vol. IV, p. 442)

Westmoreland concluded by estimating that with a force level of 565,000 men, the war could well go on for three years. With a second increment of two and one-third divisions leading to a total of 665,000 men, it could go on for two years (*The Pentagon Papers,* Vol. IV, p. 442). While McNamara concurred with Westmoreland that an increase in U.S. troops would shorten the war effort, he felt, however, that Westmoreland's analysis was too rudimentary. According to the discourse of PPB, only cost-effective solutions should be considered. Hence, in determining the proper level of U.S. forces the incremental benefits from additional troops had to be weighed against the incremental costs. In a November 17, 1966, Draft Memorandum for the President, McNamara argued that there were diminishing marginal returns from additional ground forces:

We are finding very strongly diminishing marginal returns in the destruction of VC/NVA [Viet Cong/North Vietnamese Army]. If our estimates of enemy losses (killed, captured and defected) are correct, VC/

NVA losses increased by only 115 per week (less than 15%) during a period in which we increased friendly strength by 160,000 including 140,000 U.S. military personnel and 42 U.S. and Third Country maneuver battalions. At this rate, an additional 100,000 friendly personnel deployed would increase VC/NVA losses by some 70 per week.

(*The Pentagon Papers, Vol.* IV, p. 369)

McNamara also argued that there were costs associated with a troop buildup that Westmoreland did not take into account. According to McNamara's analysis, additional U.S. troops increased the cost of the war in terms of higher inflation in the South Vietnamese economy, increased desertion rates in the Army of South Vietnam, and the negative signal sent to the communists. For example, the communists would realize that the U.S. could not afford to maintain such a large presence in Vietnam for too long and, therefore, would just wait the war out (Gibson, 1986; Palmer, 1978; *The Pentagon Papers,* Vol. IV). In a memorandum to the Joint Chiefs of Staff, McNamara stated that "excessive deployments weaken our ability to win by undermining the economic structure of the RVN [Republic of Vietnam] and by raising doubts concerning the soundness of our planning" (in *The Pentagon Papers,* Vol. IV, p. 326). In other words, victory depended upon the U.S. conducting the war in an economically rational manner. Maintaining an economically rational approach to warfare required a particular conceptualization of the enemy, the U.S. soldiers, the meaning of progress, and even the war itself. These perceptions often tragically contradicted the conditions faced by the U.S. foot soldiers.

THE USE OF STATISTICS TO MEASURE THE WAR'S PROGRESS

As noted previously, McNamara introduced PPB in order to impose his bureaucratic model of reality on the DOD. The objectification of defense made possible by PPB meant that objectives could be set, plans could be made, results could be monitored and success or failure made contingent upon whether or not goals were achieved. This created an impression that victory or defeat in Vietnam could be measured by the extent to which tangible results were realized on explicitly measurable criteria. This goal orientation towards the war is illustrated by a February 8, 1966, planning document:

Achieve results in 1966:
   Increase the population in secure areas to 60% from 50%.
   Increase the critical roads and RR open for use to 50% from 20%.
   Increase the destructions of VC/PAVN base areas to 40–50% from 10–20%.
   . . .

Attrit, by year's end, VC/PAVN forces at a rate as high as their capability to put men into the field.

(*The Pentagon Papers,* Vol. IV, p. 625)

According to this document, progress was being made in the war as long as the numbers improved. This goal orientation to the war, which made victory appear to be independent of irrational human emotions such as courage, fortitude and moral purpose, was reinforced by employing statistics to appraise the war's advancement (Appy, 1993; Edwards, 1996; Gibson, 1986). As stated previously, PPB made visible those aspects of defense problems that could be quantified. As a result, everything that could be counted in Vietnam was counted, and what could not be counted was deemed irrelevant (Appy, 1993). *The Pentagon Papers'* discussion of the war in 1966 illustrates how the U.S. leadership relied upon statistics to demonstrate progress:

The number of U.S. and FW manoeuver battalions available for operations in South Vietnam had increased from 45 to 102. ARVN had added another 24 such units, bringing its total to 163, so altogether there were 265 battalions ready to commence operations in the new year. . . . Large ground operations were mounting in number and duration, and the trend promised to continue sharply upward. . . . Kill ratios (enemy KIA vs. allied KIA) were up to 4.2 from 3.3 during the preceding six month period. . . .

(*The Pentagon Papers,* Vol. IV, p. 387)

In addition, on March 20–21, 1967, President Johnson, along with members of the White House Staff, DOD and State Department, met with the leaders of South Vietnam, General Westmoreland and other key military officials at Guam. At this meeting, General Westmoreland buttressed his optimistic views regarding the progress of the war through the use of statistical indicators. He referred to how

intensity of allied operations was up versus those of last year; that the enemy's losses had doubled; that we were taking four times the number of prisoners we had; that the number of defectors had doubled; that the enemy was losing 2 ½ times the weapons that he had in the past year; and that 18% more major roads in South Vietnam had been opened in the past three months. . . .

(*The Pentagon Papers,* Vol. IV, p. 425)

It can be seen by the above quotes that the use of statistics created an impression that U.S. actions were resulting in concrete, measurable results that were a sufficient end in themselves. Eventually, however, even McNamara (1996, p. 48) would admit that

I always pressed our commanders very hard for estimates of progress—or lack of it. The monitoring of progress—which I still consider a bedrock principle of good management—was very poorly handled in Vietnam. Both the chiefs and I bear responsibility for that failure. Uncertain how to evaluate results in a war without battle lines, the military tried to gauge its progress with quantitative measurements such as enemy casualties (which became infamous as body counts), weapons seized, prisoners taken, sorties flown, and so on. We later learned that many of these measures were misleading or erroneous.

It is interesting to note that while McNamara could admit that statistics proved to be a poor measure of progress in Vietnam, as the above quote demonstrates, he still could not relinquish the managerial model of reality—problem, plan, monitor, results—which made anything but concrete, measurable outcomes appear irrelevant.

THE ENEMY AND THE WAR AS SEEN THROUGH THE LENS OF PPB

In order to maintain the belief created by the discourse of PPB that victory depended upon conducting the war in an economically rational manner, the enemy had to be viewed as an economically rational agent that interpreted the U.S. actions as signals and based decisions upon cost/benefit analysis. This is demonstrated by the way in which the U.S. leadership believed it was fighting a limited, rather than a total, war in Vietnam. Hence, the aim of the U.S. was not to destroy North Vietnam but rather convince the North to stop infiltrating the South by demonstrating that the cost of this action far exceeded any benefits it could attain (Gibson, 1986; Kaplan, 1983; Young, 1991). General Taylor explained during the Vietnam War Hearings how "We have put in only the forces which are consistent with our limited objectives, which is the persuasion of the leadership of Hanoi to stop their aggression" (in Fulbright, 1966, p. 210). The notion of limited war was further elaborated upon in *The Pentagon Papers'* discussion of a memorandum by John McNaughton regarding the force level required to win. *The Pentagon Papers* states that

> the definition of "win," i.e., "succeed in demonstrating to the VC that they cannot win," indicates the assumption upon which the conduct of the war was to rest—that the VC could be convinced in some meaningful sense that they were not going to win and that they would then rationally choose less violent methods of seeking their goals.
>
> (Vol. IV, p. 293)

One way in which the U.S. hoped to convince the VC that they could not win was through the Rolling Thunder Campaign, in which the U.S.

selectively bombed North Vietnamese targets with the intent of signaling to the enemy the technology that could be released in full force if the North Vietnamese did not cooperate with U.S. aims (Gibson, 1986; *The Pentagon Papers*, Vol. III; Van Creveld, 1985; Young, 1991). During the Senate hearings on the air war in Vietnam, McNamara defended the military's use of discriminatory bombing as a signal rather than indiscriminate bombing for destruction alone by stating, "A selective, carefully targeted bombing campaign . . . [could] be directed toward reasonable and realizable goals . . . [in that it demonstrated] to both South and North Vietnam our resolve to see that aggression does not succeed" (Testimony of McNamara, U.S. Senate, 1967b, pp. 281–282).

The U.S. intelligence community reasoned that such a strategy would be successful in that even though Hanoi's investment in industrial plants was small, the value was inordinately great because the people had undergone incredible sacrifices to acquire it. Thus, destroying these assets should provide sufficient incentives for the North to withdraw from the war (*The Pentagon Papers*, Vol. IV). The U.S.'s belief that the VC would value their industry and consumption more than their right to self-determination is further illustrated by Walt Rostow's claim that "Ho [Chi Minh] has an industrial complex to protect: he is no longer a guerrilla fighter with nothing to lose" (*The Pentagon Papers*, Vol. III, p. 153) and Westmoreland's assertion that "these attacks by interrupting the flow of consumer goods to southern DRV [Democratic Republic of Vietnam] would carry to the NVN [North Vietnamese] man in the street, with minimum loss of civilian life, the message of U.S. determination" (*The Pentagon Papers*, Vol. III, p. 341).

Unfortunately, the conceptualization of the enemy as a rational economic man had minimal grounding in reality, for the Vietnamese were not engaged in limited war but rather total war and were willing to lose every material thing to unite North and South and maintain their independence from any form of foreign rule (Sheehan, 1988; Young, 1991). Hence, as even *The Pentagon Papers* (Vol. IV, p. 57) would admit, "The idea that destroying, or threatening to destroy, NVN's [North Vietnam's] industry would pressure Hanoi into calling it quits seems, in retrospect, a colossal misjudgment". PPB played a crucial role in masking the requirements for victory in this war.

PPB AND THE EFFACEMENT OF VIETNAMESE
SOCIAL, POLITICAL AND HISTORICAL FORCES

Given that the discourse of PPB made visible those aspects of the war that could be quantified and instrumentally related to goals, less tangible factors like the social, political and historical pressures that shaped the Vietnamese identity were rendered invisible and irrelevant. As a result, the key ingredients for victory, most especially the deeply rooted historical forces and political dynamics that fed the Vietnamese desire for independence, the social relations between the Vietnamese and the VC, the determination to fight until the end even if all was lost, were not considered by the U.S. leadership (Barnet, 1972; Gibson, 1986; Halberstam, 1992). The VC, on the other hand, held their military commanders in strict subordination to the political cadres. For the communists, the vehicle for political change was not the war, but rather the struggle to demonstrate that their way was the only true way for the Vietnamese to live (Appy, 1993; Fitzgerald, 1972).

While an effacement of the social, political and historical forces that shaped the Vietnamese identity was an outcome of the conceptual frame superimposed upon the war by the discourse of PPB, it was also a necessary ingredient for the U.S. to continue the war. According to Chomsky (1987, p. 225), "The United States openly recognized throughout that a political settlement was impossible, for the simple reason that the 'enemy' would win handily in a political competition . . .". The only way the U.S. could hope to crush the opposition was by unleashing its superior military technology on the Vietnamese (Barnet, 1972; Chomsky, 1987, 1995; Halberstam, 1992; Young, 1991). Thus, in a war where the U.S. was militarily strong, but politically weak, PPB focused the war managers' attention on what they were capable of doing—that is, dropping bombs, killing VC— and masked what they could not influence—the hearts and minds of the Vietnamese—and, hence, made their actions appear necessary and reasonable (Van Creveld, 1985).

The need for the U.S. to efface the political realities in order to maintain their involvement in Vietnam is illustrated by a controversy that occurred in 1967 between the Central Intelligence Agency (CIA) and the MACV, with support from some civilian officials, regarding who should be counted as the enemy (the order of battle) (Adams, 1975; Gibson, 1986; Moise, 1985–1986; Schneir and Schneir, 1984; Young, 1991). MACV wanted to eliminate from the order of battle all VC local guerilla and militia forces. Robert Komer, President Johnson's pacification chief in Vietnam, described these forces as "low grade part-time hamlet self-defense groups, mostly weaponless" (quoted in Schneir and Schneir, 1984, p. 572). In other words, because the local forces did not engage in the production of war full time, or wear uniforms, carry guns or possess anti-aircraft missiles, they fell outside the technological definition of the enemy. Nonetheless, the guerrilla-militia were the ones that planted most of the mines and booby traps, and in the Da Nang area these were the cause of two thirds of all U.S. Marine Corp casualties (Adams, 1975).

According to Young (1991), however, the controversy regarding whether or not local guerilla and militia forces should be counted in the order of battle was more than an argument about numbers. It was an unacknowledged political disagreement between the CIA and MACV about the very nature of the war. Young (1991, p. 214) states that "counting 'low-grade, part-time' people involved a recognition that in fighting the NLF [National Liberation Front], one fought the ordinary villagers of the country", and admitting this was tantamount to conceding that the U.S. was not fighting invaders from the North but rather the South Vietnamese themselves. Young (1991, p. 215) continues, "At its furthest logical extension, to agree to the higher figure [which included VC local guerilla and militia forces] meant that the United States, not North Vietnam, had invaded the South, was an aggressor against its people, and should withdraw". Hence, by viewing the war through the lens of PPB, which made the political loyalties of the people of the South invisible, the U.S. leaders could maintain the rationale that the North had invaded the South, which legitimized their participation in the war.

A MANAGERIAL MODEL OF WARFARE

The instrumental relationship between the inputs of the war and the outputs, which was driven by the lens of PPB, meant that if the inputs could be properly managed the desired outputs could be achieved. This managerial model of warfare is illustrated by a report written by Robert Komer discussing how to achieve results during 1967–1968:

> My prognosis of what is more likely than not to happen in Vietnam is reasonable only if we and the GVN [Government of Vietnam] mount a maximum effort in 1967–68 to make it so. The key is better orchestration and management of our Vietnam effort—both in Washington and Saigon. To me, the most important ingredient of such an outcome . . . is more effective use of the assets we already have. . . .
>
> Our most important under-utilized asset is the RVNAF [Republic of Vietnam Armed Forces]. Getting greater efficiency out of the 700,000 men we're already supporting and financing is the cheapest and soundest way to get results in pacification.
>
> (*The Pentagon Papers,* Volume IV, p. 391)

The same sentiments were reflected in a report prepared by the Systems Analysis Office in 1967 arguing against an increase in U.S. troops. The report stated:

> In brief, the additional forces are likely neither to reduce the enemy force nor contribute significantly to pacification. These goals can only be met by improving the efficiency of the forces already deployed and, particularly, that of ARVN [Army of South Vietnam]. But additional U.S. forces decrease the incentive to MACV and the GVN [Government

of Vietnam (Saigon)] to make the Vietnamese shoulder a larger portion of the burden. The RVNAF [Republic of Vietnam Armed Forces (Saigon)] appear to have done well by all statistical measures in IV CTZ, where they have been provided only logistical and combat support by the U.S., and very badly in the other areas where the U.S. has taken over the war while denying them significant support.

(The Pentagon Papers, Vol. IV, p. 459)

In other words, winning the war depended upon efficiently utilizing the assets in place. One of the assets in place was the U.S. military and, given that an attrition strategy was employed in Vietnam, the military's primary job was to kill VC. According to the managerial model of warfare, which was shown in Chapter 4 to have gained popularity in Britain in the early 20th century, this killing had to be done in a cost-effective manner in order for the U.S. to succeed. The war managers believed they could increase the productivity of the troops by using techniques derived from the managerial control systems of corporations such as incentives, standards, performance evaluations, appraisals of efficiency and monitoring.

This mindset is illustrated first by the way in which award systems were structured to encourage the troops to produce high body counts. In some cases confirmed VC kills could earn a GI a badge, a beer or additional Rest and Recreation (Caputo, 1977; Citizens Commission of Inquiry, 1972; Vietnam Veterans Against the War, 1972). Some divisions even sponsored contests. One such contest took place in 1969 and was called "Best of the Pack". The winner was determined by points, which were awarded for the following:

5—Per man per day above 25 on an operation
10—Each possible body count
10—Each 100 lbs. of rice
15—Each 100 lbs. of salt
20—Each mortar round
50—Each enemy individual weapon captured
100—Each enemy crew served weapon captured
100—Each enemy Body Count
200—Each tactical radio captured
500—Perfect score on CMMI (inspection)
1,000—Each prisoner of war

Points were deducted for the following:

50—Each U.S. WIA (wounded)
500—Each U.S. KIA (killed)

(in Emerson, 1976, p. 65)

The troops' performance was measured against standard kill ratios and other statistics. Ewell and Hunt (1974, p. 213) provide an example of how troops were hierarchically ranked based on a predetermined contact success ratio:

> In dispersed, small unit warfare, the success of a unit was largely dependent on the skill with which small units handled each individual contact. If one visualized a contact as a sighting and a success as one or more enemy casualties, the following matrix gives the general idea:

Contact Success Ratio	Skill Level of Unit
75%	Highest skill observed
65%	Very professional
50%	Unit is beginning to jell
40%	Unit has problems but correctible
Below 40%	Unit has serious deficiencies in small unit techniques. Probably does many things wrong

In addition, combat scorecards were used to evaluate the effectiveness of maneuver battalions. For example, in the 503rd Infantry a battalion's performance was measured by a weighted average approach. Positive weights were allocated to enemy kills, prisoners, enemy contacts, and a percent of first term reenlistments. Negative weights were assigned to AWOLs (absent without leave), delinquency reports, accidents, malaria cases, narcotics charges and various disciplinary actions (in Johnson, 1971, pp. 30–31). Further, MACV and the Office of Systems Analysis were continually seeking statistical means for measuring the effectiveness of the Army of South Vietnam (ARVN). Measures included: minimum present for duty, number of desertions, comparisons between U.S. and ARVN kill ratios, battalion days of operations, days of enemy contact, number of operations and weapons loss ratio, amongst others (*The Pentagon Papers,* Vol. II, pp. 507–508).

Attempts were also made to define the most efficient types of killing. According to a study done by the Office of Systems Analysis, the U.S. achieved the greatest returns, such as highest kill ratios, when the enemy attacked entrenched U.S. units (Enthoven and Smith, 1980). Further, MACV computed the efficiency of U.S. operations with and without air assets. According to Ewell and Hunt (1974, p. 55):

> With no air assets, brigade performance averaged 1.6 Viet Cong losses per field day—hardly a creditable return. With an Air Cavalry Troop, this figure rose to 5.1 Viet Cong per day: an increase in performance

of 218%. With an Assault Helicopter Company, performance averaged 6.0 Viet Cong losses per day. . . . When a brigade was supported by both an Air Cavalry Troop and an Assault Helicopter Company, brigade performance rose to 13.6 Viet Cong losses per day—an increase of 750%.

Consistent with Ewell and Hunt (1974, p. 151), this information was important because "a good general rule was to concentrate on measuring activities that culminated in meaningful results, to measure them periodically, and to stay in high efficiency areas". Lastly, production was monitored by senior officers hovering over the battlefield in helicopters (Citizens Commission of Inquiry, 1972; Van Creveld, 1985).

RESULTS FROM BODY COUNT PRESSURES

In the Vietnam War promotion in the officer corps depended on a high body count. As a result, GI's were constantly pressured by their commanding officers to produce dead VC. This resulted in the "mere gook" rule—"If its dead and Vietnamese, its VC"—becoming a rule of thumb in the bush (Caputo, 1977; Ehrhart, 1983; Gibson, 1986; Young, 1991). William D. Ehrhart (1983, p. 169), a decorated Marine Corps sergeant, related in one of his memoirs on the war how when soldiers were snipped at from a village:

> We call in an airstrike. Couple of snake-eyes, couple of napalm canisters—instant French fries. Level the whole ville. Then go in and count up the bodies. Oh, yeh, the brass likes body counts. Anything dead is VC. And you know what . . . ? I can make it read like we scored a great victory against the forces of communism and evil. It's easy! Call somebody's house an enemy structure. Call a bomb shelter an enemy fortified position. Call a helpless old man a de-tai-nee. Bingo! Facts and figures. We win. Not only can I do it—I have to do it! They don't wanna know the truth. . . . They got the whole thing all worked out, . . . and you better not be the one tell 'em we ain't getting nowhere.

This pressure for body counts not only led to the slaughter of noncombatants, but also to the systematic falsification of battle reports and the routine violation of the rules of engagement and regulations covering the treatment of prisoners (Caputo, 1977; Citizens Commission of Inquiry, 1972; Ehrhart, 1983; Gibson, 1986; Herr, 1977; Johnson, 1971). Charles David Locke, a mortar man for the American Division, relates with respect to one encounter with the enemy how

> we stopped and called the colonel and told him we had one wounded dink, you know, and that we wanted him to send a chopper. The colonel says, "Is that what I heard you say? Wounded?"

And the sergeant said, "No."

And they blew his head off.

Before we left on this mission the captain of the company had told us definitely do not take any prisoners. He didn't want to hear about any prisoners. He wanted a body count. He said he needed seven more bodies before he could get his promotion to major.

(in Citizens Commission of Inquiry, 1972, p. 228)

As early as 1962 many Americans directly involved in the war understood that the U.S.'s indiscriminate slaughter killed many more civilians than it did the VC and, as a result, created many new VC (Chomsky, 1995; Enthoven and Smith, 1980; Sheehan, 1988). Dr. Gordon Livingston, a major in the U.S. Army, referred to "the absurdity, for example, of dropping five million tons of bombs on a country that we are attempting to defend, I think is so patently obvious that only by an intense denial of what has happened can we be persuaded to live with this" (in Citizens Commission of Inquiry, 1972, p. 34). It was, in part, by denial that the U.S. leadership managed to do so.

The decision makers in Washington D.C. were insulated from the reality of the war not only by seeing it through the lens of PPB, which conflated tangible results of any kind with progress, but also, as illustrated in the above quote from Ehrhart, by the artificial and antiseptic language used in the reports. For the war managers there was no slaughter of innocent civilians with aerial bombs but rather an "air interdiction of hostiles"; what was in actuality leveling a helpless village became for reporting purposes "destroying the social infrastructure"; and as far as the U.S. leaders were concerned the Vietnamese did not live in their village but rather "infested the area" (Harris, 1996, p. 76). Further, air raids did not destroy peasants' huts or pigsties, but rather "enemy structures" which for the war managers conjured up World War II images of German barracks and ammunition plants (Sheehan, 1988). Thus, the language was distorted so that the war managers saw only what they wanted to see in exactly the way they wanted to see it, progress towards defeating an evil enemy which possessed the same war technology as the U.S.

While this artificial language masked the incredible destruction and tragedy wrought by U.S. actions and made it easier for the political elite to engage in the war, the language fostered an erosion of meaning in the foot soldier's world and even made his life more dangerous (Caputo, 1977; Gibson, 1986). According to Caputo (1977, pp. 217–218):

We were fighting in the cruellest kind of conflict, a people's war. It was . . . a war for survival waged in a wilderness without rules or laws; a war in which each soldier fought for his own life and the lives of the men beside him, not caring who he killed in that personal cause or how many or in what manner and feeling only contempt for those who sought to impose on his savage struggle the mincing distinctions of civilized warfare—that code of battlefield ethics that attempted to humanize an essentially inhuman war.

The life of the foot soldier was made even worse by the fact that in this army, which McNamara had molded into the image of Ford Motor Company, the officers became fixated on their individual career advancement (which required high body counts) with little attention paid to the welfare of the troops (Caputo, 1977; Gibson, 1986). Under such circumstances, the soldiers' lives became objectified as the raw material needed to produce a high body count (Appy, 1993; Citizens Commission of Inquiry, 1972; Gibson, 1986; Santoli, 1981). For Michael O'Mera, a captain in the army:

> The thing which seems so terrible to me was the fact that the lives of Americans were placed second to enemy dead. Body count meant more to commanders than the lives of Americans, and when this I believe takes place, when they are used as bait, when they are not used to get intelligence targets but just out there hoping to be fired upon, how can you expect a GI to feel . . .?
>
> (in Citizens Commission of Inquiry, 1972, p. 72)

Ultimately, the managerial model of reality which was imposed on the war by PPB contradicted the foot soldier's experience and contributed to the downfall of the U.S. command in Vietnam.

THE CONTRADICTIONS APPEAR

Theodore Porter (1994a, 1995) argues that representations work best if the world they aim to describe can be remade in their image. In other words, in order for people to accept a particular representation as valid, the reality the representation proposes to describe must change in response. For example, in order for IQ to be accepted as a valid measure of intelligence, notions about what constitutes knowledge, how one acquires it, have to change. If this does not occur, then people will find the representation to be inadequate and will rebel against the identity they must assume to maintain it.

The above argument implies that in order for PPB's instrumentally rational representation of warfare to produce desired results the U.S. troops would have to conform their behavior to that dictated by the representation or, in other words, accept and reproduce their instrumental identity as producers of death. However, as the following sections demonstrate, the U.S. soldiers' refusal to do so contributed significantly to the breakdown in command in Vietnam. By 1971, even the usually self-congratulatory *Armed Forces Journal* would admit that

> the morale, discipline and battle worthiness of the U.S. Armed Forces are, with a few salient exceptions, lower and worse than at any time in this century and possibly in the history of the United States.

By every conceivable indicator, our army that now remains in Vietnam is in a state of approaching collapse. . . .

(Heinl, 1971, p. 30)

The contradictions between the representation of the war through the discourse of PPB and reality began to appear with the Tet Offensive, which began on January 31, 1968, when the VC launched a series of coordinated attacks against all the major cities in South Vietnam. The Tet Offensive came as a huge surprise to the U.S. leaders. The systematic falsification of the body count reports had led Westmoreland to conclude that the "cross-over point", the point at which the VC were being killed faster than they could be reproduced, had been reached the previous autumn. The belief that the U.S. was winning the war through attrition was so overwhelming that the leaders dismissed as unbelievable captured documents indicating that the attack was forthcoming. One U.S. Army intelligence officer said, "If we'd gotten the whole battle plan, it wouldn't have been credible to us" (quoted in Gibson, 1986, p. 165).

While the U.S. soldiers were eventually able to overpower the VC in the Tet Offensive and, hence, claim a military victory, on the political side it was a complete defeat for the U.S. and Saigon. A coordinated effort this large could not have taken place without the cooperation of the people of the South, the very people the U.S. were supposedly defending from the VC (Ehrhart, 1986; Gibson, 1986; Young, 1991). Shortly after Tet, most of the U.S. troops started viewing Vietnam as a lost cause (Ehrhart, 1986). Fred Gardner (1970, p. 31) reported in the *New York Times* that

> it was in April, 1968, that I first heard a Vietnam veteran describe a seek-and-destroy mission as "seek-and-avoid." He said that most of the men in his company, an infantry unit stationed near Danang, didn't think the war seemed "worth it" in terms of life, limb and disrupted youth. "On patrol," he explained, "we were supposed to go a mile and engage Charlie, right? What we did was go a hundred yards, find us some heavy foliage, smoke, rap and sack out."

As the years progressed and a growing percentage of the U.S. ground troops were unwilling conscripts, rather than eager volunteers, the disintegration of the U.S. forces in Vietnam would become so severe that in 1970 Gardner (1970, p. 31) would conclude, "President Nixon may claim credit for phasing down the war; Congress may debate a timetable for pulling out; but the fact is that rank-and-file G.I.'s are ending the fighting on their own".

COMBAT REFUSALS, FRAGGINGS AND MORE

The difference between the soldiers' experience of the war and that of the bureaucrats is captured in the following quote from Emerson (1976, p. 65):

The soldiers had a year in Vietnam, sometimes a little less. Over and over they counted each day gone and all the days left to get through. They counted all the time and told you fifty days were left, ten days, three days. The Army counted everything else, insisted that all things be counted, until the numbers meant nothing—but still the counting kept on.

After the Tet Offensive proved that a large majority of the South Vietnamese viewed the U.S., not the VC, as the enemy, the hypocrisy of the war became clear to many U.S. soldiers. The anger expressed in the following quote by Ehrhart (1986, p. 175) was a typical GI reaction:

I'd been a fool, ignorant and naïve. A sucker. For such men (e.g., Johnson, McNamara, Nixon, etc.), I had become a murderer. For such men, I had forfeited my honor, my self-respect, and my humanity. For such men, I had been willing to lay down my life. And I had been nothing more to them than a hired gun, a trigger-man, a stooge, a tool to be used and discarded, an insignificant statistic.

Although as early as 1965 soldiers were registering their discontent with the war by refusing to follow orders, after Tet there was a rapid increase in the incidence of combat refusals (Moser, 1993). The first reported occurrence of mass mutiny took place on August 24, 1968, during the battle for Queson. For four consecutive days, Alpha Company attacked the same North Vietnamese bunker system suffering high casualties with each assault. On the fifth day, when Lieutenant Colonel Robert C. Bacon ordered the 60 men remaining in Alpha company to storm the bunkers again, the men simply refused (Anonymous, 1971a; Boyle, 1972; Cortright, 1975). The commander of Alpha Company, Lieutenant Eugene Schurtz, radioed Bacon and in a nervous voice reported the following:

"I'm sorry, sir, but my men refused to go. . . . We cannot move out." Bacon turned pale and fired back into his radio phone: "Repeat that, please. Have you told them what it means to disobey orders under fire?"
    "I think they understand," said the lieutenant, "but some of them have simply had enough, they are broken. There are boys here who have only ninety days left in Vietnam. They want to go home in one piece. The situation is psychic here."
(quoted in Boyle, 1972, p. 86)

Lieutenant Schurtz was relieved of duty and Bacon ordered two senior officers to go and speak with the men. After several more refusals, most of the 60 men grudgingly and halfheartedly began to move out. According to military code, mutiny in time of war is punishable by death. None of these men, however, received even a reprimand (Boyle, 1972; Cortright, 1975).

Later in 1968, another mutiny occurred in Cu Chi, near the Cambodian border. Twenty-one men of the 1st Platoon, B Company refused an order to advance into enemy territory (Cortright, 1975). Then, in April 1970, a mutiny took place in front of CBS television cameras. The commander of Charlie Company ordered his men down a road supposedly surrounded by VC forces. The men refused, arguing that a direct advance would almost certainly draw fire and produce casualties. As the men made a case for an alternative route, the CBS viewing audience witnessed first hand a remarkable change in combat leadership, the emergence of battlefield democracy (Anonymous, 1970a; Cortright, 1975).

After 1968, many field officers in Vietnam became painfully aware that the troops under their command might refuse to follow orders. In response, many started to abandon the age old military tradition of unilaterally issuing commands and began instead to "work it out" with the troops by discussing alternatives with the men (Anonymous, 1970b; Ayres, 1971; Cortright, 1975; Saar, 1970). In 1970, veteran Vietnam correspondent John Saar published an article in *Life* about one such officer, Brian Utermahlen, the commander of Alpha Company. Utermahlen's men respected and responded to his command because he frequently sought their opinion before making crucial decisions and because he was lenient with respect to dress code. According to Utermahlen, he relaxed his leadership style because

> These guys are no longer blindly following puppets. . . . They're thinkers and they want intelligent leadership. It's not a democracy, but they want to have a say. If I ran this company like an old-time tyrant, I'd have a bunch of rebels. There are people in the company with more experience than I have, and if they think I'm doing something grossly wrong, I'm ready to listen.
>
> (quoted in Saar, 1970, p. 32)

Not all enlisted men, however, had commanders as flexible as Utermahlen. Many of them had to resort to a much more desperate measure to ensure soldier democracy, which became known as fragging (Anonymous, 1971b; Ayres, 1971; Cortright, 1975; Linden, 1972; Moser, 1993). Fragging was the morally neutral slang term used by U.S. soldiers to describe the murder or attempted murder of a strict, unpopular or aggressive officer (Anonymous, 1971b; Heinl, 1971; Moser, 1993). Fraggings have occurred in every war in the 20th century. According to Linden (1972), however, the fraggings in Vietnam stood apart from those of World War I, World War II and Korea in their prevalence, the indifference with which they were committed, the psychological warfare GI's used to prepare the victim, and the degree to which they effectively crippled the command. Cortright (1975, p. 46) notes that

> the ultimate impact of fragging lay not with any one particular incident but with its general effect on the functioning of the Army. For every

one of the more than five hundred reported assaults, there were many instances of intimidation and threats of fragging which often produced the same result. The unexpected appearance of a grenade pin or the detonation of a harmless smoke grenade frequently convinced commanders to abandon expected military standards. Once a commander was threatened by or became the actual target of a fragging, his effectiveness and that of the unit involved were severely hampered. Indeed, as internal defiance spread within many units, no order could be issued without first considering the possibility of fragging.

Thus, the soldiers resorted to means as violent, desperate and ruthless as the war itself to gain control of their lives. They turned their instrumental identities as killers to their advantage by fighting a war with the establishment that put them in Vietnam in the first place, the U.S. Army. As Daniel Notley noted with respect to fraggings, "GI's are starting to vent their frustration on the institutions and the people that have frustrated them rather than on the Vietnamese people. I think it is really scarring them [the war managers]. They have created a monster and now it has turned on them" (quoted in Citizens Commission of Inquiry, 1972, pp. 192–193).

The level of desperation caused by fraggings can be seen in the army's attempted solution to the problem. By 1970, many officers were so afraid of the enlisted men that they started restricting access to grenades and rifles (Anonymous, 1971b; Cortright, 1975; Gardner, 1970; Jay and Osnos, 1971; Linden, 1972). It was the ultimate contradiction, for an unarmed army could not fight a war.

Outside of fraggings and mutinies, the collapse of the U.S. command in Vietnam was also evident from the GI's excessive drug use, their rapidly increasing desertion and dishonorable discharge rate, as well as the militant unrest of many African-Americans serving in Vietnam (Appy, 1993; Cortright, 1975; Heinl, 1971; Jay and Osnos, 1971; Linden, 1972). By 1971, the dissatisfaction was so great that some U.S. GI's defected to the ranks of the VC (Heinl, 1971). *Time* reported in 1971 that

> only 18 months ago, every general worth his stars was complaining that troops were being withdrawn too fast. Now, officers from Chief of Staff William C. Westmoreland on down are known to be arguing that they are not being pulled out fast enough. "If we are going to have to fight it as we are now," a Pentagon general said last week, "then let's get everyone out as fast as possible. We're just murdering ourselves sitting there."
> (Anonymous, 1971b, p. 34)

CONCLUSION

While managerial accounting has contributed to disciplining labor in capitalist societies by elevating instrumental rationality, such as the pursuit of profit, to truth, this chapter has shown that it lacks the capacity to capture and regulate all human endeavors. In fact, when it is used to represent situations for which it is ill suited, horrible aberrations can result. This chapter examined the role PPB played in changing visibilities in the DOD in such a way that war was perceived to be a rational productive process. PPB accomplished this by elevating the measurable and instrumental characteristics of war, most controversially body counts and tonnage of bombs dropped, to truth, while rendering the qualitative aspects of social relations, emotions, ingenuity, invisible. This led the U.S. war managers to take actions in Vietnam based on a lens which failed to capture the most important and relevant information.

Thus, the U.S. leaders actually thought they were fighting a limited war with an economically rational adversary. They also assumed that victory was assured as long as resources were employed in an efficient manner and statistics were improving. They further presumed that the U.S. soldiers could be manipulated through incentives and controls into producing high body counts. The Vietnamese, however, were not fighting a limited war but rather a total war, and the U.S. soldiers finally refused to conform to their instrumental identity as killers. As the war dragged on and a large percentage of U.S. ground troops became unwilling conscripts, the soldiers began to rebel against the identity imposed on them through the discourse of PPB and turned their training on the institution that put them in Vietnam. In the quintessential contradiction, the U.S. soldiers would contribute almost as much as the VC towards the defeat of the U.S. war effort.

Thus, while the economically rational discourse of accounting has improved efficiency and productivity in capitalist economies by legitimizing techniques for disciplining labor processes, this chapter has shown that it could not tame and rationalize war. For war, which is a "hurly-burly of violence" (Sheehan, 1988, p. 444), will never be amenable to rational control.

This chapter is based on the paper, "Rationality, Performance Measures and Representations of Reality: Planning, Programming and Budgeting and the Vietnam War", which originally appeared in *Critical Perspectives on Accounting,* 17 (2006), pp. 29–55. The author would like to thank the publisher, Elsevier, for permission to use this material.

7 The Holocaust, Accounting and the Denial of Humanity

INTRODUCTION

The Holocaust, which has been referred to as a "gigantic, murderous opera-tion" (Muller-Hill, 1994, p. 68) which involved the systematic annihilation of six million Jews[1] (Eisner, 1983, p. 155; Wellers, 1978, pp. 139–143), is recognized as one of the most momentous events in the 20th century, if not in recorded history (Hilberg, 1980; Dawidowicz, 1975, p. xi; Katz, 1989, p. 354). According to Pois (1989, p. 1938), "The Holocaust is the single most impor-tant phenomenon associated with a movement which . . . attempted to end history". It is widely seen amongst scholars and lay commentators as creat-ing a watershed not only in Jewish history but in what had been understand-ings of the nature of man. After the Holocaust there would never be the same level of innocence and faith in the inherent goodness of humankind or a similar understanding of the way in which social institutions worked (Hilberg, 1980, p. 102; Browning, 1988, p. 173). Wiesel (1988, p. 11) refers to the Holocaust as "a kind of black hole in history. . . . Man's attitude towards heresy and faith, language and silence, science and political science is no longer the same . . .".

Unlike other instances of genocide in history, the Holocaust was the first time when the power of the technology of the modern world had been turned on a group of people, connected only through a religious heritage, systematically and methodically to murder them to the last person (Bauer, 1989, pp. 83–84). The scale of the misery during the Holocaust, declares Habermas, creates an obligation always to remember those murdered (see LaCapra, 1994, p. 53; Talmon, 1989, Book 1, p. 185).

The Holocaust would not have been possible, argue Hilberg (1985), Goldhagen (1996) and Browning (1980, p. 183), without the enthusiastic cooperation of the German civil bureaucracy. Destruction of human life on the scale of the Holocaust "is not the work of a few mad minds. It cannot be accomplished by any handful of men. It is far too complex in its organi-zational build-up and far too pervasive in its administrative implementation to dispense with specialized bureaucrats in every segment of society" (Hil-berg, 1980, p. 99, also 1972, p. 3; Dawidowicz, 1975, p. xv). The enduring metaphor for the Holocaust is that of the operation of an efficient machine with the sole objective of processing millions of people as quickly, costlessly and effectively as possible to produce corpses. The outcome of these outputs was a world, most particularly the German Reich, without Jews; a world cleansed of what the Nazis saw as the Jewish pestilence; a world from which would be removed what the Nazis portrayed as the polluting and degrading influence of Jewish capitalism.

Accounting in the service of the German bureaucracy was not only a means of expediting the annihilation of the Jews but was also one of the means by which people who had no direct involvement in the murder of millions of Jews were able to divorce themselves from the objectives and consequences of their work. Irrespective of the then known ultimate fate of the Jews, the aggregation, reductionism and anonymity of accounting numbers allowed the forced movement of millions of people great distances from their homes to be drained of any considerations which would imply that the numbers and costings on the pieces of paper which were passed from one bureaucrat to the next related to prescient human beings. When it came time to dispose of the property taken from the Jews, the Germans attempted to purify their actions and to sanctify their motives by insisting that before any of the property could be available for use by the State it had to pass through rigorous accounting procedures. In the process, the accounts were used as the symbolic means of spiritual cleansing for those at the killing centers and directly engaged in the annihilation of the Jews.

A theme which has permeated this work is the way in which accounting has been shown to have the ability to privilege a limited set of interests and, thereby, to deny a voice for the excluded or the "Other" (Broadbent, 1995). In particular, accounting's aura of neutrality and objectivity, in part stemming from representations which emphasize accounting as a technology of inscription, has been the means to discount the subjective as something necessarily inferior to the products of the rational logic of accounting (Gallhoffer and Haslam, 1991; Francis, 1990; Miller and O'Leary, 1993, pp. 190, 192). It has also been a convenient means of isolating accounting from ethical questioning. As a significant, if mainly unheralded, participant of history, judgments about the use of accounting's calculative practices can no longer escape consideration of accounting's ethical dimensions and moral consequences (Pois, 1989, p. 1937; Lovell, 1995, p. 61; Maunders and Burritt, 1991, see p. 22). Francis's 1990 paper crystallizes the discontent in the critical accounting literature with the portrayal of accounting and accountants as socially blameless and accounting as solely a rational technology geared to ends—means relationships which is able to escape moral reckonings. Drawing upon the work on "virtue" by MacIntyre, Francis (1990, p. 6) condemns a "rationality that naively presumes to stand outside of morality by not questioning ends on the grounds that they are subjective".

Recognition of the moral and discursive character of accounting, with its ability to cause things to happen, demands that accountants desiring

to be virtuous, in a moral sense as opposed to a purely professional interpretation, take more responsibility for their work by recognizing its moral
imperatives (Francis, 1990, p. 5). Consideration of the plight of the silenced
and excluded Jews, one manifestation of the "Other", in Germany between
1933–1945 emphasizes the ethical and qualitative dimensions of accounting by recognizing the tragic consequences when these are excluded from
consideration. Previous chapters have established that conspicuous feature
of accounting information which makes it so attractive is its ability to create
new realities and visibilities (Miller, 1990, pp. 316–317). Accounting as an
instrument of the German civil bureaucracy who were responsible for the
transportation of Jews to extermination sites provided at "centers of calculation" new quantitative visibilities (Miller, 1990, p. 318), which were able
to supplant the qualitative dimensions of the Jews as individuals by commodifying and dehumanizing them and, thereby, for all intents make them
invisible as individuals with the sacred right to life.

Accounting is no longer accepted as "an innocuous mapper of reality"
(Broadbent and Laughlin, 1994, p. 4). Accounting is an active agent in social
processes, the implementation of political programs, and in the creation and
maintenance of social structures (Tinker, 1980; Tinker *et al.*, 1991; Graves
et al., 1996, p. 62; Lovell, 1995, p. 60). Accounting is no longer able to hide
behind a disguise of neutrality and disinterested objectivity. Thus,

> political rationalities accord significances and meanings to quite mun-
> dane calculative routines, allowing their practitioners to articulate their
> potential contributions in terms that extend far beyond their operation
> within individual enterprises.
>
> (Miller, 1990, p. 334)

In Nazi Germany accounting was part of a structure of controls and
practices designed to maximize the outcomes of policies contrived to deliver
efficiency and effectiveness in the service of the State, the effects of which
were tragically momentous. Consistent with the growing body of research,
which regards accounting as a social phenomenon, as opposed to a collection of sterile techniques, a broad conception of accounting will inform this
study of the Holocaust. Thus, accounting can be defined as a technology of
inscription which provides "information for decision making which leads to
action" (Broadbent and Laughlin, 1994, p. 2). When it came time to enlist
the bureaucracy in implementing the murderous policies of the Nazis, the
use of anti-Semitic propaganda by the Nazis was proven to be successful in
conditioning an already susceptible bureaucracy to regard as legitimate the
government's treatment of German citizens who were Jewish.

THE JEW IN NAZI IDEOLOGY

Anti-Semitism in Germany and the demonization of Jews as the source of
the evils of capitalism and the difficulties of Germany in the 1920s and early

1930s was not an invention of Hitler and the Nazis. Instead, in common with most other European countries Germany had a long history of antipathy towards the Jews in its midst (Winston, 1980; Langmuir, 1980; Weber, 1980; Mosse, 1970, pp. 19, 34–60). Ostracization of the Jews was sustained by emotive historical stereotypes of the predatory Jewish financier, teachings of the Christian church and spurious race theories riding on the prestige of 19th century science. In the 16th century Martin Luther, for example, had warned against the Jews and the perils which association with them would bring to Christians. Jews were seen as perennial outsiders who owed no allegiance to any country only to their religion, to the accumulation of more wealth and their own well-being (Sombart, 1913, p. 5). In the process they were accused of giving little thought of the consequences of their activities and selfishness to the non-Jewish Germans, their alleged unsuspecting and defenseless victims.

German anti-Semitism was given new life at the beginning of the 20th century with mounting opposition amongst extremist polemicists to the social transformations which accompanied capitalism. A rational economic glaze was given to anti-Semitism in the works of noted German economists, including Sombart,[2] who sought to take well-entrenched prejudices out of the realm of mythology and folklore by identifying the alleged economic perversity of Jews. Particular objection was taken with what were seen as the "mechanical", "abstract" and "artificial", and therefore to an Aryan the alien, features of capitalism which, it was suggested, particularly suited the Jew who had no empathy or understanding with the natural and the organic (Sombart, 1913, pp. 274–275, 277; Mosse, 1970, p. 9; Herf, 1984, p. 134). The Jew was the embodiment of capitalism and all its defects (Sombart, 1913, p. 50) and, therefore, epitomized everything which was foreign and not German (Sombart, 1913, p. 115; Fleming, 1985, p. 8). The German at heart was an idealist, aspiring to all that was great and pure (Mosse, 1970, p. 18). It was from this pure spirit which came "the creative force which . . . created the monuments of human culture" (Hitler, 1987, p. 271; Dawidowicz, 1975, p. 18). Set against, and the major threat to, this purity was the Jew. German romanticism was identification with the land and its embodiment of the greatness of the German nation while to the Jew it was another thing to be exploited and defiled. The result was a debasement of rural life (Hitler, 1987, p. 281). With the arrival of the Jew came urbanization, a contempt for manual work and the subservience of the German to the monied, industrial economy of the Jew (Hitler, 1987, p. 288). It was "due specifically to the Jewish spirit that these characteristics of modern economic life came into being" (Sombart, 1913, pp. 61, 115).

The Jew had created a form of modern capitalism in which everything was available for the Jew's own selfish gain. Capitalism exalted the individual; it encouraged the decoupling of the individual from their social context and trivialized all relationships by measuring them in terms of economic consequences. Accordingly, conceptions of community and self-sacrifice were allegedly never part of Jewish culture (Sombart, 1913, p. 263). Summarizing what to him was an obvious feature of the Jew, Sombart proposed that the "Jews' whole being is opposed to all that is usually understood by chivalry, to all sentimentality. . . . Politically he is an individualist. . . . It comes to this, that they behold the world not with their 'soul' but with their intellect" (1913, p. 264, also p. 271). As a result:

> The rationalization of life accustomed the Jew to a mode of living contrary to . . . Nature and therefore also to an economic system like the capitalistic, which is likewise contrary to . . . Nature. What in reality is the idea of making profit, what is economic rationalism, but the application to economic activities of the rules by which the Jewish religion shaped Jewish life? Before capitalism could develop the natural man had to be changed out of all recognition, and a rationalistically minded mechanism introduced in his stead.
>
> (Sombart, 1913, p. 238; see also Herf, 1984, pp. 136–137, 141)

Hitler (1987, pp. 262–263) believed that the Aryan was the source of all creativity and greatness. His accusation that the Jews were unable to create meant that they would have to feed off the endeavors of others. They would always be "a parasite in the body of other peoples . . ., a sponger who like a noxious bacillus keeps spreading . . ." (Hitler, 1987, pp. 276, 277). The only hope of protecting the Aryan race against the wiles of the Jew, according to Hitler (1987, pp. 195, 367), was for the State to take an active role in maintaining the purity of German blood. In this program of eugenics the State was to act "without regard to understanding or lack of understanding, approval or disapproval" (Hitler, 1987, p. 368). The purpose of the State

> lies in the preservation and advancement of a community of physically and psychically homogeneous creatures. . . . Thus, the highest purpose of the folkish State is concern for the preservation of those original racial elements which bestow culture and create the beauty and dignity of a higher mankind. . . .
>
> (Hitler, 1987, pp. 357–358)

In less than a decade after Hitler expressed his vision for the German State in *Mein Kampf* he was able to set in place the political will and the means to perpetrate the Holocaust. *Mein Kampf,* written in 1924, is often taken as the blueprint of Hitler's policy towards to the Jews and proof that Hitler had formed his intentions to annihilate the Jews as early as the end of World War I after he had been demobilized (see Hitler, 1987, p. 210; Cross, 1974, p. 87; Dawidowicz in Cesarani, 1994, p. 6). It is replete with references to the purported unhealthy influence of Jews, their debilitating effects on German society and psyche and their embodiment of all that is antithetical to what it meant to be German, wholesome and natural. The progressive exclusion and worsening persecution of Jews immediately after Hitler's rise to power is said to provide further evidence of Hitler's ultimate plans for the Jews (Dawidowicz, 1975, p. 163).

In contrast to the view that Hitler's goal of racial, Aryan purity had been formed when he was quite young and that its achievement depended upon the annihilation of the Jews, is the belief, which has assumed greatest popularity amongst historiographers, that the Final Solution, the last phase in the Holocaust, arose only as a response to the convergence of an emerging set of circumstances during World War II (Fleming, 1985, p. xviii). It is argued that there is not enough evidence to trace the idea of the Final Solution to the period immediately after World War I or even to Hitler[3] (Dawidowicz, 1975, pp. 151–153; Cesarani, 1994, pp. 7, 8; Adam in Fleming, 1985, p. xiv). In other words, it was a *function* of opportunistic events which allowed senior Nazi officials to take their Jewish policies to their ultimate conclusion (Mason, 1989). These "functionalists", therefore, do not see any long-term plan on either Hitler's part or that of other senior members of his government, including Heinrich Himmler of the SS and Reinhard Heydrich of the SD or security police. Not until the German army became enmeshed in the tragedy of the Russian campaign after December 1941 was a "final solution" put into place. It was after this time that members of the SS moved into the occupied territories behind the front lines and set about systematically to murder all Jews.

THE WILL OF THE STATE AND THE MAIN PHASES OF THE HOLOCAUST

Exclusion of the Jews in Germany 1933–1939

The powers which governments have make them supreme in all matters. In the case of elected governments these powers are given for a defined period by citizens entitled to vote. To ensure that these powers will not be used to avoid electoral censure, most systems of government have controls built into them which can be activated to reinstate the sovereignty of the people. In circumstances where governments seek to thwart the will of the people these controls can be suspended either by way of force, as in a military coup, or by stealth through the passing of laws to entrench the existing powers and deny competing groups the opportunity to govern. Often the latter approach is accompanied by a reign of terror directed towards dissidents or political groups and those who provide a convenient target to play on the fears of the nation. This form of usurpation has been most common in the 20th century in the establishment of one party states, whether socialist regimes of the far left or fascist governments of the far right, including the Nazis. In either case, the aim has been to establish systems of control which enable the sovereignty of the ruling group to be complete, entrenched and undeniable. Such was the case in Germany between 1933 and 1945, the period which the Nazis designated as the Third Reich, when the full power of the State was malevolently brought to bear on, firstly, German Jews and then all European Jewry.

In Eastern Europe throughout the 19th century Jews had been the subject of numerous pogroms, especially in Russia. Unlike the policies of the Nazis, pogroms were limited, although still often deadly, harassments of the Jews. They were not attempts to eliminate Jews or to force them to flee to other countries. Instead, they were responses by governments to the periodic venting of local hostilities towards a vulnerable minority which had become a convenient scapegoat for economic problems. The period of the Holocaust was something very different. From within the Warsaw Ghetto Chaim Kaplan described German Jewish policies as a

> gigantic catastrophe, which . . . has no parallel even in the darkest periods of Jewish history. Firstly—the depth of the hatred. This is not hatred whose source is simply in a party platform, invented for political purposes. It is a hatred of emotion, whose source is some psychopathic disease, in its outward manifestation it appears as physiological hatred, which sees the object of its hatred as tainted in body, as lepers who have no place in society.
>
> *(Extracts from the Warsaw Ghetto Diary of Chaim A. Kaplan, March 10, 1940, in Arad et al., 1981, p. 201)*

The Nazis had prepared their policy of exclusion towards the German Jews well before Hitler was appointed Chancellor and asked to form a government on January 30, 1933. In the presence of the enfeebled president, Field Marshall von Hindenburg, the passage through the Reichstag of the *Enabling Act* on March 23, 1933, gave Hitler almost dictatorial powers which, when combined with the declaration of a state of emergency soon after being elected, enabled Hitler to harass, kill and imprison his political opposition and to mute any criticism. Much of the Nazi vitriol was directed at the Jews who, on the basis of Nazi racial theories, were progressively driven out of public service occupations, the universities and the professions (*The Law for the Restoration of the Professional Civil Service, and Law Regarding Admission to the Bar,* April 7, 1933). In 1935 under the Nuremberg Laws Jews[4] were stripped of their German citizenship and deprived of the rights and benefits which all German citizens had previously enjoyed (see an example in Arad *et al.,* 1981, pp. 199–200; Bullock, 1973, p. 339). Once Jews ceased to exist as legal entities who possessed rights at law and no longer enjoyed the benevolence of the State they became easy targets for more extreme forms of Nazi attacks. After 1937 Jews were forbidden to attend most public places, including schools, libraries, swimming pools, and to use some forms of public transport. By the outbreak of World War II a comprehensive system of segregation or apartheid had been forced upon all German Jews.

Not content with excluding Jews from public life, the Nazis passed laws which excluded Jews from operating many types of businesses and gave the government the authority to seize Jewish businesses or to force their sacrificial sale (for an example, see *Regulation for the Elimination of the Jews from the Economic Life of Germany, November 12, 1938,* in Arad *et al.,* 1981, pp. 115–116). At the same time that the level of economic persecution increased, the various military arms of the Nazis became more brazen in their attacks on Jews and Jewish property. This culminated on the night of November 10, 1938, *Kristallnacht* or the Night of Broken Glass, with the widespread destruction of Jewish synagogues and property. The opportunity was also taken to round up and murder members of the Jewish community who had displeased the Nazis[5] (Klarsfeld, 1978, p. 29). With the rise in attacks sanctioned by the government and condoned by anti-Semitic legislation, those Jews who could see that while ever they remained in Germany they would be at risk attempted to settle in other countries (Klarsfeld, 1978, pp. 1–6). Almost two thirds of Germany's 500,000 Jews managed to escape. Unfortunately, most of these settled in other European countries which were soon to be overrun by the German army.

The Final Descent 1939–1945

With the declaration of war against Poland on September 1, 1939, the fate was sealed of nearly two out of every three Jews in Europe. Between the outbreak of hostilities and the end of the war two phases can be identified in the German treatment of the Jews. From 1939 to the beginning of 1942 the laws already in place were enforced with ever increasing fervor and ruthlessness. From October 1939 the Germans commenced the transportation of all Jews under their control to the east, principally to Poland. Later, an order from the Reich Security Main Office was issued on October 23, 1941, which forbade any emigration of Jews (in Arad *et al.,* 1981, pp. 153–154). From early 1942 the full effects of a policy of annihilation began to be felt.

The journey to death for most Jews began when they were loaded into, most often, railway cattle wagons and taken over large distances—a thousand miles was not uncommon—in conditions of great brutality (*Instructions for the Deportation of the Jews from the Palatinate, October 1940,* in Arad *et al.,* 1981, pp. 145–146). At first most Jews were concentrated in sealed towns or ghettos, amongst which the Warsaw ghetto is possibly the best known, where the deprivations which they were forced to endure caused the deaths of many thousands (Hilberg, 1972, pp. 40–41). Later in 1942 the policy of containment was replaced in favor of the systematic killing of Jews in the death camps of Poland[6] (Von Lang, 1983, p. 94). Goebbels (1982, pp. 147–148), in his diary on March 27, 1942, makes very clear the intentions of the Nazis towards the Jews, at the same time describing the treatment of the Jews during this period of the Holocaust as pretty barbaric . . . and not to be described here more definitely. Not much will remain of the Jews. . . . No other government and no other regime would have the strength for such a global solution of this question. Here too the Fuhrer is the undismayed champion of a radical solution necessitated by conditions and therefore inexorable. Fortunately a whole series of possibilities presents itself to us in wartime that would be denied us in peacetime.

Initially the killings were accomplished by mass shootings. However, it was soon found that killing thousands of people with bullets was very slow and complicated. A more effective method of killing a large number of Jews required the use of gas in a similar manner to the way in which it had been used extensively prior to the war to kill, it is estimated, over 75,000 Germans who suffered from incurable diseases, were mentally retarded or were persistent sexual offenders (Hilberg, 1985, p. 872). The first stage in the gassing of the European Jews was carried out by Einsatzgruppen using mobile vans modified for the purpose of using carbon monoxide from the exhaust to kill (Fleming, 1985, p. 63; Browning, 1988; Streim, 1989). These Einsatzgruppen, who were not under the control of the local army commanders, were given free rein in the early part of the campaign against Russia to carry out their work (Browning, 1985; *Special Duties for the SS in Operation Barbarossa, March 13, 1941,* in Arad *et al.,* 1981, p. 375). Mobile vans were later superseded by the establishment of the six main death camps in Poland. It was in one of these killing centers that most Jews were to die.

"A COMMERCIAL ENTERPRISE INSPIRED BY A SCHEME OF MASS MURDER": THE GERMAN BUREAUCRACY AND THE FINAL SOLUTION

The Civilian Bureaucracy

The ability of the Nazis to collect, transport, process, kill and dispose of the remains of six million Jews was due less to any extraordinary management abilities on their part and more to the presence of a very cooperative, enthusiastic and thorough German civil bureaucracy (Browning, 1980; Rosenberg, 1983; Speer, 1971, p. 5). Members of the Nazi Party of themselves could not have given Hitler the strong economy and the efficiency he needed to conduct a war on several fronts. In one of his memoirs Albert Speer (1971, p. 4) referred to the party members as people of low intellect who

> were so hidebound that they slowed down development. . . . The economic upswings after 1933 were due chiefly to the cooperation of those echelons that derived from the days of the Kaiser and the Weimar Republic . . . an excellent officialdom and outstanding technocrats in the widest sense of the word offered their services in 1933.

Rosenberg (1983, p. 13) has called these mostly anonymous technocrats the "desk-killers". The bureaucrat was

> a functionary in a vast bureaucratic organisation, who kill[ed] from behind a desk without wielding any weapons more lethal than a typewriter that issues reports dealing out death . . . along deliberately anonymous channels or through a labyrinth of bureaucratic routines and apparatus.
>
> (Rosenberg, 1983, p. 13)

In part, as a consequence of the participation of the bureaucracy, LaCapra (1994, p. 90) describes the Holocaust as being "calculated coldly and with the maximum efficiency and economy". The killing of a very large number of people in a relatively short space of time was nothing more than "an efficiency problem of the greatest dimensions. . . . With an unfailing sense of direction . . . the German bureaucracy found the shortest road to the final goal" (Hilberg, 1985, p. 9). Thus, it was in no small measure due to the professionalism of the civilian bureaucracy that the Final Solution went close to achieving its goal of the annihilation of Europe's Jews. The actions of faceless and industrious bureaucrats, and their unexceptionable identities when compared to the legacy left by the zealots who were their leaders, was for Browning and Hilberg the most alarming feature of the process of destruction (Browning, 1988, p. 172–173). Hilberg (1985, p. 25) noted that

> although the destructive work was largely embedded in administrative routines, much more was required of a bureaucrat than automatic implementation of anti-Jewish measures. Without timely proposals and initiatives, the process would have been crippled, as various complicated steps against Jewry would inevitably have been postponed, dissipated, or aborted.

Civilian bureaucrats were able to carry out their duties associated with the Final Solution separated from the ultimate consequences of their actions by distance and their indirect participation. Their work to expedite the collection, accounting for and delivery of the Jews to the death camps formed only part of their daily work. Thus, amongst the pressures of a busy day the Jews assumed a commonplaceness. They became just another cargo to be marshalled, loaded, costed and moved. In the departments responsible for the railways, for example, transportation of Jews involved largely the same considerations as other scheduling.

Even accepting that civilian, and even military, bureaucrats may not have known about the murders taking place as a consequence of devotion to their duties, they were aware that vast numbers of people were being uprooted in the most extreme and uncertain of circumstances never to be heard of again for the most part. Contrary to their protestations, Read argues that the moral duties of the person are greater than any of the duties which the individual possesses as a member of society. His moral responsibilities, both to himself and others, transcends the given social context, are conceived to be independent of the social ties which link him to his followers.

(quoted in Velayutham and Perera, 1996, p. 67; see also Rosenberg, 1983, p. 14; Lovell, 1995, p. 61)

By not actually observing and taking an active part in administering the cause of death, bureaucrats at all levels later attempted to relieve their consciences by arguing that, like their more notorious colleagues who supervized and ordered the killings, they were only following orders. In addition, they protested that they did not know the ultimate object of the orders or of their work. They may have seen orders for railway wagons, railway timetables, costings, purchase requisitions and other pieces of paper but they did not have contact with the subjects of these documents. Unlike the SS,

> most of the participants did not fire rifles at Jewish children or pour gas into gas chambers. . . . Most bureaucrats composed memoranda, drew up blueprints, signed correspondence. . . . They could destroy a whole people by sitting at their desks.
>
> (Hilberg, 1985, p. 1024)

After 30 years of examining the role of the civilian bureaucracy in the Holocaust, Hilberg was still trying to answer the question, "Why were they not inefficient?" and thereby able to slow down the rate of killing (1980, p. 101). Why did "they always . . . do the maximum" (Hilberg, 1985, p. 1003)? In an attempt to answer these questions, Browning, who has also spent much of his career studying the German bureaucracy under the Nazis, concluded that older members of the bureaucracy were tainted with anti-Semitism long before the Nazis arrived to power and, therefore, were ready to accept the Jews as a scapegoat for the problems of Germany throughout the Weimar Republic. Well before the time that the anti-Semitic laws began to bite and the Jews began to disappear in large numbers from Germany and its new territories, the German state bureaucracy had been conditioned to the consequences of Nazi policies with the result that after the Final Solution was put in place "there was no sudden crisis of conscience, no traumatic agonizing . . . virtually no foot-dragging . . ." (Browning, 1988, p. 173). Bureaucrats, whom Aly and Heim (1988, p. 8) describe as young and very ambitious, also benefited by the exclusion of a strong group of occupational competitors, the Jews (Browning, 1980, p. 195). The process of exclusion in which they colluded was achieved by accretion until a point was reached whereby the Jews had been stripped of all rights, including the right to their humanity. By the time the civil bureaucracy might have realized that they were part of a scheme of annihilation, the bureaucracy was in the control of

Nazi extremists who had infiltrated the bureaucracy's highest levels (Browning, 1980, p. 195).

While acknowledging the self-serving nature of the bureaucrats' objections, for most there is some validity in their claims of ignorance of the monstrous enterprise in which they had become an essential part. Apart from unconfirmed and dangerous rumors, the great majority of the German people had no direct knowledge of the process of annihilation in which their leaders were engaged. Indeed, the top Nazi echelons went to extraordinary lengths after the Wannsee conference in January 1942[7] to keep secret both the existence of the death camps and the eventual destiny of the Jews removed from Germany (Gilbert, 1986, p. 284). To help accomplish this, the intentions of the Nazis towards the Jews were hidden behind seemingly innocuous euphemisms,[8] sometimes referred to as "Nazi-Deutsch" (see Friedlander, 1980; Dawidowicz, 1976, pp. 14–16). Jews who were to be expelled from Germany were said to be "resettled" or "put to work" in the east (Eichmann in Von Lang, 1983, p. 93). Gassing, in deference to the Nazi preference for numbers to describe their organizations, was called Action 14f13 or *Sonderbehandlung* (special treatment) (Eichmann in Von Lang, 1983, p. 144). Most notoriously, the term "Final Solution of the Jewish Question" was successful in suppressing the true intent of the Nazi policy towards the Jews. Corruption of the German language by the Nazis, argues Dawidowicz (1976, p. 14), was designed to narrow the range of thinking and to provide "a language that concealed more than it communicated, its very nature and vocabulary buffering speaker and listener from reality".

Not only was the Nazi leadership uncertain as to the reaction of the German public if they knew that their former neighbors and associates were being systematically killed in their millions, they did not want to expose their plans to Jewish organizations which were assisting the Germans in identifying and transporting the people with whom these community groups shared a common heritage. The Nazis may have wanted to give history the legacy of a world without Jews but they did not want to publicize the process by which this was achieved. Possibly most of all, the Germans needed to keep their terrible secret hidden away from each new batch of victims. Hence, the cruel charade of the "bath houses" at Auschwitz. Jews of all ages were forced to undress and to fold neatly their clothing, to be collected by them after their shower they were told, after which they were herded into the gas chambers.

Accounting was part of this network of euphemisms and disguises to mask from the inmates, the German public and the world the eradication of an entire group of people. Accounting numbers also enabled the civil bureaucracy and their masters to control from a distance and to capture key dimensions of the extermination process without being in constant attendance (Humphrey and Scapens, 1996, p. 89; Miller, 1990, p. 318). Documents of the Holocaust, reminds Hilberg (1985, p. x), are "not merely a record of events but artefacts of the administrative machinery itself. What we call a documentary source was once an order, letter, or report. Its date, signature, and dispatch invested it with immediate consequences". In terms of Francis's (1990, p. 7) description of accounting, as with all sectors and resources within a ruthless totalitarian State, accounting in Nazi Germany was above all else a political practice which was not value free. Rather, "the rationality of accounting—what we account for, how we account, to whom we account, about whom we account, when we account, and so on—are value choices made with respect to relations between members of the *polis*" (Francis (1990, p. 7). The theme of interdependency when an account is given is also emphasized by Schweiker (1993, pp. 234, 240), who describes accounting as

> a discursive act of saying or writing something about intentions, actions, relations and outcomes to someone—even if this is ourselves—. . . in such a way that an identity is enacted as intrinsically interdependent with others. . . . As *moral* agents we give various accounts of those actions, relations and sufferings in a way that binds us to others. . . .

Accounting as a moral practice, therefore, means that the accountant is never acting in isolation; there will always be others affected by the accountant's actions.

ACCOUNTING IN THE SERVICE OF THE HOLOCAUST

Accounting for the Invisible

The Holocaust involved the extension of functional reasoning from the factory, where it assists management in the transformation of inputs into desired outputs, to the processing of human beings and their property (see Rubinoff in Rosenberg, 1983, p. 13). More particularly, according to Rosenberg (1983, p. 14), it resulted in the "corruption of rationality into ideological forms of functional reasoning". At the heart of functional reason is the use of technologies of calculation, most importantly accounting. A great advantage of these technologies, now well recognized in accounting research (Francis, 1990), is the perception that they are amoral, value-free and that of themselves they cannot be made to be responsible or to have prescience. In the service of the Holocaust they were used to

> reduce human beings to quantified objects, thus eliminating their troublesome qualities of humaneness. . . . Functional reason must treat people as objects, as things, as mere numbers that can be easily manipulated and casually disposed of. . . . It allows individuals to manipulate fellow human beings as things until they were done away with when no longer perceived as useful or needed.
>
> (Rosenberg, 1983, p. 12)

A prominent claim in the critical management accounting literature is the ability of accounting information to create visibilities which had not previously existed, with the result that control is enhanced (Broadbent and Laughlin, 1994, p. 4; Miller and O'Leary, 1987). The visibilities created by accounting enhance control by making possible modes of control tailored to the smallest level of activity and resource within an organization (see Hopwood, 1983; Humphrey and Scapens, 1996, p. 87). Velayutham and Perera (1996, p. 76) also refer to the ability of accounting to create organizational visibilities. Broadbent (1995, p. 1) has shown how these visibilities created by accounting have contributed to an entrenched discourse with its persuasive logic which has led to the exclusion of other criteria to assess value. She proposes that by "making certain aspects of reality 'visible' it creates the possibility of controlling these elements. It is this partiality in representation and its control potential which constitutes its real social influence as well as its social danger" (Broadbent, 1995, p. 4).

Creation of visibilities by accounting, as has been demonstrated here with the preparations for nuclear war and the Vietnam War, will be at the expense of other things moving into the shadows and becoming or remaining invisible (Easthope and McGowan, 1992; Gallhoffer and Haslam, 1991, p. 492). That which does not possess the dimensions captured by accounting records is excluded. Thus, accounting provides a partial rendition of reality whereby "visibilities created by accounting become reality and, thereby, those issues that have been stripped away in order to create the metaphor become invisible" (Broadbent, 1995, p. 71). To be invisible is to risk becoming valueless. Unfortunately for those adversely affected by the bifurcation of reality by accounting into that which is visible and that which is invisible, by definition that which is not captured by accounting must be without value.

The consequence of creating particular visibilities is that some things are allowed to be seen as tangible and therefore to exist. As a result "they can more easily be decoupled from the social milieu in which they are embedded and discussion of these issues in the 'public' sphere is enabled" (Broadbent and Laughlin, 1994, p. 7). The conversion of Jews to an extreme one-dimensional metric, an integer as a component of tabulations which could be arithmetically manipulated, stripped the identity and all other qualities from the Jews and gave their tormentors the anonymity for the subjects of their work which enabled them to avoid divulging the human correspondence of their accounts. The Jew was recognized no longer as a social being and, thereby, in the absence of this measure they became invisible and ceased to exist. They could then be discussed in the public domain through their surrogates found in the calculations on accounting reports. Unlike other social participants they no longer had a life history, the potential to make worthwhile contributions, responsibilities as family members or the capacity to love and have feelings. Debased numbers are not able to experience emotions, nor do they have a past. Numbers are contrived for a purpose and then cease to have the same importance beyond that purpose.

As one who later had cause to regret the bureaucracy's pedantic ways, Eichmann derisively complained that "the various departments defended every inch of their competency tooth and nail. . . . The bureaucracy . . . stuck to the regulations with an obstinacy, a punctiliousness" (quoted in Von Lang, 1983, p. 146; Arendt, 1964). In the records of the bureaucracy, as the next section illustrates, accounting as a technology of management is clearly implicated in all stages of the destruction of European Jews. From the creation of lists of victims used to plan railway rolling stock needs and the timetabling of transports, to the disposal of Jewish property left outside the gas chambers or near the shooting pits, accounting can be seen to have fulfilled an essential part at each step. Thus, those who diligently used accounting precisely to track and account for over six million people cannot escape their share of responsibility for the results of their undertaking. Fleming (1985, p. 46) notes that the "planned killing" of the Holocaust "required a procedure thought out with absolute precision down to the smallest detail". In a similar manner to production in a factory, the Holocaust was killing based on the detailed organization and principles of the assembly line.

Extermination Accounting

From the time that the Jews were mustered for deportation they ceased to exist as individuals and instead took on the sole identity of a numbered Jew. The creation of lists of deportees was the final stage in a process which had grown from the Nuremberg Laws in 1935 to make the Jews non-existent. They were not recognized as anything other than an input, of varying degrees of value, in a conversion process. As a member of a class of objects they were denoted as a number; a number which formed the basis of a system whereby the Germans could account for the progress of their policy of extermination. Thus, in reports to Hitler and Himmler, for example, the emphasis is on reporting the *number* of people who had been killed and the number yet to be killed. As an example, in a report prepared by the head of the Statistics Department in Himmler's office in March 1943, detailed figures are given of the number of "moves" from the Sudetenland, Austria and other areas under German control. It concludes that total "evacuations" for Special Treatment were 1,786,356 (*SS Statistics of the Final Solution*, in Arad *et al.*, 1981, pp. 333–334).

This process of accounting, and accountability, was made possible by the detailed lists of Jews living in most areas which had been kept or created for the Germans by Jewish community organizations. Well before preparations for the Final Solution were put into place the Germans knew the extent of their task. They knew that in Poland there were 2,284,000 Jews, 2,994,684 in the Ukraine and 742,800 in Hungary. With their lists of Jews all that remained was for the Germans to count the number killed and to deduct this from the number available to be killed. Wellers (1978, p. 139) calls this "macabre accounting". The lists of Jews were often so accurate that with the assistance of Jewish community leaders the Germans knew precisely how many people lived in each house. If they did not collect the correct number of people from each house then Jewish community representatives would be arrested to make up the numbers. Thus, far from being innocuous, documents which specified numbers of Jews to be collected were effectively death warrants in the form of charge–discharge accounting. Jewish leaders would be charged with the number on requisition documents and would be held personally liable until the charge was discharged with a corresponding number of people transported.

As if they knew that the owners would never return, civilian government employees immediately confiscated and meticulously accounted for all property left by the Jews including "personal property, apartments, community assets, blocked accounts, . . . sequestered securities, firms . . . credits and debts, pensions, insurance. . . . All these odds and ends . . . were now dropped into the laps of the Finance Ministry's experts" (Hilberg, 1985, p. 471). The process, which was systematic, well organized and extremely thorough, was greatly enhanced by the existence of detailed lists of property and wealth which had been required by the *Decree Regarding the Reporting of Jewish Property* (April 26, 1938). The key provisions of this decree stated that

> s.1(1) Every Jew . . . must report and assess his entire domestic and foreign property as of the effective date of this decree, in accordance with the regulations that follow. . . .
> s.3(1) Each item of property is to be assessed, in reporting, at its common value on the effective date of this decree. . . .
> s.4(1) . . . the property must be tentatively reported with an estimated value by June 30, 1938.

All property disclosed was liable to be used in the interests of the State (s.7) according to the wishes of the Reich Minister of the Interior, Herman Goering. In cases where property was not disclosed according to the Decree, the owner risked imprisonment for a period of up to ten years and immediate confiscation of all property, including that previously disclosed. Conforming to the Decree was in essence an accounting exercise whereby each Jew had to draw up a truncated balance sheet containing nothing but assets. In order to produce the list, the Decree made it clear that only values which could be substantiated were to be placed on the property. For Jews with extensive fixed property holdings this and the final compilation of the lists would have entailed the assistance of professionals with accounting skills, both to arrive at valuations and to create the reports in conformity with the legislation. Accounting, therefore, was involved in the spread of State surveillance, both of domestic and foreign affairs, and in the identification of resources in the possession of condemned Jews, which could be made available to the State.

After the passage of the 11th Ordinance of Reich Citizenship Law in November 1941, the property of any Jew who left Germany was immediately lost to the State. Prior to this, confiscation of property could only occur after the courts pronounced, in each case, the Jew to be an enemy of the State (Hilberg, 1985, p. 471). With the prospect of the inevitable seizure of their property, many Jews were induced to sell their property and businesses in an attempt to gain at least something. At the forefront of this process "accountants and bookkeepers . . . could busy themselves with contracts that were products of pressure put on Jewish owners to sell their property. . . . The accountants could always say to themselves that acquisitions were acquisitions" (Hilberg, 1993, p. 65).

Crucial to the success of Nazi extermination policies was the ability to gain access to railway rolling stock to transport the Jews and to schedule these transports. Once a train had been allocated it was up to the bureaucrats on the railways and the Gestapo to ensure that each train was fully utilized and that the time for each shipment was rigorously met (Hilberg, 1985, pp. 455–465; Hilberg, 1989). Prior to the trains being made available it was the responsibility of the Traffic Division of the Reichsbahn and its accountants to set the rates to charge for the transports. The Gestapo, who was primarily responsible for providing the cargo for the death camp trains, was charged the third-class one-way fare of 4 pfenning per track kilometer for each adult carried. A fare of 2 pfenning was charged for children under ten while children under four travelled free. A discount of half the normal third-class fare was offered for groups of 400 or more.

Sometimes transportation bills would be sent to the Gestapo through the official Nazi travel agency, the Mittelewopaische Reiseburo. As the scale of the deportations grew, however, the Gestapo found it more difficult to meet the costs of transportation out of their budget. To deal with this problem a charge was levied on the Jewish community for each person deported (Hilberg, 1985, pp. 467–468). They in turn charged the deportees 25% of their liquid assets. Thus, in effect the Jews were paying for their own death. This money was to be deposited into a special SS account called Account W at the Reichsbank. At the conclusion of each transport a detailed account was required of movements into and out of Account W associated with the transport (*Instruction of Reich Association of the Jews in Germany to Jewish Community Associations, December 3, 1941*, in Hilberg, 1972, pp. 115–116).

Accounting was the essential ingredient which allowed sequestration of Jewish property by the Nazis to be comprehensive and exhaustive. In a State where terror was an institutionalized practice of the government, where infractions of onerous laws directed against the Jews were met with retribution which was severe and disproportionate to the offence, accounting provided another weapon of threat and intimidation to police easily decrees such as the *Decree Regarding the Reporting of Jewish Property*. Without the complicity of accountants, laws and decrees which firstly catalogued Jewish property and then denied Jews their rights to the property which had been identified would have been far less effective if not unenforceable. It was also accounting which provided the linkages and transitions which cohered the different phases of annihilation without the need to divulge to each the specifics of previous stages.

In occupied countries the Germans paid for the use of the State railway infrastructure. If there were insufficient funds in accounts which contained proceeds from the sale of confiscated Jewish property a charge might be made on the Reich Finance Ministry. Examination of correspondence between the Ministry of Transport and the High Command of the Army in March 1944, which referred to difficulties being experienced by the Greek State Railways in being paid 1,938,488 Reichmark for shipments of Jews to Auschwitz, provides details of payment arrangements and, possibly more importantly, gives a good idea of the business-like approach of those responsible for the transports. The Ministry of Transport officer writing the request for payment, presumably well after those who had been transported had been killed soon after arriving at Auschwitz, concludes by asking that

> this matter be cleared up with the Reichsfuhrer-SS and Chief of the German Police/Command Security Police and possibly the Reich Economy Minister and that care be taken to assure transmittal of the transport costs to the Directorate of the Greek State Railways. Kindly inform me about the progress of negotiations.
>
> (in Hilberg, 1972, pp. 164–165)

Directing the logistics of transportation was Eichman's office, which referred to the trains as *Sonderzuge* or "special passenger trains" (Hilberg, 1985, pp. 410–415). Eichmann confirmed that organizing the transports and ensuring that they were all paid for was an extremely complicated process which became increasingly more difficult towards the end of the war. Consequently, the cooperation of a number of German agencies was required for "no matter how large a German force was present, they couldn't just round up people, put them in freight cars, and ship them out. . . . We had to requisition the trains . . . and contract Administration and Supply headquarters" (Eichmann in Von Lang, 1983, p. 99).

Upon arrival at the camps, the inmates came under the control of the SS Economic Administration Main Office under Obergruppenfuhrer Oswalf Pohl. In Auschwitz inmates who were allowed to live long enough to work in the camp were given numbers which were tattooed onto their forearms. They were called *figuren* or simply numbers (*Evidence Given at the Nuremberg Trials*, in Arad et al., 1981, pp. 358–360), with the numbers recorded in a *Totenbuch* or "death book". Other dimensions of their being as individuals were thereby displaced by their number for "once they had been tattooed, the only thing that was important about them was their number. Whatever productive work that was to be had from them was as if from a machine" (Gilbert, 1986, p. 824).

As part of the efforts to delude the Jews as to their ultimate fate prior to deportations, everyone was permitted to take a small amount of money and some clothing. After each batch of killings the belongings which remained were carefully sorted, including gold extracted from teeth, and sent back to Germany. Great care was taken to account for everything. Hilberg notes how everything was collected, "to the last hairpin" (1985, p. 473). Himmler insisted that there be "painstaking exactness" in all dealings with and accounting for Jewish property, warning that "we cannot be accurate enough" (quoted in Hilberg, 1985, p. 951). As an example, in a secret report in June 1943 from the Commander of the SS in Galicia, a detailed inventory is provided of all property confiscated from Jews, including:

25.580kg	copper coins
97.190kg	gold coins
20.952kg	wedding rings
11.730kg	gold teeth
343.1kg	cigarette cases
6.166kg	pocket watches, various
3.425kg	pocket watches, silver
7.495kg	fountain pens and propelling pencils

(Final Report by Katzman, Commander of the SS in Galicia, in Arad *et al.,* 1981, pp. 335–341).

Himmler's demand for meticulous accounting was mainly to ensure that all possible proceeds found their way into the accounts of the SS. He was also concerned that in the absence of clear accountability the way would be open for theft which would be detrimental to the spiritual well-being of his troops (Hilberg, 1985, p. 951). By enforcing stringent standards of accountability Himmler believed that "in carrying out this most difficult of tasks . . . we have suffered no harm to our inner being, our soul, our character" (*Speech by Himmler to SS Officers, October 4, 1943,* in Arad *et al.,* 1981, p. 345). Indicating the seriousness with which meticulous accounting was regarded, Himmler threatened that

> anyone who takes so much as a single Mark, of this money is a dead man. . . . There will be no mercy. We had the moral right, we had the duty towards our people, to destroy this people that wanted to destroy us. But we do not have the right to enrich ourselves by so much as a fur, as a watch, by one Mark or a cigarette or anything else.
> *(Speech by Himmler to SS Officers, October 4,*
> *1943, in Arad et al., 1981, p. 345)*

The Nazis endeavored to transform accounting into the means by which they could be purged of impure motives and avoid being contaminated by a difficult task which the Jews had "forced" upon the Nazis. Himmler's insistence on punctilious accounting for property seized in the concentration camps and killing centers was the use of accounting for the purpose of *sanctification*. The stolen wealth of the Jews had to pass through the accounts of the SS to transform its corrupt nature, which threatened the purity of those with whom it came in contact, into something which was wholesome and which could be a consecrated servant of the State. The seizure of Jewish property could be blessed by rigorous accounting to demonstrate that the acts which produced the property were motivated not by the material results but by the need to purify the German race. For members of the SS and others, to benefit materially in an indiscriminate, avaricious manner allegedly similar to those who had previously owned the property, and probably obtained it by methods injurious to the German people, would be to become one of the fallen race and to put into question the right of the Nazis to conduct the crusade against the Jews. Thus, in addition to ensuring that the State benefited from property seizures, accounting offered the means of redemption, a clear conscience and the protection of the inner self.

All cash seized both before and after death was deposited in accounts at the Reichsbank along with the safe keeping of a vast amount of precious metals and jewelry (Dawidowicz, 1975, p. 147). According to Eichmann (in Von Lang, 1983, p. 123), the Swiss assisted in the sale of jewelry and watches in Switzerland and in the safekeeping of the proceeds for all of which there had to be a detailed accounting. In addition to benefiting financially from the disposal of property, the SS established an extensive business empire centered on the death camps. Inmates who were not immediately chosen for the gas chambers were employed in SS factories and hired out to private business firms. Of the latter, the most notorious was I.G. Farben, the chemical and dye manufacturer. Zyklon B, the trade name for hydrogen cyanide, which was used extensively in the gassing chambers of Auschwitz, was produced by a subsidiary of I.G. Farben, which also manufactured a stabilizing agent for transportation of the gas, but sold to the SS through another company in which Farben had a major share. I.G. Farben's association with the SS and the Final Solution provided them with an unbroken series of high profits throughout the last years of the war.[9] Other German companies benefited through the construction of the dormitory buildings, gas chambers and crematoria (Klarsfeld, 1978, p. 111). These profits found expression in company accounts but without any ethical qualifications.

CONCLUSION

The Nazis took advantage of a long history of German romanticism which portrayed the Aryan race as the source of creativity, spiritual strength and purity and therefore a sure bulwark against the deprecations which the Jew had introduced into German life. What was in reality a campaign to bring about the political bondage of the German people to the National Socialists was masqueraded as a religious crusade against the Jews. Hitler was the savior who would release the German people from the destructive influences of the Jews. By definition the defiler could not be tolerated if Aryan Germans were to be brought back to their simple roots and innocent happiness. The program to achieve this progressively coalesced around more extreme measures against the Jews to constitute the Holocaust. Accounting has been shown to have been involved at all stages in the Holocaust to facilitate the efficient implementation of the Nazis' program of firstly the exclusion of Jews and later their annihilation. In particular, accounting provided an unassuming and uncontested means to objectify Jews and to hallow the motives of the Nazis.

This chapter is based on the paper, "Accounting in the Service of the Holocaust", which originally appeared in *Critical Perspectives on Accounting*, 9 (1998), pp. 435–464. The author would like to thank the publisher, Elsevier, for permission to use this material.

NOTES

1. Adolf Eichmann during his interrogation after his capture agreed that six million was close to the number of Jews killed by all methods (Von Lang, 1983, p. 110). Eichmann admitted being responsible for the transportation of the Jews to the killing centers but denied involvement with their deaths (Von Lang, 1983, p. 103–104).
2. Landes described Sombart's *The Jews and Economic Life* as "a pseudo-scholarly hoax, a pedantic effort to confer by the lavish use of polyglot footnote references, an academic respectability to errant nonsense . . ." (quoted in Herf, 1984, p. 135).
3. Disagreement still exists amongst scholars as to whether Hitler gave the order which unleashed the Final Solution or even whether he knew about what was happening in the further reaches of the Reich. Amongst those who give Hitler the benefit of the doubt is David Irving. He argues, and is supported even by his most strident opponents, that no written evidence has yet come to light directly to link orders for a Final Solution with Hitler (Breitman, 1994, p. 73). Eichmann thought that it was "inconceivable" that Himmler or Hitler would put in writing an order of this nature (Von Lang, 1983, p. 93). Albert Speer, Hitler's armaments minister and chief architect, was in no doubt as a result of his close association with the top Nazis that orders for the Final Solution came from Hitler with contributions from Goebbels and Borman (Speer, 1971, p. 6). Eichmann at his trial also believed that his superior, Himmler, had received his orders from Hitler and that Himmler would not have dared to have conducted such a massive campaign of destruction which required a great many resources without Hitler's explicit approval (Eichmann in Von Lang, 1983, pp. 81, 93; see also Friedlander in Fleming, 1985, pp. xxv–xxvi; Klarsfeld, 1978, p. 35).
4. The *Reich Citizenship Law* and the *First Ordinance to the Reich Citizenship Law*, in November 1935, defined a Jew as someone who had three grandparents who were "fully Jewish by race" (Article 5). The second law decided upon in Nuremberg by the Nazi party was *The Law for the Protection of*

German Blood and Honor. The law prohibited marriages between Jews and Aryan Germans, permitted annulment of existing marriages, prohibited sexual intercourse between Jews and pure blood Germans and limited the household employment of Jews.

5. This persecution was not limited to the Jews. Jehovah's Witnesses, homosexuals, gypsies and most other minority religious groups suffered similar privations to those of the Jews.

6. The death camps were: Belzec, Sobibor, Treblinka, Chelmno, Majdanek and Auschwitz-Birkenau. The first train to the death camps left Germany on October 18, 1941 (Fleming, 1985, p. 67).

7. It was at the town of Wannsee on January 20–21, 1942, that the implementation of the Final Solution was discussed (Muller-Hill, 1994, p. 68). This had been preceded by a conference on October 10, 1941, amongst members of the RSHA, the Reich Security Main Office created by Reinhard Heydrich.

8. SS participating in extermination operations were required to sign an oath of silence (see Arad *et al.*, 1981, pp. 274–5).

9. I.G. Farben was also an enthusiastic supporter of the elimination of Serbians by the Croatian Ustasha who were an ally of the Nazis (Aly and Heim, 1988, p. 13).

8 Rendering Death and Destruction Visible
Counting the Costs of War

INTRODUCTION

Accounting has allowed political elites to legitimize the use of force by creating the visibilities and invisibilities needed to do so. In the previous chapter accounting was shown to have assisted the Nazis with the attempted systematic annihilation of the Jewish people by reducing individuals to anonymous, numbered units, thus dehumanizing them. This chapter confirms the way in which accounting makes war a more viable option for the U.S. political elite by excluding the social and human costs of war. While horror and devastation dominate personal accounts of war, these same subjects almost never appear in the strategic or political rhetoric of warfare. This is achieved by war planners using a techno-strategic discourse that renders the impact of fighting on humans invisible (Cohn, 1987; Scarry, 1985). If death and destruction is vanquished from official representations, then it must be the case that a State's ability to convince its citizens to wage war depends on silencing these horrors. According to Nordstrom (2004, p. 34):

> Part of [the modern state's] power rests on the optics of deception: focusing attention on the need for violence while drawing attention away from both the war-economy foundations of sovereign power and the price in human life this economy of power entails. This is the magician's trick: the production of invisible visibility.

Government accounting practices contribute to the creation of the invisible visibilities needed by the state to promote violence by concealing the human and social costs of war. When the Executive branch of the U.S. Government requests appropriations for war it only has to account for the short-term financial expenditures, making warfare appear to cost the nation a few extra dollars for salaries, ammunition or transportation.[1] The long-term social, political, physical, psychological, environmental, and economic costs to both the victor and the vanquished are ignored by these official accounts. Yet, it is these latter costs that matter the most. To a mother such as Cindy Sheehan, the Iraq War has been far more costly than the monetary resources the U.S. Government expended to transport her son to Iraq. Szymanski (2005, p. 1) has eloquently reminded us that

> there is nothing more painful or more heart breaking than a parent losing a child. And for Sheehan to lose her 24-year-old son, Casey, must have been like someone taking her very own heart and soul and, without warning, ripping them out and throwing them into the depths of hell. No one should have to experience such pain, but the cold reality of war is that someone's child actually dies and there are actual parents left living with the hopeless task of trying to cope with the pain.

Rendering visible the toll of war on humans and society contributes to the emancipatory potential of social accounting by addressing "what really matters to people" (Gallhofer and Haslam, 2003). Social accounting covers all forms of accounts and surpasses the purely economic in order to challenge the elitist interests served by the dominant discourses of instrumental rationality and economic efficiency that conventional accounting sustains (Gray, 2002; Mathews, 1997; Parker, 2005). This chapter argues that if the U.S. Government was required to do a social account for war, the tremendous human costs would become visible to the president, Congress and U.S. citizens, making it difficult to use a discourse of abstraction to hide the serious consequences from using violence.

No attempt will be made to monetize the social and human costs, for doing so would structure war as an economic rather than a human problem. The following quotes illustrate how the moment war is discussed within the dominant discourse of economy, production, contracting and costs, the travesty and human tragedy disappear:

> What the American military is good at knocking down—bridges, telephone exchanges, silos—the Army Corps of Engineers and their commercial contractors, such as Halliburton and Bechtel, are good at building back up.
>
> (Anonymous, 2004, p. 1)

> Iraq's defeat would add 3 million to 5 million barrels a day of production to world supply, and actually be good for the world economy, Lindsey said.
>
> (Neikirk, 2002, p. 1)

> Why is Iraq such a prize? Not only does it have the potential to become the world's largest producer, but no other country can do it as cheaply.
>
> (Barlett and Steele, 2003, p. 2)

Financing an invasion of Iraq would cause an already hobbling economy to fall on its face, right? Maybe not. Consider the war as a hostile
takeover with an upside, where you eventually recoup the costs—in
lower, more stable oil prices that result from toppling Saddam, lifting
sanctions and raising production.

(Cook, 2003, p. 48)

RENDERING THE COST OF WAR INVISIBLE

If a topic is invisible in a given discourse, it cannot become political. According to Scarry (1985, p. 12):

The relative ease or difficulty with which any given phenomenon can
be verbally represented also influences the ease or difficulty with which
that phenomenon comes to be politically represented. . . . While the central activity of war is injuring and the central goal in war is to out-injure
the opponent, the fact of injuring tends to be absent from strategic and
political descriptions of war. . . .

In order for wars to be rationally discussed, the horrific consequences
must not be contained in strategic discourses. One method by which this is
accomplished is through the use of obfuscating language. In the case of the
Nazis, they did not commit the mass murder of the Jews during World War II;
they enacted the "Final Solution". The U.S. did not slaughter innocent civilians with aerial bombs during the Vietnam War; they engaged in "air inter-
dictions of hostiles". Nor did they drop bombs on Iraqis during Operation
Desert Storm; they "delivered the ordnance" (Harris, 1996; Jensen, 2004;
Kingsolver, 1998). Lastly, dead soldiers are no longer returned to the U.S. in
"body bags" but rather "transfer tubes" (Harper, 2003).
    In the strategic discourse of war, if killing and injury are mentioned it
is in relation to things not people. Accordingly, an arsenal of tanks can
receive "massive injuries", the government can "kill a base" and nuclear
weapons can commit "fratricide". However, soldiers, enemy combatants, and civilians remain unscathed in the banter of war (Cohn, 1990;
Scarry, 1985). Language which obfuscates death and destruction loses its
ability to touch us morally and disables our capacity to care. Ruddick
(1990, pp. 247–248) emphasizes how "dying bodies stumble, smell, for-
get, swell, waste away, fester and shake. But whereas military ideology
masks these realities, the practice of care depends upon grasping them
accurately". Hence, the strategic discourse of war enables the enactment of
unspeakable horrors towards others by denying human agency in actions
or consequences.
    Another way in which the government denies human agency in war is by
creating an abstract and dehumanized entity against which war is waged,
"the enemy" (Bethke Elshtain, 1985; Keen, 1986). This is done in order to

distinguish as sharply as possible the act of killing from the act of murder. For acknowledging that war kills living, breathing people with hopes and dreams just like us, and not some lifeless abstraction, would bring into full relief the horrendous consequences of our actions.

The extent to which the U.S. Government needs to annihilate death in order to rationalize and justify war to the civilian population is evident in the actions the Bush Administration took to minimize the public's aware-ness of the Iraq War's carnage. Thus, journalists were prohibited from pub-lishing photographs of coffins of dead soldiers returning from Iraq until Russ Kick filed a Freedom of Information Act request and won permission (Harper, 2003; Kamiya, 2005; Kirschbaum, 2003; Stark, 2004; www.mili tarycoffins.bootnetworks.com). President Bush never attended a funeral of a soldier killed in Iraq or sat at the bedside of a wounded soldier in the Walter Reed Army Hospital in Washington, D.C. (Harper, 2003; Kamiya, 2005; Stark, 2004). Meanwhile, there was virtually no national coverage of the stories of wounded soldiers. If their stories were told at all they were in hometown papers (Harper, 2003; Stark, 2004). Further, the U.S. Gov-ernment did not maintain official statistics on the number of dead and wounded Iraqis. According to General Tommy Franks of the U.S. Central Command, "We don't do body counts" (quoted in Dority and Edwards, 2004, p. 16). It is as if the Bush Administration was trying to replace the reality of the war with an idea of reality that is bloodless and bodiless and, hence, not political.

The official discourse and actions of war disavow death, destruction, crime and inhumanity, and in so doing makes war appear to be emotion-ally and physically costless to the perpetrator and their victims. Yet, as the following sections will show, this is a great untruth for there is a divergence between what is accounted for and what is not. The concealed costs have particular political importance.

THE COSTS OF WAR

Budgetary Deceptions

In September 2002, President Bush's former chief economic advisor, Law-rence Lindsey, created a stir when he estimated that a war with Iraq would cost between $100 and $200 billion. This was much higher than the pre-liminary Pentagon estimate of $50 billion (Davis, 2002). However, history has proven that even Lindsey was conservative, for by November 24, 2006, the official cost of the Iraq War had exceeded $344.9 billion (www.costof war.com). According to the Congressional Budget Office, by 2010 autho-rized war expenses were expected to total $600 billion (Grier, 2005).

The official U.S. budget for war includes only incremental costs, or those additional funds expected to be expended due to the war (Congressional

Budget Office, 2002; Nordhaus, 2002; www.costofwar.com). Thus, the basic pay of active-duty military personnel is not included. Soldiers receive the same basic pay if they are in North Carolina or Iraq. However, the additional combat pay for these soldiers as well as the pay for reservists recalled to full-time duty are included. The budget also includes the incremental costs associated with operating and maintaining air, land and sea forces such as the increased fuel consumption from additional flying hours and ship steaming days created by the war (Congressional Budget Office, 2002; Nordhaus, 2002). In March 2003, when the Bush administration requested an additional $62.6 billion for the military operations in Iraq and the global war on terror, Secretary of Defense Rumsfeld outlined some of the expenditures as follows:

> $7.1 billion for the round trip costs of transporting our forces and equipment to and from the theater of operations;
> $13.1 billion to provide war fighters in theater with the fuel, supplies, repair parts, maintenance and other operations support they need to prevail;
> $15.6 billion for incremental personnel costs, such as for special pay and compensation for mobilized reservists;
> $7.2 billion to start reconstituting our forces by replacing the cruise missiles, smart bombs, and other key munitions being expended in the course of the conflict . . . (Rumsfeld, 2003, pp. 2–3).

Obvious future costs such as veterans' benefits for soldiers wounded in war, postwar reconstruction and equipment replacement are not included in the incremental short-term costs of the official budget (Bender, 2005; Hartung, 2003).

The Cost of Injury

Stevens's (1976) research into the full economic cost of the Vietnam War to the U.S. demonstrates the extent to which the official budget undercosts war. Stevens (1976, p. 164) included in his estimate four categories of costs:

> The budgetary cost to the U.S. Government incurred at the time of fighting the war.
> Budgetary costs that the government will have to meet in the future because the war was fought.
> The various extra-budgetary economic costs that the war imposed upon the American people and the American economy.
> Some indirect social costs and burdens that are properly attributable to the war.

At the height of the Vietnam War, Stevens (1976, p. 187) estimated that the budgetary cost incurred (category one) for the Vietnam War was between $128.4 and $171.5 billion; future budgetary costs (category two), which consisted predominantly of war veterans' benefits, totaled $304.8 billion; extra-budgetary costs (category three), which included the cost of drafting service personnel and the foregone earnings of personnel killed, were $70.7 billion; and lastly, indirect costs and burdens (category four), primarily as a result of the Vietnam War recession and excess inflation, were $378 billion. This meant that the total economic cost to the U.S. from the Vietnam War was between $882 and $925 billion, which is approximately 687% of the official budgeted cost. Of the future unaccounted-for costs, war veterans' benefits estimated to be $232 billion were the largest (Stevens, 1976, p. 181).[2]

While it is obvious that veterans' benefits are a huge unacknowledged cost of war, the 1991 Persian Gulf War probably illustrates this more than any other. The Persian Gulf War at first appeared to be a relatively low-cost conflict for the U.S. because most of the direct costs were paid for by foreign pledges. The estimates of costs to the U.S. ranged from a $7 billion loss to an $8 billion profit (Quinn, 1994, p. 41). However, shortly after the war ended many service members began experiencing "fatigue, muscle and joint pain, gastrointestinal complaints, headaches, memory loss and sleep disturbances" (General Accounting Office, 1999, p. 2). This sickness became dubbed Gulf War Illness or Syndrome. As of September 10, 2002, of the 572,833 veterans of the Persian Gulf War, more than one-third filed claims for medical disabilities. This far exceeds the rate for World War II (6.6%), Korea (5%) or Vietnam (6.6%) (Hartung, 2003, p. 9). According to Taxpayers for Common Sense, the cost of just treating Gulf War Syndrome is more than $2 billion a year (Taxpayers for Common Sense, 2002). Further, as of October 2003, the Federal Government had sponsored 224 studies related to Gulf War Syndrome costing approximately $213 million (Department of Veterans Affairs, 2003). Hence, the Persian Gulf War did not turn out to be that great of a bargain for the U.S.

By ignoring veterans' benefits in the official cost of war, the U.S. Government removes from view the disfigured bodies that will need long-term care and masks the fact that injury is the primary purpose and consequence of physical conflict. In order to include such costs, the government would need to estimate the number of mutilated bodies the conflict would produce, the cost of treating one missing arm versus two, and other similar unsettling disfigurements. The Secretary of Defense would have to request additional war funds when the number of injuries or seriousness of the injuries was greater than expected. Congress would have to debate whether the cause was worth the large number of disabled soldiers the war would produce. In other words, one of the concrete horrors of war, injury, would need to be acknowledged and addressed upfront. War would no longer be an abstract fight against an evil enemy taking place in a distant land.

The Value of Life

Death is the ultimate cost of war and this is not unknown to politicians.[3] Ever since the carnage of the two world wars, and the rising resistance of the American people to using youth as cannon fodder, lowering the number of casualties in warfare has become a serious preoccupation of politicians and the military (Markusen and Yudken, 1992). Yet, while the U.S. Government knows in essence that death is the definitive cost, it does not estimate the value of the lives that will be lost when it budgets for war. This is not because the government hesitates to put a dollar value on something as precious as life, for in other contexts it does do so. In the case of the Environmental Protection Agency, when it estimates the costs and benefits of regulations it incorporates the value of a statistical life in its calculations. While the value of a statistical life varies across analyses, when the Environmental Protection Agency estimated the benefits and cost of the clean air act, for instance, it considered one human life to be worth $4.8 million (Environmental Protection Agency, 1999).

Other types of economic analysis incorporate a monetary value of life. In 2004, the World Health Organization summarized peer-reviewed articles on the economics of interpersonal violence. In order to calculate the cost of aggression, many of the studies had to place a dollar value on life ranging from $3.1 to $6.8 million (World Health Organization, 2004, p. 9). This allowed researchers to quantify the economic effect of child abuse and neglect, intimate partner violence, sexual violence, workplace violence and youth violence (World Health Organization, 2004). A study by Caldwell found that child abuse cost the U.S. $1 billion annually when the following costs were included: direct medical, incarceration, policing, lost earnings and opportunity cost; lost investments in human capital; and psychological costs (World Health Organization, 2004, p. 16). If it is possible to estimate the cost of a rape, homicide, suicide and death from environmental pollutants, it is also possible to estimate the cost to the nation of a death from war.[4] However, doing so would politicize the ultimate cost of war and make it less palatable.

It is difficult to imagine the president of the U.S. submitting to Congress when seeking the political approval and finance necessary to embark on a war an estimate of the dollar value of lives the country would lose to a war. Congress would have to debate whether the value of a statistical life the Executive office used was correct and whether the estimated number of dead was correct. This would bring forth questions such as: How many deaths is a war worth? How many young people is the country willing to sacrifice? The ultimate cost of war could no longer be silenced and the production of invisible visibility no longer possible.

THE HIDDEN PSYCHOLOGICAL COST

Post-traumatic stress disorder (PTSD) has been called a "hidden wound of war" in that it cannot be bandaged, stitched up, operated on, receives no purple heart, yet festers over a lifetime (Lyke, 2004). While PTSD was not officially recognized as a clinical condition until 1980, the symptoms were documented in the historical medical literature since the U.S. Civil War. Prior to 1980, it was called "soldier's heart", "Da Costa's syndrome", "shell shock", "battle fatigue" and "combat neurosis" (Epstein and Miller, 2005; Hallock, 1998; National Center for PTSD, 2005). Symptoms of PTSD include: depression, alienation, isolation, anxiety, rage-reactions, intrusive thoughts, problems with intimacy, psychic numbing, emotional constriction, self-defeating and deceiving behavior, frequent nightmares and trouble sleeping (Hallock, 1998; Hedges, 2003). Harris (1997, p. 272) notes

> Death by no means exhausts the effects of war on humans. Apart from physical wounding, the experience of war may result in post traumatic stress disorder. . . . People damaged as a result of war will be less productive and may require assistance from others. Economists typically place a cost on such effects by valuing the potential output foregone as a result of the death or disability.

Yet again, when the U.S. Government budgets for war it does not take into account the future costs to society of the psychologically damaged people the war will create. These costs include both the direct costs, mainly treatment and disability compensation, and the indirect costs. Thus, in 2004, 25,000 World War II veterans and 161,000 Vietnam War veterans were still receiving disability compensation from the Veterans Administration for PTSD (Epstein and Miller, 2005). According to Robinson's (2004, p. 8) calculations, the economic impact of these benefits can be very significant:

> If a 24-year-old married male soldier with one child were to develop PTSD to the degree of unemployability, that solder could receive compensation payments from the VA of over $2,400 per month for the remainder of his life. Over an average male lifespan, such costs could amount to more than $1.3 million, not counting inflation.

The indirect costs of PTSD include higher rates of domestic violence, child abuse, divorce, unemployment, incarceration, psychiatric illness and alcohol and drug abuse (Hedges, 2003; Lifton, 1992; National Center for PTSD, 2005). For example, an exhaustive study of Vietnam War veterans found that those with PTSD were five times more likely to be unemployed, twice as likely to have been divorced, two to six times more likely to abuse drugs or alcohol, and almost half had been arrested or in jail at least once (Hedges, 2003; Lifton, 1992). Further, spouses of veterans with PTSD experience serious emotional difficulties and the children are more likely to have behavioral problems. In addition, PTSD is linked to increased physical illness in the form of circulatory, digestive, musculoskeletal, respiratory and infectious problems (Hallock, 1998; Hedges, 2003; Lifton, 1992).

Given that soldiers in the Iraq War are experiencing the most sustained combat operations since Vietnam, it is expected that this war will exact a heavy psychological toll on the veterans, their families and society (Litz, 2005; Robinson, 2004). According to an army survey published in the *New England Journal of Medicine* on July 1, 2004, 15.6% to 17.1 % of soldiers returning from Iraq showed signs of anxiety, major depression or PTSD (Hoge *et al.,* 2004; Litz, 2005; Lyke, 2004; Robinson, 2004). These results were reconfirmed in a survey of paratroopers who served in Iraq, 17.4% of whom showed symptoms of PTSD (Lyke, 2004; Robinson, 2004). They also confirm that PTSD is a consequence of war which creates huge psychological, physical, economic and social costs. Some of these costs could be monetized and estimated by the U.S. Government and hence incorporated into a war budget. Yet, doing so would acknowledge that wars have a lasting impact not only on soldiers and their families but on the lives of U.S. citizens as well through increased crime, drug abuse and family discord. Including the costs of PTSD in a war budget would require asking questions such as how many soldiers will be psychologically shattered by the war and what will be the impact on their families or how will the war increase the domestic unemployment rate or crime rate, and what will all this cost. The "hidden wound of war" would no longer be hidden.

OPPORTUNITY COSTS

According to a classic cost accounting textbook, managers must take into account the opportunities foregone when making a decision (Horngren, *et al.,* 2006). Yet, the U.S. budget for war contains no analysis of opportunity costs. The government does not ask whether a dollar spent on war would bring more benefit to the U.S. than a dollar spent on some alternate activity. However, with respect to the Iraq War, other organizations have asked this question.

The Center for American Progress (2004) did an extensive analysis of how the $144.4 billion spent on the Iraq War as of August 2004 could have been used to better protect the U.S. from terrorists. They estimated that for $144.4 billion the U.S. could have: safeguarded ports and waterways; upgraded the Coast Guard fleet; improved cargo security; protected commercial airliners from shoulder fired missiles; equipped airports with state-of-the-art baggage screening machines and walk through explosive detectors; hired 100,000 more police officers; increased funding for fire departments; integrated the emergency radio system nationwide; secured roads and rails; added two divisions to the army; doubled the Special Operations Forces; helped to rebuild Afghanistan; bought Afghanistan's opium crop; increased assistance to the neediest countries and enhanced public diplomacy (Center for American Progress, 2004).

What is probably most damaging is that the money could have been spent to stop the proliferation of weapons of mass destruction, one of the stated aims of the war with Iraq. For example, a $30.5 billion investment would secure the world's nuclear weapons-grade fissile material from theft, and $2.25 billion per year would double the amount spent on the Nunn-Lugar Cooperative Threat Reduction program designed to reduce the danger from "loose nukes" in the former Soviet Union (Center for American Progress, 2004; Hartung, 2004).

A study by Bennis and Leaver (2005, p. 52) demonstrated how egregious it was to spend $224.5 billion, as of December 6, 2005, on death and destruction in Iraq when a mere $24 billion per year would reduce world hunger in half; $10 billion annually could launch a global program to respond to HIV/AIDS; $2.8 billion annually would immunize every child in the developing world; and $37 billion would provide clean water and functioning sewage systems to the world's population. Alternatively, the National Priorities Project (2005) estimates that with the then budget for the Iraq War of $204.6 billion, 46,458,805 people could receive health care, 1,841,833 affordable housing units could be built or 361,892,756 homes could be retrofitted for renewable electricity.

By spending hundreds of billions on the Iraq War, the U.S. has foregone opportunities to secure the nation from real terrorist threats or eliminate terrorists by responding to human security needs. Spending money on war can only appear reasonable if the alternatives remain hidden from public view. If the rationality of accounting dictates that managers take into account opportunity costs when analyzing alternatives, war requires irrationality to remain legitimate.

COST OF WAR TO THE VICTIMS

In order for a government to convince its citizens to engage in war, it must distinguish the act of killing from the act of murder. Most often this is achieved by the government waging war not on people but on an abstract entity, the enemy. By creating this abstraction the barbarous acts of war and the consequences on people are masked. Thus, perhaps more than any other, the cost of war to the victims must be silenced. Yet, war has serious outcomes for the vanquished. Harris (1997) summarizes the cost of war to the victims as follows: direct and indirect human casualties; long term impacts on humans from forced relocations such as post-traumatic stress disorder and loss of skills; childhood malnutrition; development of a protracted culture of violence; loss and damage to physical capital and infrastructure; breakdown of government and institutions; and extensive environmental damage. Further, Nordstrom (1999, p. 154) notes that

> while statistics chronicle the destruction of lives and social infra-structure, they cannot capture one important aspect of the war. War's destruction of cultural integrity—the undermining of knowledge and action frameworks necessary to life—remains an often unrecognized casualty of civilian-targeting warfare.

If the U.S. Government was forced to take into account the costs to the victims before waging a war, it would have to determine whether abstract goals like freedom and democracy were worth the human carnage and despair required. However, while civilian death is inevitable in modern war, the U.S. Government goes to great lengths to deny complicity in killing non-combatants. For instance, during the 1991 Persian Gulf War the U.S. military, in essence, disavowed civilian deaths by promoting the notion that their use of smart bombs made it possible to find and strike only military targets. Yet, as the Research Unit for Political Economy (2003, p. 37–38) reports, "The reality was far different. . . . About 70% of bombs and missiles missed their targets, frequently destroying private homes and killing civilians". In one particularly horrendous incident, the U.S. "accidentally" destroyed a civilian bomb shelter in a populated residential area of Baghdad. The bomb shelter held over four hundred women and children; boys over the age of fifteen were not allowed (Research Unit for Political Economy, 2003; Riverbend, 2005). Riverbend (2005, pp. 46–47) reports

> watching images of horrified people clinging to the fence circling the shelter, crying, screaming, begging to know what had happened to a daughter, a mother, a son, a family that had been seeking protection within the shelter's walls. I remember watching them drag out bodies so charred, you couldn't tell they were human. I remember frantic people, running from corpse to corpse, trying to identify a loved one. I remember seeing Iraqi aid workers, cleaning out the shelter, fainting with the unbearable scenes inside. I remember the whole area reeked with the smell of burnt flesh for weeks and weeks after.

During the most recent war in Iraq, the U.S. Government disavowed civilian deaths by refusing to do body counts. Early in the war, the Iraqi Health Ministry ordered morgues and hospitals to count the number of war dead and wounded, but the American Coalition Provisional Authority ordered them to stop counting. After the interim Iraqi government took over, the Iraqi Health Ministry started counting again. This time they were ordered to stop releasing the figures (Bennis and Leaver, 2005; Coburn, 2005). Given that the U.S. Government must either fabricate stories to deny civilian deaths or simply refuse to acknowledge them, it is obvious that conceding to the fact that war kills innocent women, children and men could jeopardize the whole institution. Thus, any official accounting for war must render civilian death invisible.

Other researchers and organizations have attempted to fill the void left by the U.S. Government's denial of noncombatant deaths in Iraq. The Iraq Body Count (2005), based on a comprehensive analysis of over 10,000 media reports published between March 2003 and March 2005, estimates that 24,865 civilians were killed in the first two years of the war. U.S. led forces were responsible for the largest percentage of deaths, 37.3%, followed by predominantly criminal killings, 35.9% (Iraq Body Count, 2005). In a controversial study published in the British medical journal *The Lancet,* Roberts *et al.* (2004) estimated that there were nearly 100,000 excess deaths in Iraq during the first eighteen months of the war (see also Anonymous, 2005). The Geneva-based Graduate Institute of International Studies re-examined the raw data gathered for *The Lancet* study and estimated that some 39,000 Iraqis had been killed at the time of their study as a result of combat or armed violence since the U.S. invasion in March 2003 (Arieff, 2005).

As these numbers indicate, civilian deaths do occur and are a high cost of war. Unfortunately, violent death is just the beginning, for wars seriously disrupt food supplies and damage the infrastructure required for proper maintenance of health and well-being (Medact, 2004). According to the World Health Organization (2002), collective violence results in increased rates of infant mortality and deaths from communicable and non-communicable diseases. Prior to the 1991 Persian Gulf War, Iraq was quite an urbanized and mechanized society with one of the healthiest and best educated populations in the world (Medact, 2002; Pilger, 2002). However, during Gulf War I, the U.S. led coalition systematically bombed and destroyed Iraq's civilian infrastructure including roads and bridges, as well as electrical, communication, water and sanitation facilities (Medact, 2002; Research Unit for Political Economy, 2003). According to Medact (2002), the Persian Gulf War wrought "near-apocalyptic results" on Iraq in that it turned a post-industrial country into a pre-industrial country, yet the population relied on the life support systems of a modern society to survive.

Many years of U.N. imposed sanctions combined with the damage wrought by the most recent Iraq War, postwar looting and insurgent sabotage has left most Iraqis with inadequate sources of electricity, water and sewage treatment after President Bush declared the end of major combat operations (Medact, 2004; Moussa, 2005; Murphy, 2005; Ureibi, 2005). Lack of electricity, potable water and sanitation has led to a surge in typhoid, tuberculosis, cholera and hepatitis (Chelala, 2005; Laurance, 2004; Ureibi, 2005). Further, since the U.S. led invasion toppled Saddam Hussein, acute malnutrition among the youngest Iraqis has doubled. One-quarter to one-third of children under the age of five suffer from chronic malnutrition and

7.7% suffer from acute malnutrition (Bennis and Leaver, 2005; Chelala, 2005; Fowler, 2005; Laurance, 2004). Crumbling health care facilities, short-ages of drugs, equipment and supplies, lack of electricity, refrigeration and potable water has seriously hampered the ability of health care professionals to take care of the Iraqi people (Jamail, 2005; Medact, 2002, 2003, 2004).

SOCIAL COSTS

While the physical infrastructure has a significant direct and indirect impact on health, the social infrastructure, although less tangible, is equally impor-tant to human well-being. Violence, poverty, unemployment, disruptions to family and community relations all impact prospects for healthy individual, community, cultural, social and political development (Medact, 2003; Nor-dstrom, 2004). Nordstrom (2004, pp. 59–60) notes how

> violence is set in motion with physical carnage, but it doesn't stop there. Violence reconfigures its victims and the social milieu that hosts them. It isn't a passing phenomenon that momentarily challenges a stable system, leaving a scar but no lasting effects. Violence becomes a determining fact in shaping reality as people will know it, in the future. So while a study of violence may begin with direct and immediate car-nage, it shouldn't end there.

Wars destroy the knowledge and action frameworks that hitherto guided people's behavior, rendering illegitimate old patterns that pro-vided stability to daily life. In their stead, heightened fear, dread, worry, hopelessness, insecurity, hunger and discomfort become the norm (Nor-dstrom, 1999, 2004). As such, wars leave deep wounds on the individ-ual and social psyche, which if left unacknowledged and untreated fester rather than heal (Medact, 2003). In postwar Iraq, "fear is the subtext of life . . ." (Reitman, 2004, p. 66). What was once the birthplace of civiliza-tion now lies in ruin: occupied, corrupt, impoverished, chaotic, a swel-tering bed of criminal mayhem, religious fundamentalism, and armed resistance (Glantz, 2005; Parenti, 2004). This chaos and insecurity has created an extremely fearful and traumatized population (Abdul-Ahad, 2005; Baker, 2005; Reitman, 2004).

One of the first acts of the U.S. Coalition Provisional Authority was to disband Iraq's military and dismantle much of the state bureaucracy. This resulted in a surge in unemployment—estimates range between 60% and 70%—and created a security vacuum (Bennis and Leaver, 2005; Medact, 2003; Riverbend, 2005). The consequences were manifold. First, the high levels of unemployment fueled the resistance by putting "too many angry young men, with no hope for the future, on the street" (U.S. Army offi-cer quoted in Bennis and Leaver, 2005, p. 29). Second, a state of rampant crime has emerged. Initially, after the U.S. capture of Baghdad, there was widespread looting. This has now transformed into something much more sinister, organized crime (Kallio, 2005; Riverbend, 2005). The organized crime networks have made carjacks, rape and abduction of women and children, human trafficking and kidnappings for ransom daily occurrences (Integrated Regional Information Networks, 2005; Medact, 2003, 2004; Parenti, 2004).

Women and children are suffering perhaps more than anyone else as a result of the social breakdown from the war and occupation. The dangers of kidnapping and sexual violence have prevented women and girls from participating in public life, going to work, school, seeking medical treatment or even leaving their homes (Amnesty International, 2005; Human Rights Watch, 2003; Medact, 2004; Parenti, 2004; Riverbend, 2005). According to Hana Ibrahim (2005, p. 4):

> From the day that the occupation started in Iraq there was a systematic violation of women and their rights. They were kidnapped, raped and even taken to other countries in order to work in networks. I talked to one of these people who was in a gang that picked up these women. He told me that if a woman is not a virgin she would not cost more than 2,000 or 3,000 dollars but if the woman was a virgin then she would cost much more. If that woman can be used for her organs because she is a healthy subject then her price could go up to 10,000 dollars, whereas in Iraq this does not have a price at all. Now this kind of crime is being committed on a daily basis in a systematic manner by an organized, mafia-type organization. That kind of thing did not exist in Iraq before the occupation.

In addition to heightened insecurity, women in Iraq are suffering from the Islamic fundamentalist backlash unleashed by the war and occupation. In toppling Saddam, the U.S. destroyed an essentially Western regime, militant in secularism. Radical Islam emerged to fill the void left by violence and despair (Glantz, 2005; Parenti, 2004; Riverbend, 2005). Whereas prior to the war it was an individual woman's decision whether or not to wear a hijab (headscarf), now a woman risks being attacked, abducted or insulted if she does not wear one. Some prominent women, such as Hana Aziz, an electrical engineer, have been assassinated simply for going to work (Parenti, 2004; Riverbend, 2005; Amnesty International, 2005). Death and destruction are not the only hidden costs of war to the victims. Wars unleash cultures of violence that impact the daily life of the living to such an extent that survival may be a worse fate than death.

Given that the legitimacy of war depends upon disavowing civilian death, it is not surprising that the indirect deaths from war must be a secret as well. It is not difficult to imagine the political consequences if the U.S.

Government was required to announce the number of Iraqi children that starved to death, died from diarrhea, were kidnapped and murdered as a result of the war, or the number of women murdered, raped or beaten as a consequence of the misogynist impulses released by the initial violence. In order for wars to retain their legitimacy, they must appear to be the province of rational militaries attempting to control irrational forces that can be clearly defined and contained (Nordstrom, 2004). Accounting for the costs to the victims would demonstrate the charade of rationality, placing the institution of war in jeopardy of extinction.

CONCLUSION

While horror and devastation dominate personal accounts of war, they are vanquished from the official representations. It is through mystifying the human and social consequences of war that the U.S. Government is able to convince the citizens that conflict is a reasonable means to achieve an end. Conventional accounting contributes to the mystification by limiting the costs of war to short-term expenditures, such as for salaries, fuel and ammunition, thereby ignoring the long-term human and social costs. Thus, hidden are those aspects of war that touch us emotionally: the debilitated and dead bodies, the deep psychological and social wounds, the increased misogyny and crime, the starving and dehydrated children. The deceptions, thereby, disable our capacity to care and quarantines the political elite from retribution by a disillusioned public. However, given that "the central activity of war is injuring and the central goal in war is to out injure the opponent" (Scarry, 1985, p. 12), the primary purpose of war is to create human misery. A more thorough accounting for war, as presented in this chapter, brings this fact to the forefront. If we are to eliminate war as an institution, understanding and publicizing the physical, psychological and social cost of war to the victor and the vanquished would be a first step.

Given that conventional accounting serves the interests of the political and economic elite who benefit from making the death and destruction in war invisible, conventional accounting will not be the vehicle through which the human and social consequences of war will be addressed. We must rely, instead, on radical forms of social accounting to publicize the pain of war. Non-profit organizations such as the National Priorities Project, the Iraq Body Count, the Center for American Progress, Global Policy Forum and Medact, Amnesty International, each individually detail costs of war that official accounts hide. However, what is lacking is a unified report that amalgamates these distinct perspectives into a whole.

A complete alternative account for war would describe, amongst others: the number of men, women, children and elderly that have died from violence and from disease caused by the war; the estimated number of women that have been raped and kidnapped; the number of U.S. soldiers and contractors killed, maimed and psychologically wounded; personal testimonies of soldiers living with PTSD; firsthand accounts of the atrocities of war, such as watching a child die, a wife raped or your neighbor's home explode; descriptions of starvation, dehydration, living on the streets, insecurity, turmoil, fear; and disruptions of routines needed to survive.

Creating such a social report would require an organization of people dedicated to bringing the pains of war to light. If this can be done, perhaps the true costs of war would be rendered visible and comprehensible, infiltrating the social consciousness in such a way that war could no longer be viewed as an abstraction with no real consequences, revealing social accounting's potential to emancipate us from warfare.

This chapter is based on the paper, "Rendering Death and Destruction Visible: Counting the Costs of War", which originally appeared in *Critical Perspectives on Accounting*, 19 (2008), pp. 573–590. The author would like to thank the publisher, Elsevier, for permission to use this material.

NOTES

1. In addition, unlike other government projects, the Department of Defense is not required to subject war to rigorous cost-benefit analysis (Bilmes and Stiglitz, 2006; Wallsten and Kosec, 2005).
2. Stevens (1976) derived his estimate of war veterans' benefits from research done by Professor James L. Clayton and presented to the Joint Economic Committee of Congress in June 1969. Professor Clayton estimated veterans' benefits as a percentage of the original cost of war for eight different U.S. wars fought over a period of two hundred years, starting with the American War for Independence and ending with the Korean War. The estimates ranged from 53% for the War of 1812 to 1,500% for the Spanish-American War. The un-weighted average for the eight wars was 319% (Stevens, 1976, p. 171). Further, according to Dr. Al Nofi, if military pension costs are factored in, the ultimate outlays associated with major American wars tends to triple (Hartung, 2003, p. 9).
3. According to statistics compiled by Al Nofi (n.d.), approximately 3.7 million U.S. soldiers have died in conflicts starting with the Revolutionary War and ending with the Persian Gulf War. By February 14, 2006, the Iraq War has cost the U.S. 2,272 soldiers (icasualties.org/oif/).
4. A recent working paper from the AEI-Brookings Joint Center for Regulatory Studies estimated that from March 20, 2003 to August 25, 2005, the Iraq War cost the U.S. $14 billion in lost lives (Wallstin and Kosec, 2005).

9 Commodifying State Crime
Accounting for "Extraordinary Rendition"

INTRODUCTION

On September 11, 2001, al Qaeda terrorists destroyed the World Trade Center and part of the Pentagon, killing close to three thousand people. Six days later, President Bush signed a Memorandum of Notification giving the CIA the authority to kill, capture and detain al Qaeda operatives (Gellman, 2001; Johnston, 2006; Mayer, 2009; Siems, 2011). In response to this Memorandum of Notification, the CIA set up a program, known as "extraordinary rendition", to secretly apprehend supposed al Qaeda agents and render them to countries known for torturing prisoners, such as Egypt or Morocco, or to U.S. controlled black sites where euphemistically termed "enhanced interrogation techniques" were used (Danner, 2009; Mayer, 2009; Siems, 2011).[1] Extraordinary rendition subjected the victims to violations that are considered illegal, such as forced disappearance, prolonged arbitrary detention and torture (American Civil Liberties Union, 2005a, 2007a). Hence, extraordinary rendition could be considered a state crime. This chapter identifies the role accounting played in reconstructing state crime into a commodity that could be costed, billed and argued about. It does so by analyzing the privatization of the U.S. Central Intelligence Agency's (CIA) extraordinary rendition program.

In a speech given to a joint session of Congress and the nation on September 20, 2001, President Bush declared a War on Terror (Bush, 2001). The War on Terror would be unique in its expansionary logic, that there is no end to terrorism, and the degree to which it would be outsourced (Hughes, 2007; Klein, 2007). During the Vietnam War, the CIA had used a wholly government owned proprietary company, Air America, to assist with its secret missions in Vietnam and Southeast Asia (Grey, 2007; Hughes, 2007). However, by the War on Terror neoliberalism had created such a permissive environment that even aspects of a covert operation, like extraordinary rendition, could be privatized.

Similar to the Vietnam War, the CIA initially used a proprietary company, Aero Contractors, to perform the rendition flights. However, by October 2002 Aero Contractors' capacity was reached and the CIA started outsourcing the flights to private companies (European Parliament, 2006; Grey, 2007; Weissman, 2012). In the case examined here, the CIA hired DynCorp, a major private military company, as the prime contractor for the privatized rendition flights. DynCorp subcontracted with Sportsflight, an airline broker, who in turn hired a Gulfstream IV aircraft from Richmor Aviation, a privately owned luxury jet charter service. Richmor chartered a Gulfstream IV from the owner, Phillip Morse, vice-chairman of New England Sports Ventures (Richmor Aviation, Inc. v. Sportsflight Air, Inc., 2011).

In 2009 Richmor Aviation sued Sportsflight in civil court over a billing dispute. As a result, 1,700 pages of court files, including contracts and flight invoices, were released into the public domain (Richmor Aviation, Inc. v. Sportsflight Air, Inc., 2011). Based on the information in the court files, this chapter examines how accounting transformed state crime into just another business opportunity for these companies by focusing attention on what was important—profit—while masking the act that generated the income. Richmor Aviation, Inc. v. Sportsflight Air, Inc. also demonstrates the absolute mendacity of accounting. While the U.S. Government invoked the "state secrets privilege" to dismiss court cases filled on behalf of the victims of "extraordinary rendition", the government did not intervene in Richmor Aviation, Inc. v. Sportsflight Air, Inc.

EXTRAORDINARY RENDITION

On September 16, 2001, Vice President Dick Cheney appeared on the television program *Meet the Press*. In reply to a question regarding the U.S.'s response to Osama bin Laden, Cheney set the tone for the War on Terror by stating:

> We also have to work, through, sort of the dark side, if you will. We've got to spend time in the shadows in the intelligence world. A lot of what needs to be done here will have to be done quietly, without any discussion, using sources and methods that are available to our intelligence agencies, if we're going to be successful. That's the world these folks operate in, and so it's going to be vital for us to use any means at our disposal, basically, to achieve our objective.
>
> (NBC News Meet the Press, 2001, pp. 6–7)

The next day, President Bush signed a Memorandum of Notification giving the CIA the authority to kill, capture and detain al Qaeda operatives (Gellman, 2001; Johnston, 2006; Mayer, 2009; Siems, 2011). In response, the CIA set up an extraordinary rendition program. It was "extraordinary" in that the intent was not to capture fugitives and return them to the U.S. or a foreign country to stand trial, but rather to apprehend individuals suspected of having links to terrorist organizations and imprison them indefinitely in order to exploit them for intelligence (Grey, 2007; Johnson, 2007; Mayer, 2009).

The Bush Administration was convinced that in order to prevent future catastrophic attacks from occurring, there was a need to gather intelligence quickly from the detainees seized by the CIA (Gonzales, 2002). Bush signaled his administration's tolerance for harsh interrogations when he signed a memorandum on February 7, 2002, stating that the Geneva Convention did not apply to the conflict with al Qaeda (Bush, 2002). Then, on August 1, 2002, Jay Bybee, head of the Office of Legal Council, determined that it was legal for the CIA to use ten "enhanced interrogation techniques" on captured terrorists, namely attention grasp, walling, facial hold, facial slap, cramped confinement, wall standing, stress positions, sleep deprivation, insects placed in a confinement box, and waterboarding (Bybee, 2002, p. 2). George Bush demonstrated his bravado attitude towards torture in his memoir, *Decision Points,* when he remembered how

> George Tenet asked if he had permission to use enhanced interrogation techniques, including waterboarding, on Khalid Sheikh Mohammed. I thought about my meeting with Danny Pearl's widow, who was pregnant with his son when he was murdered. I thought of the 2,973 people stolen from their families by al Qaeda on 9/11. And I thought about my duty to protect the country from another act of terror. "Damn right," I said.
> (Bush, 2010, p. 170)

The CIA classified detainees as either "high value" or "medium value" based on the quality of intelligence they could provide. Senior al Qaida planners and operators were considered "high value" detainees (Central Intelligence Agency Inspector General, 2004). Due to the sensitivity of the intelligence, high value detainees were interrogated by CIA agents using "enhanced interrogation techniques" in black sites located in places such as Thailand, Afghanistan and Morocco (Mayer, 2009; PBS, 2007; Priest, 2005). Medium value detainees were individuals who were believed to have less direct knowledge of threats but still possessed information of intelligence value (Central Intelligence Agency Inspector General, 2004). Intelligence gathering from medium value detainees was outsourced to countries that were notorious for torturing prisoners such as Morocco, Jordan and Egypt (Grey, 2007; Mayer, 2009; Priest, 2005).

While the extraordinary rendition program was exposed by Priest and Gellman (2002) in an article in the *Washington Post* in December 2002, it would not be until September 2006 that the Bush Administration would publicly acknowledge that it existed (Bush, 2006). In that same month the Bush Administration transferred 14 "high value" detainees out of secret CIA black sites to American controlled Guantanamo (International Committee of the Red Cross, 2007). Based on interviews with these detainees, the International Committee of the Red Cross (2007, p. 26) concluded that the ill-treatment they were subjected to while held by the CIA constituted "torture" and "cruel, inhuman or degrading treatment".

Public opinion polls taken between 2001 and 2009 consistently showed that the U.S. population was opposed to torture (Gronke and Rejali, 2010). Shortly after taking office, President Obama signed an Executive order forcing the CIA to close all "black sites" and follow the Army Field Manual for interrogations (Isikoff, 2009; Shane *et al.*, 2009). However, Obama ruled out prosecutions against those involved in the extraordinary rendition program, stating it is a "time for reflection, not retribution" (quoted in MacAskill, 2009, p. 1) and "we need to look forward as opposed to looking backwards" (quoted in Johnston and Savage, 2009, p. 1).

While Bush Administration officials will probably never be held accountable for torture in the U.S., outside of the U.S. they may not be immune from prosecution. In February 2011 Bush cancelled a trip to Switzerland over concerns of protests linked to his administration's treatment of detainees and the threat of legal action against him for torture. Human rights groups had compiled a 2,500-page criminal complaint against Bush, which they would have filed with the Swiss courts if Bush had entered the country (Anonymous, 2011; Center for Constitutional Rights, 2011; Dwyer, 2011; MacAskill and Hirsch, 2011). Katherine Gallagher, an attorney at the Center for Constitutional Rights, which was party to the complaint, stated that "The reach of the Convention against Torture is wide—this case is prepared and will be waiting for him wherever he travels next" (Center for Constitutional Rights, 2011, p. 1).

"EXTRAORDINARY RENDITION" AS STATE CRIME

The American Civil Liberties Union (ACLU) filed two lawsuits on behalf of the victims of extraordinary rendition, El-Masri v. Tenet and Mohamed *et al.* v. Jeppesen Dataplan, Inc. (American Civil Liberties Union, 2005a, 2007a). In the initial complaints, the ACLU argued that the depravities endured by the victims of rendition, such as forced disappearance, prolonged arbitrary detention, torture and other cruel, inhuman and degrading treatment violated international norms. These norms were codified in conventions, declarations and other international instruments such as

1. United Nations General Assembly, "Declaration on the Protection of All Persons from Enforced Disappearances"
2. Inter-American Convention on Forced Disappearance of Persons, International Convention for the Protection of All Persons from Enforced Disappearance
3. United Nations Convention Against Torture and Other Cruel, Inhuman or Degrading Treatment or Punishment, Universal Declaration of Human Rights

4. International Convention on Civil and Political Rights (American Civil Liberties Union, 2007a, pp. 7–8)
5. Universal Declaration of Human Rights, the International Convention on Civil and Political Rights
6. Geneva Convention relative to the Treatment of Prisoners of War
7. Geneva Convention relative to the Protection of Civilian Persons in Time of War (American Civil Liberties Union, 2005a, p. 5)

Given that the U.S. is a signatory to the conventions, the ACLU and many legal experts from around the world are of the opinion that extraordinary rendition is illegal (American Civil Liberties Union, 2005b; Galella and Esposito, 2012; The Rendition Project, n.d.).

The first lawsuit filed by the ACLU on behalf of victims of extraordinary rendition was El-Masri v. Tenet (American Civil Liberties Union, 2005a). On December 31, 2003, Khaled El-Masri, a German citizen of Lebanese descent, embarked on a holiday to Macedonia. At the border he was detained by law enforcement officials, who confiscated his passport and held him incommunicado for 23 days in a hotel. On January 23, 2004, he was rendered by the CIA to a black site in Afghanistan called the "Salt Pit" (American Civil Liberties Union, 2005a). The CIA stripped, hooded, shackled and sodomized El-Masri with a suppository while in Macedonia, and then subjected him to abuses in Afghanistan including total sensory deprivation, solitary confinement, forced feeding, physical assault, sleep deprivation and inadequate food and water (American Civil Liberties Union, 2005a; Frankel, 2012; Kulish, 2012; Singh, 2012).

Not long after the CIA abducted El-Masri, officials realized they had abducted an innocent man. Yet, his unlawful detention and inhumane treatment continued for two additional months (American Civil Liberties Union, 2005a). On May 27, 2004, El-Masri was released from the "Salt Pit" and flown to Albania and then flown home to Germany. In the initial complaint filed by the ACLU, they stated that

> El-Masri brings this action against Mr. Tenet, who promulgated this unlawful policy and who directed the agents and subordinates who carried out the unlawful acts described herein; against current and former employees of the Central Intelligence Agency who participated directly in Mr. El-Mari's abduction, detention, and interrogation; and against the aviation corporations that supplied the aircraft and personnel used in the unlawful transfer, knowing that they were to be used in Mr. El-Masri's secret detention and interrogation in Afghanistan, thereby conspiring in and aiding and abetting the violation of Mr. El-Masri's rights under the United States Constitution and the law of nations, including his right to be free from prolonged arbitrary detention, torture and other cruel, inhuman, or degrading treatment.
>
> (American Civil Liberties Union, 2005a, p. 2)

In May 2006 the U.S. Government succeeded in having El-Masri v. Tenet dismissed, arguing that allowing the case to proceed would jeopardize state secrets (American Civil Liberties Union, 2011a). However, the illegality of the actions by Macedonia and the CIA were affirmed in December 2012, when the European Court of Human Rights found that El-Masri's abduction and detention did amount to an "enforced disappearance", and that the CIA's treatment during the rendition constituted "torture", both acts in violation of the European Convention on Human Rights (European Court of Human Rights, 2012). The court awarded El-Masri EUR 60,000 for damages (European Court of Human Rights, 2012, p. 79). It is interesting to note, that while Aero Contractors performed the rendition flight from Skopje, Macedonia, to Kabul, Afghanistan, Richmor Aviation completed the reverse rendition, flying El-Masri from Kabul to a military airbase in Albania called Bezat-Kucova Aerodrome (American Civil Liberties Union, 2005a, 2008).

The second lawsuit brought by the ACLU was Mohamed *et al.* v. Jeppesen Dataplan, Inc. (American Civil Liberties Union, 2007a). Jeppesen Dataplan, a subsidiary of Boeing, was contracted by the CIA to arrange the complex logistics required for a rendition flight including such things as landing clearances, flight plans, crews, hotel rooms and catering (American Civil Liberties Union, 2006a; Mayer, 2006). The ACLU filed this lawsuit on behalf of five victims of "extraordinary rendition": Binyam Mohamed, Abou Elkassim Britel, Ahmed Agiza, Mohamed Farag Ahmad Bashmilah, and Bisher Al-Rawi. These victims were kidnapped from Pakistan, Sweden, Jordan or Gambia and rendered to Morocco, Egypt, or Afghanistan in 2002 or 2003. Once imprisoned they were subjected to torture such as scalpel cuts to their penises, electric shocks, sleep deprivation and beatings (American Civil Liberties Union, 2007a).

The ACLU argued that Jeppesen, in providing services to the CIA, knew that the plaintiffs would be subjected to forced disappearances, detention and torture. They used as evidence an article written by Jane Mayer in which a former employee of Jeppesen claimed that Bob Overby, a managing director, stated at a meeting that "we do all of the extraordinary rendition flights—you know, the torture flights. Let's face it, some of these flights end up that way" (quoted in Mayer, 2006, p. 2). In addition, the ACLU provided evidence that Jeppesen submitted "dummy flights" to various aviation authorities in Europe to conceal the flight paths of the rendition planes (American Civil Liberties Union, 2007a). The ACLU stated in their complaint that

> Mr. Mohamed, Mr. Britel, Mr. Agiza, Mr. Bashmilah, and Mr. al-Rawi bring this action against Jeppesen because in knowingly providing flight and logistical services to the CIA for the rendition program, the company facilitated and profited from Plaintiffs' forced disappearance, torture, and other inhumane treatment.
>
> (American Civil Liberties Union, 2007a, p. 6)

As with El-Masri v. Tenet, the U.S. Government intervened, asserting "state secrets privilege", claiming the litigation would undermine national security interests (American Civil Liberties Union, 2011b). In addition to the two ACLU lawsuits, the Center for Constitutional Rights filed a lawsuit against former Bush Administration officials on behalf of Maher Arar. Maher Arar, a Syrian born Canadian citizen, was detained during a layover at JFK Airport in September 2002 and rendered to Syria where he was tortured. In addition, the U.S. Government had this lawsuit dismissed based on the "state secrets privilege" (Center for Constitutional Rights, n.d.a).

THE CASE OF ABU OMAR

On February 17, 2003, Abu Omar, an Egyptian national with refugee status in Italy, was abducted by the CIA in Milan. The CIA drove him to a U.S. Air Force Base in Aviano and from there he was flown by military jet to a U.S. Air Force Base in Ramstein, Germany. Richmor Aviation would complete the final stage of the rendition from Ramstein to Cairo. In Cairo, he was taken to the Torah prison compound and tortured. He was placed in a cell with no light or windows, subjected to extreme changes in temperature and hung upside down and given electrical shocks to sensitive parts of his body, including his genitals. After four years in prison, in February 2007 an Egyptian court ruled his imprisonment unfounded and he was released (Bergen, 2008; Foot, 2007; Grey, 2007; Mazza, 2012).

An Italian police investigation into Abu Omar's disappearance would eventually lead to the indictment and conviction in absentia of 23 U.S. citizens, almost all CIA operatives, for kidnapping (Danadio, 2009; Rome, 2009; Whitlock, 2009). It was the first ever criminal case to be tried against extraordinary rendition. Armando Spataro, the deputy chief prosecutor of Milan and coordinator of all terrorism investigations, built the case against the CIA agents. Spataro had independently been investigating Abu Omar for terrorism offenses at the time of his abduction (Bergen, 2008; Grey, 2007; Rome, 2009). In an interview with Spataro, Bergen (2008, p. 4) asked why he pushed so hard to prosecute the CIA agents for kidnapping given he was about to indict Abu Omar himself. Spataro explained that "kidnapping is a serious crime. It is important for European democracy that all people are submitted to the law. It is possible to combat terrorism without extraordinary means". Abu Omar, who now lives in Alexandria, is jobless and taken care of by his family (Bergen, 2008; Mazza, 2012). In an interview with Amnesty International, he referred to the way in which he could not

> walk alone in the street. I expect to be kidnapped again, to face fabricated charges or even to be killed. . . . My prison experience has changed my life, as torture left some sternness in me. . . . I am always

afraid, and suffer from health problems, tension and eat with greed. . . .
I do not want to see or receive visitors. All night long, I suffer nightmares, and all day long I remember torture so I shake. . . .

(quoted in Mazza, 2012, p. 145)

Given that Richmor Aviation transported Abu Omar to Cairo, according to the Italian courts, Richmor abetted kidnapping. Firms such as Dyn-
Corp, Sportsflight, Richmor and Jeppesen not only aided and abetted state
crime, they also profited from it. To achieve this, accounting assisted with
creating the visibilities and invisibilities needed in order for corporations to
unabashedly participate in crimes against humanity.

ACCOUNTING AS A POLITICAL ACT

Accounting is a form of representation and, hence, is a political act in
that descriptions determine our social understanding of a phenomenon,
therefore what actions are appropriate and which are not (Eagleton, 1990;
Edwards, 1996; Hall, 1982). Depictions succeed in guiding actions in particular directions by rendering some aspects of a phenomenon visible and,
thus, worthy of attention, and others invisible (Morgan and Willmott,
1993; Shapiro, 1988). However, it is not by happenstance that a particular
representation of an event or object gains prominence. Rather, meanings
are historically and socially determined and, as such, frequently reflect the
value systems necessary for perpetuating the existing distribution of wealth
and power in society (Chomsky, 1987; Eagleton, 1990). For example,
budgets and cost-benefit analysis presuppose financial scarcity, which is
integral for rationalizing a capitalist society premised on an unequal distribution of wealth.

In a seminal article on accounting as social practice, Burchell *et al.* (1980,
p. 16) noted that "by creating a new pattern of organizational visibility,
computational practice (or accounting) can often significantly change organizational participants' perceptions of the problematic and the possible". By
focusing attention on that which can be accounted for, certain debates are
foreclosed. For instance, given that accounting assumes a capitalist economy, it is impossible to discuss alternative social arrangements for the provision of goods and services within this discourse. Accounting derives its force
and tenacity from appearing to be self-evident and, in so doing, ensures
that the distribution of wealth and power that it sustains goes unexamined
(Covaleski and Dirsmith, 1988).

Further, accounting only reports on those aspects of an organization
that can be represented quantitatively. One result of this is that issues of
equity, justice and even survivability are lost (Rose, 1991). For example,
by reducing myriad political issues such as race relations, nuclear disarmament, or carbon emissions to arguments over numbers, their political

content is effectively erased (Covaleski and Dirsmith, 1988, 1995; Hall, 1982; Rose, 1991). However, that which an emphasis on numbers excludes is frequently the most important. Hence, as demonstrated in Chapter 6, the U.S.'s use of statistics to measure progress in the Vietnam War effaced the social, political and historical forces that shaped the enemy's identity, leading to highly misguided policies that prolonged a conflict in which many lost their lives for no reasonable purpose. Thus, equally important to the visibilities created by accounting are the invisibilities. From the Holocaust, to war, to the genocide of indigenous people, accounting has served the status quo distribution of power by rendering invisible the acute human trauma suffered by the victims (Neu, 2000). Dehumanization is essential for squelching moral inhibitions against committing violent acts towards others (Bauman, 1989). Accounting assisted the Nazis with the attempted systematic annihilation of the Jewish people by dehumanizing them. Accounting reduced a Jewish person to an anonymous, numbered unit that could either provide some temporary value to the German war effort as slave labor or were expensive debris to be disposed of in a cost-effective manner.

With respect to war, the previous chapter demonstrated that accounting renders invisible those aspects that touch us emotionally by limiting costs to short-term expenditures on such items as salaries, fuel and ammunition. Dying bodies, starving children and psychologically distraught soldiers are not represented in the accounts. As a result, accounting contributes to sustaining war as a viable institution by ensuring that the profound social and human costs are left out of any political debate. Similarly, accounting assisted with the genocide of Canada's first nations by making progress towards the goals of the dominant race, which were measured financially, the only metric that was important (Neu and Graham, 2006). Issues of equity and justice disappeared, and cultural differences were effaced as accounting translated into practice policies of containment and assimilation which led to genocidal outcomes (Neu, 2000). Hence, accounting enables the perpetuation of extreme violence by ensuring that the horrors suffered by the victims disappear behind a discourse that elevates financial success to the only thing of value.

Neoliberalism has greatly enhanced the privileging of calculative practices as a preferred way of knowing the world by positioning the values and norms of the market as the primary means by which people measure themselves, others and things (Ilcan and Phillips, 2010). Human relations have become increasingly commodified, in that solutions to problems that used to be ameliorated through the community can now be purchased, such as security (Garland, 2001; Gill, 2003; Johnson, 2000). Hence, concepts which previously relied on communal relations for their merit now pass through an autonomous market for valuation. Neoliberalism holds that the role of the state is to create and preserve an institutional framework which will enable the functioning of free markets (Harvey, 2005; Funnell, 2001).

Under neoliberalism, the provision of goods and services by the state is ideologically constructed as inferior in that private entities are presumably more flexible, adaptable and creative and, hence, can perform these functions at lower costs (Felts and Jos, 2000). However, once a state function is privatized, political accountability, most importantly making political leaders responsive to popular wishes, is subordinated to managerial accountability, making sure the work is done efficiently (Funnell *et al.*, 2009). Further, the implementation becomes proprietary and cannot be influenced by the community (Box, 1999; Box *et al.*, 2001; Christensen and Laegreid, 2002; Ventris, 2000). Thus, discussions of justice, equity and fairness are displaced by performance metrics which determine if the contract is being fulfilled (Funnell, 2001).

Hughes (2007) argues that the privatization of government functions was first tested out on a marginal group of society, prisoners, before becoming the norm for mainstream applications. Through privatizing prisons, emphasis has been placed on procedural accountability, reducing society's treatment of criminals to an activity that needs to be monitored with metrics such as the number of drug tests administered or violent incidents contained (Andrew, 2007). Broader and more important political debates regarding the purpose and intent of incarceration have disappeared as a result (Andrew, 2007, 2011). Further, similar to extraordinary rendition, given that incarcerating people is a use of force, the privatization of prisons has made the pain and suffering of individuals a legitimate business opportunity (Andrew, 2007).

PROFITING FROM "EXTRAORDINARY RENDITION"

While organizations such as the Center for Constitutional Law and the ACLU were attempting to find justice for victims of extraordinary rendition, Richmor Aviation, Inc. v. Sportsflight Air, Inc. was about money. Richmor initially entered into a six-month contract with Sportsflight that guaranteed payment for 250 flight hours, whether or not the hours were used. In exchange, Richmor provided exclusive use of Phillip Morse's Gulfstream, with tail number N85VM (later changed to N227SV), at a discounted rate of $4,900 per hour. Mr. Richards (Richmor) contended that at the end of the contract he and Mr. Moss (Sportsflight) entered into a verbal agreement that guaranteed a minimum of 50 flight hours per month as long as Sportsflight continued chartering the Gulfstream IV from Richmor. When Richmor billed Sportsflight for $1,119,650 for the unused hours, Sportsflight refused to pay. Sportsflight claimed the minimum guaranteed hours ended with the first six-month contract (Richmor Aviation, Inc. v. Sportsflight Air, Inc., 2011).

The lawyer for Sportsflight alleged that Richmor was seeking additional compensation to make up for the negative publicity it started receiving once the public associated the company with the CIA's rendition flights (Richmor Aviation, Inc. v. Sportsflight Air, Inc., 2011, pp. 4–5). The lawyer used a letter written by Mahlon Richards to Don Moss requesting payment for the unused hours to support his claim. In the letter Richards stated:

> Richmor has become the target of negative publicity and hate mail. In the future, whenever the name "Richmor" is googled this will come up.
>
>   GIV N227SV will always be linked to renditions. No tail number change will ever erase that. . . .
>
>   Our crews are not comfortable leaving the country. The owners of N227SV are afraid to fly in their own aircraft. We are losing a management customer due to this association.
>
>   (Richmor Aviation, Inc. v. Sportsflight Air, Inc., 2011, p. 320)

As is evident by the letter, Richard's concern was with the negative impact the association with renditions was having on the company. Nowhere in the court documents does Richards express remorse for aiding kidnapping and torture.[2] It was the potential loss of profit, not humanity, that provided the incentive for the court case. Richard's apparent indifference to the plight of the detainees was expressed in an exchange that occurred in court. When Richards was asked, "Who or what was Richmor transporting in the Gulfsteam IV aircraft?" he responded, "We were transporting government personnel and their invitees" (Richmor Aviation, Inc. v. Sportsflight Air, Inc., 2011, p. 60).

A former member of a CIA transport team reported to Mayer (2009, p. 272) that the "takeout" of prisoners was "a carefully choreographed twenty-minute routine, during which a suspect was hog-tied, stripped naked, photographed, hooded, sedated with anal suppositories, placed in diapers, and transported by plane to a secret location". During the transport, the detainee was blindfolded, had earphones over his ears, was shackled by hands and feet, was not allowed to use the toilet, and on some occasions was required to lay flat on the floor with hands cuffed behind their backs (International Committee of the Red Cross, 2007). These were the government's "invitees" Richards referred to.

Richmor received the Columbia County Chamber of Commerce's Excellence in Business Award for 2008. They were hailed for being a great employer, for providing a generous benefits package and profit sharing to its employees, and for being an exceptional corporate citizen, giving both monetary and volunteer contributions to local organizations (Richmor.com, n.d.). Many of Richmor's employees and customers have been with the company for over 20 years. Further, the company is proud of its strong tenet of family. Mahlon Richard's son works as a mechanic, his daughter in charter sales and her husband is a chief pilot (Richmor.com, n.d.). That such a company would only worry about the financial impact of participating in kidnapping and torture is testament to accounting's ability to mask the human ramifications of business transactions. Accounting ensures that the profitability of the entity takes precedence to all other considerations. Through the lens of accounting, it did not matter whether Richmor chartered a plane to a rock star to fly to a concert or to the CIA to fly a detainee to torture. The reason for the flight only became relevant once it interfered with profitability.

Accounting's emphasis on profitability also ensured that progress towards the CIA's goals was the only relevant consideration for Richmor and Sportsflight. The pain and suffering endured by the detainees was overshadowed by performing well and generating more business. Don Moss explained to Mahlon Richards in a letter written after extraordinary rendition started receiving extensive media coverage, "I believe our best strategy is to provide the highest level of service, where the client will appoint us as the sole vendor in the best interests of confidentiality" (Richmor Aviation, Inc. v. Sportsflight Air, Inc., 2011, p. 738). Richmor did, indeed, provide the CIA with the highest quality service, frequently receiving praise from DynCorp for a job well done. For example, in an email sent by Stephan Lee, Program Manager for DynCorp National Security Program, to Richmor and Sportsflight on October 23, 2002, regarding the need to charter a plane during a time when Phillip Morse's Gulfstream IV was scheduled for maintenance, Lee stated:

> While this request may seem a little burdensome, it's actually a nod to the great job you all have been doing to meet the client's needs during this time of increased need for executive aviation services. They trust the DynCorp-Richmor team and wish to increase the opportunities for more and different kinds of charter business with your fleet.
> (Richmor Aviation, Inc. v. Sportsflight Air, Inc., 2011, p. 772)

In another email sent by Stephan Lee to Sportsflight, Lee praised Richmor's professionalism, stating, "DynCorp and the U.S. Government have been extremely satisfied with this project, in large measure due to Richmor's excellent service and the professionalism of Richmor's management and flight teams" (Richmor Aviation, Inc. v. Sportsflight Air, Inc., 2011, p. 342). Hence, the end, that is, kidnapping and torture, was displaced by a focus on performing the work professionally in order to please the client and maintain their business. Mahlon Richards's dominant concern with keeping Philip Morse's Gulfstream IV productive was evident in court testimony. When Richards was asked what happened at the end of the initial term of the contract, he responded:

> Don Moss, Sportsflight called, and said that: "I realize that we're short of the 50 hours for the initial term of the contract. The client would like you to roll that time over because we're going to be very busy, we want to continue the contract of the 50 hours a month.

Would you agree to letting us make up that time as we proceed with the contract?"

I said: "Okay, if that's what they want to do, we'll agree to do that; but let's have an agreement between us that whenever the contract ends, we need to have flown 50 hours a month for every month during that term."

He said: "That's no problem. The client says we're going to be very, very busy, we're going to fly more than 50 hours a month."

I said: "Based on that agreement, then we'll continue it."
(Richmor Aviation, Inc. v. Sportsflight Air, Inc., 2011, p. 58–59)

Hence, for Richmor, ensuring the productivity of their asset, Philip Morse's Gulfstream IV, took precedence to any concern regarding what the asset was being used for, the enactment of a state crime. However, during the court case the judge became very aware of the disregard for the rendition victims. When Mahlon Richards was asked if Richmor's services were accepted, he responded, "Oh yes. We were complemented all the time". The court interrupted, asking, "By the invitees for the government or Mr. Moss?" Richards responded, "Not the invitees, the government. And Mr. Moss" (Richmor Aviation, Inc. v. Sportsflight Air, Inc., 2011, p. 77).

MINUTIA WAS IMPORTANT

While the ACLU and Center for Constitutional Rights cases brought to the forefront the torture and torment suffered by the victims of rendition, in Richmor Aviation, Inc. v. Sportsflight Air, Inc. the pain and agony of the detainees disappeared behind minutia. The focus of the case was not the crime of kidnapping and torture, but rather whether or not a contract was breached and money was owed. Thus, such things as the contract terms, the billable hours, and the aircraft used were in contention. For example, in his preliminary statement, Sportsflight's attorney took issue with the unreimbursed hours from the original contract for which Richmor was seeking payment. When the original contract expired, Richmor had flown 81 hours less that the 250 hours guaranteed. However, on one occasion N85VM was unavailable and Sportsflight had to charter an aircraft from a different provider for 34.7 hours. As per the original contract, these 34.7 hours should have been credited against the 250 hours guaranteed. In addition, Sportsflight gave Richmor a 30-hour initial deposit. Sportsflight's lawyer argued that taking into account the 64.7 hours, Sportsflight only owed Richmor for 15.3 unused hours on the original contract (Richmor Aviation, Inc. v. Sportsflight Air, Inc., 2011, p. 12). With respect to the 30-hour initial deposit of $147,000, Richmor's lawyer countered:

Plaintiff, on the other hand, established [via its business records] that the $147,000 amount was credited [in 2002] towards both Defendant's

total obligation and the amounts billed in the previous invoices. For example, $146,410 of the initial deposit was credited towards the $240,643.95 balance on an invoice dated November 26, 2002 [regarding 44.5 flight hours]. As reflected by Plaintiff's business records, the $146,410 credit reduced the November 26, 2002 invoice's balance to $94,233.95, which Defendant paid on February 14, 2003 in cash.
(Richmor Aviation, Inc. v. Sportsflight Air, Inc., 2011, p. 10)

Further, in his preliminary statement Sportsflight's lawyer argued that after the initial contract expired, Richmor used a plane other than N85VM and charged a different rate than $4,900 on ten different occasions, listing the details in a footnote (Richmor Aviation, Inc. v. Sportsflight Air, Inc., 2011, p. 12). Therefore, the parties had not continued their relationship under the same terms of the original contract and Sportsflight was not bound to the 50 hours per month guarantee. Richmor's lawyer countered, "Although Plaintiff occasionally used a different (substantially-similar) plane, it received no complaints and satisfactorily performed its standby duties" (Richmor Aviation, Inc. v. Sportsflight Air, Inc., 2011, p. 7).

Pain and suffering cannot be expressed in a vocabulary of invoices, business records, hours used, initial deposits and credits. Scalpel cuts or electro shocks to genitals faded away as planes used and hours or money credited became the focus of attention. Accounting moved the companies' gaze away from the acute human trauma they profited from to the minutia that determined whether or not money was owed.

BUSINESS AS USUAL

The business of rendition had few differences from the day-to-day activities of the firms involved. Sportsflight had previously brokered planes for the U.S. Department of Defense and the White House Travel Office, so working with government agencies was not new (Richmor Aviation, Inc. v. Sportsflight Air, Inc., 2011, pp. 622–623). The bulk of Richmor's business was in charter flights. While their typical customers were families, businessmen, athletes, movie and rock stars (Richmor.com, n.d.), Mahlon Richards never asked his "customers why they go anywhere, whether it's West Palm Beach or the moon" (quoted in Crewdson and Hundley, 2005, p. 4). Hence, the nature of the customer and their purpose was not important to Richmor.

There were a few unique aspects to the CIA's contract, including Richmor needed to commit Phillip Morse's aircraft to the project. Further, letters of transit from the State Department were required. The letters informed "To Whom It May Concern" that the aircraft and accompanying personnel were under contract with the U.S. Government and were traveling to the destination in support of that contract (Richmor Aviation, Inc. v. Sportsflight Air, Inc., 2011, pp. 243–259). Lastly, Richmor was granted rights to land at U.S. military bases worldwide, a right that is issued to few civil aircraft providers (European Parliament, 2006; Johnson, 2007). However, outside of these differences, rendition was business as usual for Richmor and Sportsflight.

The chapter on the Holocaust demonstrated, with respect to the Nazis' train transportation of the Jewish people to Auschwitz, that accounting facilitated a business-like approach to the gruesome reality of moving people to their death. Accounting allowed the railways participating in the transportation to discuss it in terms of bills and payments, rendering the purpose irrelevant and invisible. Similarly, Richmor sent Sportsflight over two hundred invoices for chartering the aircraft and associated costs, as well as handling fees for takeoff and landing, and inflight communications, for which Sportsflight tendered payment (Richmor Aviation, Inc. v. Sportsflight Air, Inc., 2011). For instance, Abu Omar's abduction and rendition to Egypt for torture converted into a bill totaling $138,389.70 for a flight that went from Washington to Ramstein, Ramstein to Cairo, Cairo to Shannon, Shannon to Washington. The charges included 24.1 hours use of the chartered aircraft, per diems for the flight crew, communications, catering, de-icing, landing fees and extra crew (Richmor Aviation, Inc. v. Sportsflight Air, Inc., 2011, p. 272). The business-like approach to the transaction was demonstrated by the fact that the bill was stamped paid on April 4, 2003. Accounting transformed a crime into a matter of making the appropriate debits and credits to the correct accounts.

The importance to the contracting parties of getting the accounting right is evident in an email sent by Capital Aviation, who worked for DynCorp, to Don Moss of Sportsflight early in the contract. Capital took issue with Richmor's vague invoices, stating:

> On Richmor's invoice C41355 they have to tell us in detail what the "Charter Extra Crew" of $8,000.00 represents. DynCorp will be looking for number of crew members and the daily rate per the contract. There is no way that they will pay this $8,000.00 bulk amount without a breakdown and explanation. Also, what is "Charter Ground Transportation" of $610.50? . . . DynCorp will not process this vague information. It is now clear to me that they operate very much like the government which means that everything has to be specifically applied to the contract terms or they'll reject it.
>
> (Richmor Aviation, Inc. v. Sportsflight Air, Inc., 2011, p. 775)

Hence, similar to the Nazis' train transportation of Jewish people to their death, accounting sustained a business as usual approach to the transportation of CIA detainees to torture. Accounting focused attention on the appropriate debits and credits and the correct breakdown of costs, ensuring that no one had to confront the purpose of the flights.

THE MENDACITY OF ACCOUNTING

Richmor Aviation, Inc. v. Sportsflight Air, Inc. also demonstrated how accounting renders everything so mundane that a billing dispute, which would release "state secrets" into the public domain, completely escaped the attention of the Federal Government. William Ryan, a lawyer who acted on behalf of Richmor, told the *Guardian* that

> what happened here was that Richmor Aviation entered into a contract with Sportsflight to provide rendition flights for detainees and after I got involved in it and I saw the various invoices from Richmor that were submitted to Sportsflight it was amazing to me that no one from the United States government ever said boo to me about any of this. So I just went about prosecuting the case for the client.
> (quoted in Quinn and Cobain, 2011, p. 2)

The court documents released in Richmor Aviation, Inc. v. Sportsflight Air, Inc. contained myriad "state secrets". First, the case revealed that Dyn-Corp was the prime contractor for the privatized rendition flights. Second, flight invoices that provided details on dates and locations of possible rendition flights were released into the public domain. Third, communication logs with phone numbers were entered into evidence and made publicly available. Fourth, contracts and correspondence between Richmor, Sports-flight and DynCorp were revealed (Richmor Aviation, Inc. v. Sportsflight Air, Inc., 2011). Lastly, during Donald Moss's initial deposition, he disclosed the names of other companies, such as First Flight Aviation, International Group, Vision Aviation and Classic Design, involved in the CIA's rendition program (Richmor Aviation, Inc. v. Sportsflight Air, Inc., 2011, p. 664–666).

As noted earlier, the U.S. Government used the "state secrets privilege" to dismiss El-Masri v. Tenet, Mohamed *et al.* v. Jeppesen, and Arar v. Ashcroft *et al.* According to the Center for Constitutional Rights (n.d.b, p. 1), "The state secrets privilege is a common-law privilege that allows the head of an executive department to refuse to produce evidence in a court case on the grounds that the evidence is secret information that would harm national security or foreign relations interests if disclosed". The modern use of the "state secrets privilege" is derived from a 1953 landmark Supreme Court case, United States v. Reynolds, in which three widows filed a wrongful death action against the government when their husbands were killed in a military airplane crash. In response to the widows' request for the accident report, the government asserted the "state secrets privilege", arguing that disclosure would hamper national security, flying safety and the development of secret military equipment (American Civil Liberties Union, n.d.; Bazzle, 2012; Garvey and Liu, 2011).

Between 1953 and 2000, the U.S. Government invoked the "state secrets privilege" a total of 65 times. During the Bush Administration, a period of eight years, the privilege was invoked 48 times and during the first four years of the Obama Administration, nine times (OpenTheGovernment.org, 2013, p. 19). Both the Bush and Obama Administrations used the "state secrets privilege" to dismiss legal challenges to highly controversial government programs, such as extraordinary rendition, the National Security Agency's terrorists surveillance program, and targeted assassinations (Bazzle, 2012; Garvey and Liu, 2011). Critics argue that the Bush and Obama Administrations have used the "state secrets privilege" to cover up the government's illegal actions and disable the court's ability to provide a check on the power of the Executive branch (American Civil Liberties Union, n.d.; Center for Constitutional Rights, n.d.a).

In El Masri v. Tenet, the U.S. Government argued that the lawsuit had to be "terminated at its outset because further litigation would expose means, methods, and operational details of the CIA's overseas operations" (American Civil Liberties Union, 2006b, p. 10), "as well as secret contracts with transportation companies" (Garvey and Liu, 2011, p. 9). For Mohamed *et al.* v. Jeppesen, the U.S. Government contended that litigation of the plaintiffs' claims would reveal intelligence "sources and methods" (American Civil Liberties Union, 2007b, p. 40) and risked "disclosure of privileged information" (Garvey and Liu, 2011, p. 8).[3] In Arar v. Ashcroft, the U.S. Government asserted that the reason Mr. Arar was believed to be a member of al Qaeda and sent to Syria was a "state secret". Litigating the case would reveal intelligence gathering methods (Center for Constitutional Rights, n.d.b).

Given that Richmor Aviation, Inc. v. Sportsflight Air, Inc. revealed "means, methods, and operational details of the CIA's overseas operations" (American Civil Liberties Union, 2006b, p. 10), "secret contracts with transportation companies" (Garvey and Liu, 2011, p. 9), and disclosed "privileged information" (Garvey and Liu, 2011, p. 8), this case should have been shut down as well by the Federal Government. The fact that the case completely escaped the government's attention is a testament to the mendacity of accounting. How could something as mundane as an invoice possibly threaten national security?

CONCLUSION

The victims of "extraordinary rendition" suffered extreme deprivations, including kidnapping, prolonged arbitrary detention and torture. Yet, private companies profited from providing the plane transportation that enabled this state crime and did so with no apparent remorse until the bad publicity threatened profits. This chapter demonstrated that accounting focused the companies' attention on what is important in a capitalist economy, profit, even when supporting a state crime. The pain and suffering endured by the CIA's detainees disappeared as the profitability of the entity and progress towards the CIA's goals took precedence to all other considerations, and minutia, such as hours flown and credits made, became contentious. Further, accounting enabled a business as usual approach to the commission of a state crime by reducing aiding and abetting kidnapping and torture to the appropriate debits and credits and breakdown of costs. Lastly, Richmor Aviation, Inc. v. Sportsflight Air, Inc. demonstrated the absolute mendacity of accounting in that a billing dispute which would release "state secrets" into the public domain completely escaped the attention of the Federal Government.

However, Richmor Aviation, Inc. v. Sportsflight Air, Inc. also demonstrated the emancipatory potential of accounting (Gallhofer and Haslam, 2003) in that the invoices released into the public domain have been used by organizations such as Reprieve and The Rendition Project to investigate corporate complicity into "extraordinary rendition" (Reprieve, n.d.; The Rendition Project, n.d.). Nonetheless, as Bauman (1989) demonstrated, the principles of rationality that guided the Nazis' extermination of the Jewish people during the Holocaust ensured that moral considerations did not interfere with the pursuit of the objective, a pure Arian society. Similarly, accounting as a technology of rationality provides no means for companies to confront the injustices and horrors that the quest for profit can support.

This chapter is based on the paper, "Commodifying State Crime: Accounting and 'Extraordinary Rendition'", which is forthcoming in *Critical Perspectives on Accounting*. The author would like to thank the publisher, Elsevier, for permission to use this material.

NOTES

1. "Enhanced interrogation techniques" included such things as attention grasp, walling, facial hold, facial slap, cramped confinement, wall standing, stress positions, sleep deprivation, insects placed in a confinement box and waterboarding (Bybee, 2002, p. 2).
2. While it is impossible to know the impact on Richmor's employees of participating in "extraordinary rendition", it should be noted that the pilots, in particular, did not experience rendition through the lens of accounting and, hence, may have been traumatized by their work.
3. While the government was not a defendant in Mohamed *et al.* v. Jeppesen, it did intervene to assert privilege and simultaneously moved to dismiss the case (Garvey and Liu, 2011).

10 Conclusion

A core theme of critical accounting research is the interested nature of accounting. Accounting is not a neutral, mechanistic activity for which the primary concern and consequence is the accumulation and reporting of financial and other information to enhance the efficiency of activities. Instead, accounting is used to benefit individuals, institutions or social groups by providing the means by which particular meanings and visibilities which are favorable to them are created and accepted. In the realm of politics the use of accounting is particularly well known in the promotion of the interests of the dominant political elite. It is also used to deny those who are governed the ability to realize the partial, biased nature of the information provided, which is used to create meanings and renditions of events that favor the aims and position of the political elite. Governments came to appreciate that especially at times of war accounting could be used to justify and disguise political motives, that is, to deceive, especially when victory was threatened. There was the realization that for governments to gain continued support and acceptance of their decision to engage in war, accounting could be used to create meanings, visibilities and understandings which favored their interests and those of their allies. This has been especially obvious since the 19th century in Europe and the U.S. with the rise of liberal democratic governments which have realized the importance of accounting as a political tool; a means to gain the acceptance of a particular set of beliefs and to deny competing interpretations the opportunity both to be heard and recognized as credible alternatives. Thus, although accounting has the potential to be both a means of illuminating and enhancing performance, it provides the means to deceive; about what should be achieved, what is being achieved and who this mostly benefits.

The use of accounting to deceive becomes especially important in times of major economic and political crises, most especially war, when those who control the financial and political destinies of nation states will, if necessary, ruthlessly seek to enlist whatever means they can to protect their position of power which may come under threat. *Accounting at War* has established that the deceptions which accounting makes possible have been a prominent feature of the relationship between the state and military forces and in the conduct and justification of war. Ultimately all political power is dependent upon control over public finances for, at its most basic level, control over finances ensures the ability to marshal and use military force, either against external foes or, if necessary, to stifle internal discontent, to maintain political dominance. This nexus between political hegemony, the military and public finances has been shown to lie at the heart of the constitutional battles between Parliament and the Executive in the evolution of the English Constitution.

From the late 17th century until the late 19th century in both Britain and the U.S. accounting by governments was a means to ensure that the elected who governed were not deceived by the intentions and capability of the military. The enduring lesson of the English Civil War and the "Glorious" Revolution in the 17th century was the need to ensure that, by controlling the military's finances, never again would they be able to reign supreme and liberty be denied to those who were oppressed. Prior to the 17th century constitutional crises, poor accounting meant that Parliament was easily deceived into believing that it had the means to know the intentions and to control the aspirations of those who sought to harness military forces for their own purposes, most especially the Crown. In an attempt to eliminate the possibility that the Nation would be deceived about threats to its liberty, the English Parliament introduced constitutional controls, later adopted by the Americans, which denied the military the opportunity to control its finances by making this the exclusive concern of civilians and requiring that there be a detailed accounting for military expenditures. It was not until nearly a century after these constitutional protections against the military were introduced that similar accounting requirements were introduced for the civil service, which was the province of the Crown.

Although governments had clearly appreciated the importance and effectiveness of accounting in controlling the military as a political threat, this created the deception that there would be no deleterious consequences for the military when engaged in war. Ensuring that the military was financially ignorant but also financially accountable made them dependent upon the decisions of others who may be far from the front line of battle and whose first priority was to ensure a detailed accounting for spending according to approvals and mandatory procedures. The terrors and uncertainties of battle were not to be allowed to diminish the constitutional authority of Parliament. The results of this were clearly seen in many wars, including the Crimean War, when military forces struggled to adapt to the uncertainties of war and their interests were frequently jeopardized by the rising political influence of businesses which sought to benefit from opportunities provided by the panics of war to reap huge rewards. These intentions were easily disguised as patriotic contributions to the war effort. This was to become especially obvious in the many wars in the 20th century when increasingly the scale of war meant that military conflicts provided the opportunity for private individuals and businesses to influence and collude with governments.

This so concerned President Eisenhower that he felt compelled in his farewell address in January 1961 to warn against the threat to our liberties that could arise when there is a close association and an identity of interests between government and the interests of business:

> We have been compelled to create a permanent armaments industry of vast proportions. We annually spend on military security alone more than the net income of all United States corporations. . . .
>
> In the councils of government, we must guard against the acquisition of unwarranted influence, whether sought or unsought, by the military-industrial complex. The potential for the disastrous rise of misplaced power exists and will persist. We must never let the weight of this combination endanger our liberties or democratic processes.

The influence of business was also recognized by the adoption of business measures of performance by governments when planning and evaluating the progress of military campaigns. In the case of the Vietnam War, *Accounting at War* has shown how program planning and budgeting was used to transfer from the world of business to government a set of understandings about how to describe and manage war which promoted and justified the concentration of authority in the office of the Secretary of Defense. These both denied the importance of the human cost of war and the means for others to realize that this was the consequence of the way the war was being managed. Accounting information was used to deny a presence to other interpretations of events, thereby deceiving the American people and Congress about true costs of the war in terms of human suffering. The introduction of commercially derived financial planning and management practices was meant to create an interpretation of what constituted success in battle and how this was to be achieved which was political in its intent and operation. This logical, mathematical precision of commercial management practices such as PPB contradicted the experience of service personnel in the field and denied them a presence in military decisions.

Secrecy and deception have long been characteristics of government. Societies controlled by privileged and powerful interest groups, class or party prefer secrecy to disclosure. Apart from disclosing the extent and variety of the advantages which they enjoy, they particularly do not relish the exposure of their faults. Wherever possible they will

> resist being checked. . . . [They] are not inclined to want others examining their conduct closely, second guessing their judgments, or questioning how well they reconcile pursuit of the public interest with furtherance of their personal aims and ambitions. Few power holders operate under conditions of full disclosure. To the contrary, most expend considerable effort deciding what to withhold and how to present what they do.
>
> (Stone, 1987, p. 240)

Accounting has been shown within the context of war to have provided a powerful means for governments to prevent and avoid full disclosure, including the nature of the relationship that they might have with service providers in the private sector. Relying upon a number of excuses for their secrecy including, as shown here in relation to the extraordinary rendition program, the protection of information which could endanger the security of the state, that is, "state secrets", governments have shown themselves adept at protecting their actions with innovative forms of concealment. Thus, exposure of the intimate relationship between the U.S. Government and business in carrying out extraordinary rendition showed how the hegemonic influence of neoliberal beliefs from the latter decades of the 20th century has meant that citizens can now find themselves abandoned by government in preference for the privacy rights of contractors. While concerted efforts by governments to prevent embarrassing and potentially harmful information getting into the hands of their adversaries may be an understandable, even a natural, consequence of the seductions of political power, it cannot be tolerated in a liberal democracy for the way in which it precludes informed consent. Worse still, premeditated efforts, in which accounting is able to play a critical role, to keep the public ignorant confer a license

> upon deceit. . . . [W]hen there are no independent means of verifying official accounts of public transactions, an invaluable check is removed. It becomes relatively safe for authority to publicise such a version of an event as lends the most luster to government, or the least discredit. . . . The temptation to sugar-coat each disaster and gild every triumph will prove almost irresistible to officials who are secure against contradiction.
>
> (Wiggins, 1964, preface)

The ability of citizens to obtain information about the actions of government is a critical guarantee of liberty. Should this right be threatened and citizens are deceived, then all are vulnerable to the self-serving threats of a potentially despotic government. President James Madison (1809 and 1817) was convinced that "knowledge will forever govern ignorance. And a people who mean to be their own governors, must arm themselves with the power knowledge gives" (Madison to W.T. Barry, August 4, 1822, in Padover, 1953, p. 337). In the absence of the right to be informed, individuals remain unaware of the true nature of the existence which holds them hostage to a false consciousness and could place them in peril in times of war when secrecy can become the pre-eminent concern of governments.

References

Abdul-Ahad, G. (2005). "We are living in a state of constant fear." *The Guardian,* March 1. Available from: www.globalpolicy.org/security/issues/iraq/attack/conse quences/2005/0302fear.htm (Accessed October 1, 2005).

Adams, S. (1975). "Vietnam cover-up: playing war with numbers." *Harpers,* May, 41–44, 62–73.

Advisory Board (1911). *Report of the Advisory Board, London School of Economics, on the fifth course at the London School of Economics, 3rd October 1910 to 22 March 1911, for the training of officers for the higher appointments on the administrative staff of the army and for the charge of departmental services.* London: HMSO.

Advisory Board (1912). *Report of the Advisory Board, London School of Economics, on the fifth course at the London School of Economics, 5th October 1911 to 27 March 1912, for the training of officers for the higher appointments on the administrative staff of the army and for the charge of departmental services.* London: HMSO.

Airey, R. (1913). "The London School of Economics and the Army." *Army Review,* IV, April, 465–473.

Alison, A. (1869). *On army organisation.* London: William Blackwood & Son.

Aly, G., and Heim, S. (1988). "Economics of the Final Solution." *Simon Wiesenthal Centre Annual, 5,* 3–48.

American Civil Liberties Union (2005a). "Khaled El-Masri, plaintiff, v. George J. Tenet; Premier Executive Transport Services, Inc.; Keeler and Tate Management LLC; Aero Contractors Limited; Does 1–20, Complaint." Available from: www. aclu.org/files/safefree/rendition/asset_upload_file829_22211.pdf (Accessed July 15, 2013).

American Civil Liberties Union (2005b). "Fact sheet: extraordinary rendition." Available from: www.aclu.org/national-security/fact-sheet-extraordinary-rendition (Accessed July 18, 2013).

American Civil Liberties Union (2006a). "ACLU fact sheet on 'air CIA.'" Available from: www.aclu.org/national-security/aclu-fact-sheet-air-cia (Accessed January 16, 2013).

American Civil Liberties Union (2006b). "Khaled El-Masri v. United States of America. Reply brief for plaintiff-appellant." Available from: www.aclu.org/files/pdfs/ safefree/elmasri_reply_brief_for_plaintiff-appellant.pdf (Accessed July 22, 2013).

American Civil Liberties Union (2007a). "Binyam Mohamed; Abou Elkassim Britel; Ahmed Agiza; Mohamed Farag Ahmad Bashmilah; Bisher Al-Rawi, plaintiffs v. Jeppesen Dataplan, Inc., defendant, first amended complaint." Available from: www.aclu.org/files/pdfs/safefree/mohamed_v_jeppesen_1stamendedcomplaint. pdf (Accessed July 16, 2013).

American Civil Liberties Union (2007b). "Binyam Mohamed; Abou Elkassim Britel; Ahmed Agiza; Mohamed Farag Ahmad Bashmilah; Bisher Al-Rawi, plaintiffs v. Jeppesen Dataplan, Inc., defendant, memorandum of plaintiffs in opposition to the United States' motion to dismiss or, in the alternative, for summary judgment." Available from: www.aclu.org/files/pdfs/safefree/mohamed_v_jeppesen_opposition_motiontodismiss.pdf (Accessed July 25, 2013).

American Civil Liberties Union (2008). "Petition alleging violations of the human rights of Khaled El-Masri by the United States of America with a request for an investigation and hearing on the merits." Available from: www.aclu.org/files/pdfs/safefree/elmasri_iachr_20080409.pdf (Accessed July 16, 2013).

American Civil Liberties Union (2011a). "El-Masri v. Tenet." Available from: www.aclu.org/national-security/el-masri-v-tenet (Accessed July 2, 2013).

American Civil Liberties Union (2011b). "Mohamed et al. v. Jeppesen Dataplan, Inc." Available from: www.aclu.org/national-security/mohamed-et-al-v-jeppesen-dataplan-inc (Accessed December 20, 2011).

American Civil Liberties Union (n.d.). "Background on the state secrets privilege." Available from: www.aclu.org/national-security/background-state-secrets-privilege (Accessed April 22, 2014).

Amery, L. (1902). *The Times history of the war in South Africa*, Vols. 1 and 2. London: Sampson Low & Co.

Amery, L. (1903). *The problem of the army*. London: Edward Arnold.

Amery, L. (Ed.) (1907). *The Times history of the war in South Africa*, 7 Vols. London: Sampson Low and Co.

Amery, L. (1909). *The Times history of the war in South Africa*, Vol. 7. London: Sampson Low & Co.

Amery, L. (1953). *My political life*. London: Hutchinson.

Amnesty International (2005). *Iraq: decades of suffering, now women deserve better*. London: Amnesty International.

Anderson, O. (1967). *A liberal state at war*. New York: Macmillan.

Andrew, J. (2007). "Prisons, the profit motive and other challenges to accountability." *Critical Perspectives on Accounting*, 18, 877–904.

Andrew, J. (2011). "Accounting and the construction of the cost effective prison." *Journal of Australian Political Economy*, 68, 194–212.

Anonymous (1970a). "Just downright refusal." *Newsweek*, April 20, 51–52.

Anonymous (1970b). "Cambodia: we're cache counters." *Newsweek*, May 25, 43–45.

Anonymous (1971a). "General won't punish G.I.'s for refusing orders." *New York Times*, March 23, A1–A9.

Anonymous (1971b). "South Vietnam: the war within the war." *Time*, January 25, 34–35.

Anonymous (2004). "How to get ahead in Bremer's Iraq." *The Economist*, February 10, 1.

Anonymous (2005). "Iraq war takes heavy toll on civilians." MSNBC, July 19. Available from: www.msnbc.msn.com/id/8628614/ (Accessed September 2, 2005).

Anonymous (2011). "Bush cancels visit to Switzerland due to threat of torture prosecution, rights groups say." *The Huffington Post*, February 5. Available from: www.huffingtonpost.com/2011/02/05/bush-switzerland-torture_n_819175.html (Accessed June 12, 2014).

Appy, C.G. (1993). *Working class war: American combat soldiers and Vietnam*. Chapel Hill: The University of North Carolina Press.

Arad, Y., Gutman, Y., and Margarliot, A. (1981). *Documents on the Holocaust: selected sources on the destruction of European Jewry*. Jerusalem: Yad Vashem.

Arendt, H. (1964). *Eichmann in Jerusalem: a report on "the banality of evil."* New York: Viking.

Arieff, I. (2005). "39,000 Iraqis killed in fighting since March '03—new study." Reuters, July 12. Available from: www.globalpolicy.org/security/issues/iraq/attack/consequences/2005/0712study.html (Accessed August 3, 2005).

Armacost, M. (1969). *The politics of weapons innovation.* New York: Columbia University Press.

Armstrong, P. (1987). "The rise of accounting controls in British capitalist enterprises." *Accounting, Organizations and Society,* 12(5), 415–436.

Art, R.J. (1968). *The TFX decision: McNamara and the military.* Boston: Little, Brown and Company.

Ayres, B.D. (1971). "Army is shaken by crisis in morale and discipline." *New York Times,* September 5, A1–A40.

'B' (1899). "The state burden of a standing army." *The United Services Magazine,* XIX, 64–71.

'B' (1907). "The Army Service Corps." *The United Services Magazine,* XXXV, 665–673.

Badcock, G. (Lieut.-Col). (1925). *The army course at the London School of Economics.* LSE Archives, Unregistered Documents 20/5/36.

Badcock, G. (Lieut.-Col.) (1926). "The London School of Economics." *The R.A.S.C. Quarterly,* July, 104–106.

Baker, L. (2005). "Iraq's national psyche traumatized." *Armenian Medical Network,* August 4. Available from: www.health.am/psy/more/Iraqs_national_psyche_traumatized_doctor/ (Accessed October 1, 2005).

Barker, A. (1971). *The war against Russia.* New York: Holt, Rinehart and Winston.

Barlett, D.L., and Steele, J.B. (2003). "Iraq's crude awakening." *Time,* 161(20), 49.

Barnes, J., and Nicholson, D. (1980). *The Leo Amery diaries: volume I, 1896–1929.* London: Hutchinson.

Barnet, R.J. (1972). *Roots of war: the men and institutions behind U.S. foreign policy.* New York: Penguin Books.

Barnett, C. (1970). *Britain and her army 1509–1970.* London: Penguin Press.

Barnett, C. (2000). *Britain and her army.* London: Cassell and Co.

Bauer, Y. (1989). "Genocide: was it the Nazis' original plan?" In M. Marrus (Ed.), *The Nazi Holocaust: historical articles on the destruction of the European Jews,* Vol. 1. Westport, CT: Meckler.

Bauman, Z. (1989) *Modernity and the Holocaust.* New York: Cornell University Press.

Bazzle, T. (2012). "Shutting the courthouse doors: invoking the state secret privilege to thwart judicial review in the age of terror." *Civil Rights Law Journal,* 23(1), 29–71.

Bender, B. (2005). "War's 'hidden cost' called heavy." *Boston.com,* January 14. Available from: www.boston.com/news/nation/washington/articles/2005/01/14/wars_hidden_cost_called_heavy.html (Accessed August 3, 2005).

Bennis, P., and Leaver, E. (2005). *The Iraq quagmire: the mounting costs of war and the case for bringing home the troops.* Washington, D.C.: Institute for Policy Studies.

Bentley, M. (1984). *Politics without democracy, 1815–1914.* London: Fontana.

Bergen, P. (2008). "Exclusive: I was kidnapped by the CIA." *Mother Jones,* March/April. Available from: www.motherjones.com/politics/2008/03/exclusive-i-was-kidnapped-cia (Accessed January 28, 2013).

Bethke Elshtain, J. (1985). "Reflections on war and political discourse: realism, just war, and feminism in a nuclear age." *Political Theory,* 13(1), 39–57.

Biddulph, R. (1904). *Lord Cardwell at the War Office.* London: John Murray.

Bilmes, L., and Stiglitz, J.E. (2006). "The economic costs of the Iraq war: an appraisal three years after the beginning of the conflict." Columbia University. Available from: www2.gsb.columbia.edu/faculty/jstiglitz/Cost_of_War_in_Iraq.htm (Accessed January 15, 2006).

Birks, J.W., and Ehrlich, A.H. (1990). "If deterrence fails: nuclear winter and ultraviolet spring." In A.H. Ehrlich and J.W. Birks (Eds.), *Hidden dangers: environmental consequences of preparing for war*. San Francisco: Sierra Club Books, 119–143.

Black, J. (2001). "Full circle: the cost accounting experiment in the British Army 1917–25 and the corps of military accountants." *Journal of the Society for Army Historical Research*, 79(318), 145–162.

Blum, W. (1995). *Killing hope: U.S. military and CIA interventions since World War II*. Monroe, ME: Common Courage Press.

Bond, B. (1972). *The Victorian army and the Staff College 1854–1914*. London: Eyre Methuen.

Bottome, E. (1986). *The balance of terror: nuclear weapons and the illusion of security, 1945–1985*. Boston: Beacon Press.

Box, R. (1999). "Running government like a business: implications for public administration theory and practice." *The American Review of Public Administration*, 29, 19–43.

Box, R., Marshall, G., Reed, B., and Reed, C. (2001). "New public management and substantive democracy." *Public Administration Review*, 61, 608–619.

Boyer, P. (1984). "From activism to apathy: the American people and nuclear weapons, 1963–1980." *The Journal of American History*, 70, 821–844.

Boyer, P. (1985). *By the bomb's early light: American thought and culture at the dawn of the atomic age*. New York: Pantheon Books.

Boyle, R. (1972). *The flower of the dragon: the breakdown of the U.S. army in Vietnam*. San Francisco: Ramparts Press.

Breitman, R. (1994). "Himmler: the architect of genocide." In D. Cesarani (Ed.), *The final solution: origins and implementation*. London: Routledge.

Brighton, C., and Uhl, M. (1995). "Bombing for the hell of it." *The Nation*, June 12, 822–826.

Broadbent, J. (1995). "The values of accounting and education: some implications of the creation of visibilities and invisibilities in schools. *Advances in Public Interest Accounting*, 6, 69–98.

Broadbent, J., and Laughlin, R. (1994). *Moving towards an accounting that will be enabling: accounting, Habermas and issues of gender*. Seminar paper, Department of Accounting and Finance, University of Wollongong.

Browning, C. (1980). "The government experts." In H. Friedlander and S. Milton (Eds.,), *The Holocaust: ideology, bureaucracy, and genocide*. Millwood, NY: Kraus International Publications.

Browning, C. (1985). *Fateful months*. New York: Holmes & Meier.

Browning, C. (1988). "Bureaucracy and mass murder: the German administrator's comprehension of the final solution." In A. Cohen (Ed.), *Comprehending the Holocaust*. Frankfurt am Main: Peter Lang.

Bullock, A. (1973). *Hitler: a study in tyranny*. London: Book Club Associates.

Bunbury, H. (1924) "Financial control within government departments." *The Journal of Public Administration*, 2, 131–137.

Burchell, S., Clubb, C., and Hopwood, A. (1980). "Accounting in its social context: towards a history of value-added." *Accounting, Organizations and Society*, 5(1), 5–27.

Bush, G.W. (2001). "Text: President Bush addresses the nation. September 20, 2001." *The Washington Post*, September 20. Available from: www.washington post.com/wp-srv/nation/specials/attacked/transcripts/bushaddress_092001.html (Accessed July 3, 2012).

Bush, G.W. (2002). "Memorandum: humane treatment of al Qaeda and Taliban detainees." *American Civil Liberties Union*, February 7. Available from: www. aclu.org/files/assets/2010065_dos_release_1_doc_0_already_released.pdf (Accessed August 8, 2012).

Bush, G.W. (2006). "Trying detainees: address on the creation of military commissions." *PresidentialRhetoric.com,* September 6. Available from: www.presidential rhetoric.com/speeches/09.06.06.html (Accessed March 27, 2012).

Bush, G.W. (2010). *Decision points.* New York: Crown.

Business Week (1969). "Putting a dollar sign on everything." In J.W. Davis (Ed.), *Politics, programs and budgets: a reader in government budgeting.* Englewood Cliffs, NJ: Prentice Hall, 155–160.

Buxton, J. (Major) (1883). *The elements of military administration.* London: Kegan Paul, Trench & Co.

Bybee, J. (2002). "Memorandum for John Rizzo Acting General Counsel of the Central Intelligence Agency." *The Guardian,* August 1. Available from: http://image. guardian.co.uk/sys-files/Guardian/documents/2009/04/16/bybee_to (Accessed April 20, 2009).

Canan, J.W. (1975). *The supperwarriors.* New York: Weybright and Talley.

Caputo, P. (1977). *A rumor of war.* New York: Ballantine Books.

Carter G. (1972). *The Government of the United Kingdom.* New York: Harcourt Brace Jovanovich.

Center for American Progress (2004). *The opportunity costs of the Iraq war.* Washington, D.C.: Center for American Progress.

Center for Constitutional Rights (2011). "CCR announces Bush indictment for Convention Against Torture signatory states." February 7. Available from: http:// ccrjustice.org/newsroom/press-releases/human-rights-groups-announce-bush-indictment-convention-against-torture-sign (Accessed June 14, 2014).

Center for Constitutional Rights (n.d.a). "Arar v. Ashcroft et al." Available from: http://ccrjustice.org/ourcases/current-cases/arar-v-ashcroft (Accessed on July 3, 2013).

Center for Constitutional Rights (n.d.b). "100 days: end the abuse of the state secrets privilege." Available from: www.ccrjustice.org/learn-more/faqs/100-days%3A-end-abuse-state-secrets-privilege (Accessed April 22, 2014).

Central Intelligence Agency Inspector General (2004). "Special review: counterterrorism detention and interrogation activities." *American Civil Liberties Union,* May 7. Available from: www.aclu.org/torturefoia/released/052708/052708_ Special_Review.pdf (Accessed April 2, 2012).

Cesarani, D. (Ed.) (1994). *The final solution: origins and implementation.* London: Routledge.

Chelala, C. (2005). "Unending health disaster for Iraqi kids." *Japan Times,* June 18. Available from: www.globalpolicy.org/security/issues/iraq/attack/consequences/ 2005/0618kids.htm (Accessed September 10, 2005).

Chomsky, N. (1987). *The Chomsky reader.* New York: Pantheon Books.

Chomsky, N. (1995). "Memories." *Z Magazine,* July/August, 28–40.

Christensen, T., and Laegreid, P. (2002). "New public management: puzzles of democracy and the influence of citizens." *The Journal of Political Philosophy,* 10, 267–295.

Chubb, B. (1952). *The control of public expenditure: financial committees of the House of Commons.* Oxford: Clarendon Press.

Churchill, R. (1959). *Lord Derby: "King of Lancashire."* London: Heinemann.

Churchill, S. (Maj.) (1895). "Army financial reform." *The United Services Magazine,* XI(797), 36–46.

Churchill, S. (Lieut.-Col.) (1903). "Financial lessons from the late war, part I." *The Journal of the Royal United Services Institute,* XLVII, 278–288.

Churchill, W. (1906). *Lord Randolph Churchill,* 2 Vols. London: John Murray.

Churchill, W. (1962). *A history of the English speaking peoples,* Vol. II. London: MacMillan.

Citizens Commission of Inquiry (1972). *The Dellums Committee Hearings on war crimes in Vietnam.* New York: Vintage Books.

Clode, C. (1869). *The military forces of the crown: their administration and government,* Vols. I and II. London: John Murray.

Coburn, J. (2005). "Iraqi casualties: unnamed and unnoticed." *Mother Jones,* July. Available from: www.motherjones.com/commentary/columns/2005/07/unnamed__and_unnoticed.html (Accessed October 3, 2005).

Cohn, C. (1987). "Sex and death in the rational world of defense intellectuals." *Signs: Journal of Women in Culture and Society,* 12, 687–718.

Cohn, C. (1990). "'Clean bombs' and clean language." In J. Bethke Elshstain and S. Tobais (Eds.), *Women, militarism and war: essays in history, politics and social theory.* Savage, MD: Rowman & Littlefield Publishers, 33–55.

'Colonel' (1914). "Administrative commanders and their staff." *The United Services Magazine,* XLVIII, 71–80.

Committee of Administration of, and Accounting for, Army Expenditure (Lawrence Committee) (1924). *British Parliamentary Papers,* (Cmd.2073), VII, 707.

Committee on War Office Organisation (Dawkins Committee) (1901). *British Parliamentary Papers,* (Cmd.580), XI, 179; Evidence XI, 207.

Committee to Consider Decentralisation of War Office Business (Brodrick Committee) (1898). *British Parliamentary Papers,* (Cmd.8934), XII, 123.

Congress and the Nation, Vol. II, 1965–1968 (1969). Washington, D.C.: Congressional Quarterly Service.

Congressional Budget Office (2002). "Estimated costs of a potential conflict with Iraq." September 30. Available from: www.cbo.gov/showdoc.cfm?index=3822& sequence=0_ (Accessed July 2, 2005).

Constitutionalist (1901). *Army administration in three centuries.* London: Edward Stanford.

Cook, L.J. (2003). "The war dividend." *Forbes,* 171(7), 48a.

Cortright, D. (1975). *Soldiers in revolt: the American military today.* Garden City, NJ: Anchor Press.

Covaleski, M., and Dirsmith, M. (1988). "The use of budgetary symbols in the political arena: a historically informed field of study." *Accounting, Organizations and Society,* 13(1), 1–24.

Covaleski, M., and Dirsmith, M. (1995). "The preservation and use of public resources: transforming the immoral into the merely factual." *Accounting, Organisations and Society,* 20(2/3), 147–173.

Crew, G. (1970). *The Royal Army Service Corps.* London: Leo Cooper.

Crewdson, J., and Hundley, T. (2005). "Jet's travels cloaked in mystery." *The Chicago Tribune,* March 20. Available from: http://articles.chicagotribune.com/2005-03-20/news/0503200504_1_31st-fighter-wing-suspects-abuomar (Accessed January 30, 2013).

Crosland, A. (1918). *Notes on cost accounting,* Director of Army Finance.

Cross, C. (1974). *Adolf Hitler.* London: Coronet Books.

Dahrendorf, R. (1995). *A history of the London School of Economics and Political Science.* Oxford: Oxford University Press.

Danadio, R. (2009). "Italy convicts 23 Americans, most working for C.I.A., of abducting Muslim cleric." *The New York Times,* November 5, A15.

Danner, M. (2009). "U.S. torture: voices from the black sites." *The New York Review of Books,* April 9. Available from: www.nybooks.com/articles/archives/2009/apr/09/us-torture-voices-from-the-black-sites/?pagination=false (Accessed November 4, 2010).

Davies, G. (1954). "The army and the Restoration of 1660." *Journal of the Society for Army Historical Research,* XXXII(129), 26–29.

Davis, B. (2002). "Bush economic aide says cost of Iraq war may top $100 billion." *Wall Street Journal,* September 16, A1.

Dawidowicz, L. (1975). *The war against the Jews 1933–1945.* London: Weidenfeld and Nicholson.

Dawidowicz, L. (1976). *A Holocaust reader.* New York: Behrman House Inc.

de Wet, C. (1902). *Three years war.* Westminster: Archibald Constable and Co.

Department of Veterans Affairs (2003). *Gulf War research: a report to veterans* (IB10–42, October 2003, P93101). Washington, D.C.: Department of Veterans Affairs.

Dicksee, L. (1915). *Business methods and the war.* Cambridge: Cambridge University Press.

Dictionary of National Biography (1922–30). Oxford: Oxford University Press.

Digby, J. (1989). *Operations research and systems analysis at RAND, 1948–1967* (RAND Corporation Rep. No. N-2936-RC). Santa Monica, CA: RAND Corporation.

Dority, B., and Edwards, F. (2004). "Humanism versus the militarization of America." *The Humanist,* 64(4), 12–17.

Durell, A. (Col.) (1917). *The principles and practice of the system of control over Parliamentary grants.* Portsmouth: Gieves Publishing.

Dwyer, D. (2011). "George W. Bush cans Swiss trip as groups promise prosecution for war crimes." ABC News, February 7. Available from: http://abcnews.go.com/Politics/george-bush-cancels-swiss-trip-rights-activists-vow/story?id=12857195 (Accessed June 12, 2014).

Eagleton, T. (1990). *The significance of theory.* Oxford: Basil Blackwell.

Eagleton, T. (1991). *Ideology.* London: Verso.

Easthope, A., and McGowan, K. (Eds.) (1992). *A critical and cultural theory reader.* Sydney: Allen and Unwin.

Editor (1907). "The experimental course at the London School of Economics and Political Science." *Army Service Corps Quarterly,* October, 304–320.

Edwards, P. (1996). *The closed world: computers and the politics of discourse in Cold War America.* Cambridge, MA: MIT Press.

Ehrhart, W.D. (1983). *Vietnam-perkasie: a combat marine memoir.* Jefferson, NC: McFarland.

Ehrhart, W.D. (1986). *Passing time: memoir of a Vietnam veteran against the war.* Amherst: University of Massachusetts Press.

Ehrman, J. (1969). *Cabinet government and war 1890–1940.* London: Archer Books.

Einzig, P. (1959). *The control of the purse.* London: Secker and Warburg.

Eisner, J. (1983). "The genocide bomb." In R. Braham (Ed.), *Perspectives on the Holocaust.* Netherlands: Springer.

Ellison, G. (Major-General) (1918). "Cost accounting committee address." In War Office Cost Accounting Committee, *Addresses and explanatory remarks to officers and N.C.Os charged with the preparation of cost accounts in certain units,* 26th to 29th June 1918, London: War Office.

Elton, G. (1963). *England under the Tudors.* London: Methuen & Co.

Emerson, G. (1976). *Winners and losers: battles, retreats, gains, losses and ruins from the Vietnam War.* New York: Harcourt Brace Jovanovich.

Emy, H. (1973). *Liberals, radicals and social politics.* Cambridge: Cambridge University Press.

Enthoven, A.C. (1963). "Defense and disarmament: economic analysis in the Department of Defense." *The American Economic Review,* 53(2), 413–423.

Enthoven, A.C. (1969). "The systems analysis approach." Reprinted in *Planning-Programming-Budgeting: hearing before the Subcommittee on National Security*

and International Operations of the Committee on Government Operations,
United States Senate, 91st Cong., 1st Sess. 5, 565–574.

Enthoven, A.C., and Smith, K.W. (1980). *How much is enough: shaping the defense program, 1961–1968*. Millwood, NY: Kraus Reprint.

Environmental Protection Agency (1999). *The benefits and costs of the Clean Air Act 1990 to 2010* (EPA-410-R-99–001). Washington, D.C.: Environmental Protection Agency.

Epstein, J., and Miller, J. (2005). "U.S. wars and post-traumatic stress disorder." *SFGate*, June 22. Available from: www.sfgate/cgi-bin/article.cgi?f=/c/a/2005/06/22/MNGJ7DCKR71.DTL&type=health (Accessed August 15, 2005).

European Court of Human Rights (2012). "Case of El-Masri v. the former Yugoslav Republic of Macedonia, judgement." December 13. Available from: http://hudoc.echr.coe.int/sites/eng/pages/search.aspx?i=001-115621#{"ite mid":("001-115621")} (Accessed July 16, 2013).

European Parliament (2006). "Working document no. 8: on the companies linked to the CIA, aircraft used by the CIA and the European countries in which CIA aircraft have made stopovers." November 16. Available from www.europarl.europa.eu/comparl/tempcom/tdip/working_docs/pe380984_en.pdf (Accessed December 12, 2011).

Ewell, J.J., and Hunt, I.A. (1974). *Sharpening the combat edge: the use of analysis to reinforce military judgment*. Washington, D.C.: Department of the Army.

Fallows, J. (1981). *National defense*. New York: Random House.

Felts, A., and Jos, P. (2000). "Time and space: the origins and implications of the new public management." *Administrative Theory & Praxis*, 22, 519–533.

Finer, A. (1937). *The British civil service*. London: George Allen & Unwin.

Fitzgerald, F. (1972). *Fire in the lake: the Vietnamese and the Americans in Vietnam*. New York: Vintage Books.

Fleetwood, W.G. (1922). *Letters to somebody*. London: Cassell & Co. Ltd.

Fleming, G. (1985). *Hitler and the final solution*. London: Hamish Hamilton.

Foot, J. (2007). "The rendition of Abu Omar." *London Review of Books*, 29(15), 25–35.

Fortescue, J. (1930). *A history of the British army, vol. XIII, 1852–1870*. London: Macmillan & Co.

Fortescue, J. (1931). *The Royal Army Service Corps: a history of transport and supply in the British Army*, Vol. I. Cambridge: Cambridge University Press.

Fowler, J. (2005). "Expert: malnutrition affects Iraq kids." Associated Press, March 30. Available from: www.globalpolicy.org/security/issues/iraq/attack/conse quences/2005/0330malnutrition.htm (Accessed October 2, 2005).

Francis, J. (1990). "After virtue? Accounting as a moral and discursive practice." *Accounting, Auditing and Accountability Journal*, 5(5), 5–17.

Frankel, A. (2012). "European court: U.S. extraordinary rendition 'amounted to torture.'" *American Civil Liberties Union*, December 13. Available from: www.aclu.org/blog/national-security-human-rights/european-court-us-extraordinary-rendition-amounted-torture (Accessed January 29, 2013).

Friedlander, H. (1980). "The manipulation of language." In H. Friedlander and S. Milton (Eds.), *The Holocaust: ideology, bureaucracy, and genocide*. Millwood, NY: Kraus International Publications.

'Frugalitis' (1905). "The army council and army economy." *The United Services Magazine*, XXXI, 10–14.

Fulbright, W.J. (1966). *The Vietnam hearings: the complete statements of Dean Rusk, James M. Gavin, George F. Kennan, Maxwell D. Taylor with extensive excerpts from their testimony*. New York: Vintage Book.

Funnell, W. (1997). "Military influences on public sector accounting and auditing 1830–1880." *Accounting History*, 2(2), 9–31.

Funnell, W. (2001). *Government by fiat: the retreat from responsibility.* Sydney: University of NSW Press.

Funnell, W. (2004). "Victorian parsimony and the early champions of modern public sector audit." *Accounting History,* 9(1), 25–60.

Funnell, W., Jupe, R., and Andrew, J. (2009). *In government we trust: market failure and the delusions of privatisation.* London: Pluto Press.

Furse, G. (1894). *The organisation and administration of the lines of communication in war.* London: William Clowes and Sons.

Galella, P., and Esposito, C. (2012). "Extraordinary renditions in the fight against terrorism. Forced disappearances?" *SUR: International Journal on Human Rights,* 9(16), 7–31.

Gallhofer, S., and Haslam, J. (1991). "The aura of accounting in the context of a crisis: Germany and the First World War." *Accounting, Organizations and Society,* 16(5/6), 487–520.

Gallhofer, S., and Haslam, J. (2003). *Accounting and emancipation: some critical interventions.* London: Routledge.

Gardner, F. (1970). "War and G.I. morale." *New York Times,* November 21, A31.

Garland, D. (2001). *The culture of control: crime and social order in contemporary society.* Chicago: The University of Chicago Press.

Garvey, T., and Liu, E. (2011). "The state secrets privilege: preventing the disclosure of sensitive national security information during civil litigation." Washington, D.C.: Congressional Research Service.

Gellman, B. (2001). "CIA weights 'targeted killing' missions." *The Washington Post,* October 28, A01.

General Accounting Office (1999). *Gulf War illness: procedural and reporting improvements are needed in DOD's investigative processes* (GAO/NSIAD-99–59). Washington, D.C.: General Accounting Office.

Gibson, J.W. (1986). *The perfect war: the war we couldn't lose and how we did.* New York: Vintage Books.

Giffen, R. (1901). "A business war office." *The Nineteenth Century,* 193, July, 1–11.

Gilbert, E. (1961). *Sir Halford Mackinder 1861–1947: an appreciation of his life and work.* London: G. Bell and Sons.

Gilbert, M. (1986). *The Holocaust: the Jewish tragedy.* London: Collins.

Gill, S. (2003). *Power and resistance in the new world order.* New York: Palgrave Macmillan.

Glantz, A. (2005). *How America lost Iraq.* New York: Penguin Group.

Glover, R. (1963). *Peninsular preparation: the reform of the British army 1795–1809.* Cambridge: Cambridge University Press.

Goebbels, J. (1982). *The Goebbels diaries, 1939–1941.* London: H. Hamilton.

Goldhagen, D. (1996). *Hitler's willing executioners: ordinary Germans and the Holocaust.* London: Little, Brown and Company.

Gonzales, A.R. (2002). "Decision re application of the Geneva Convention on Prisoners of War to the conflict with al Qaeda and the Taliban." January 25. Available from: www2.gwu.edu/~nsarchiv/NSAEBB/NSAEBB127/02.02.25.pdf (Accessed August 8, 2012).

Gordon, H. (1935). *The War Office.* London: Putnam.

Graves, O.F., Flesher, D.L., and Jordan, R.E. (1996). "Pictures and the bottom line: the television epistemology of U.S. annual reports." *Accounting, Organizations and Society,* 21(1), 57–88.

Gray, J. (2004). "Power and vainglory." In *Abu Ghraib: the politics of torture.* Berkeley: North Atlantic Books, 47–55.

Gray, R. (2002). "The social accounting project and *Accounting, Organizations and Society:* privileging engagement, imaginings, new accountings and pragmatism over critique?" *Accounting, Organizations and Society,* 27, 687–708.

Great Britain (1829). "Report of the commissioners appointed to inquire into and to state the mode of keeping the official accounts." *British Parliamentary Papers,* VI, part 290, 1–155.

Great Britain (1856). "Second report of the Royal Commission into the supplies of the British army in the Crimea." *British Parliamentary Papers,* XX, 715.

Great Britain (1904). "Report of the Committee on the War Office Reconstuction" (Esher Committee). *British Parliamentary Papers,* VIII, 1.

Grey, S. (2007). *Ghost plane: the true story of the CIA rendition and torture program.* New York: St. Martin's Griffen.

Grier, P. (2005). "The rising economic cost of the Iraq war." *The Christian Science Monitor,* May 19. Available from: www.csmonitor.com/2005/0519/p01s03-usmi.html (Accessed August 2, 2005).

Griffiths, A. (1900). "The conduct of the war." *The Fortnightly Review,* CCCXCVII, New Series, 1–10.

Grimwood, J. (Lieut.-Col.) (1919). "Costing in relation to government control, efficiency and economy." *The Incorporated Accountants Journal,* March, 114–120; April, 133–138; May, 156–161.

Gronke, P., and Rejali, D. (2010). "U.S. public opinion on torture, 2001–2009." Reed College, July. Available from: www.academic.reed.edu/poli_sci/faculty/rejali/articles/US_Public_Opinion_Torture_Gronke_Rejali.pdf (Accessed March 17, 2014).

Gross, B.M. (1971). "The new systems budgeting." In A. Westin (Ed.), *Information technology in a democracy.* Cambridge, MA: Harvard University Press, 357–374.

Halberstam, D. (1992). *The best and the brightest.* New York: Ballantine Books.

Haldane, R. (1929). *Richard Burdon Haldane: an autobiography.* New York: Doubleday, Doran & Co.

Hall, S. (1982). "The rediscovery of 'ideology': return of the repressed in media studies." In M. Gurevitch, T. Bennett, J. Curran, and J. Woollacott (Eds.), *Culture, society and the media.* New York: Methuen & Co., 56–90.

Hallin, D.C. (1986). *The uncensored war: the media and Vietnam.* Berkeley: University of California Press.

Hallock, D. (1998). *Hell, healing and resistance: veterans speak.* Farmington, PA: The Plough Publishing House.

Hamer, D. (1972). *Liberal politics in the age of Gladstone and Rosebery: a study in leadership and policy.* Oxford: Clarendon Press.

Hamer, W. (1970). *The British army: civil-military relations 1885–1905.* Oxford: Clarendon Press.

Hanham, H. (1969). *The nineteenth century constitution, 1815–1914.* Cambridge: Cambridge University Press.

Harper, T. (2003). "Pentagon keeps dead out of sight." *The Toronto Star,* November 4. Available from: www.commondreams.org/cgi-bin/print.cgi?file=/headlines03/1102–08.htm (Accessed August 10, 2005).

Harris, C. (1911). "Army finance." *Army Review,* I, July, 55–76.

Harris, C. (1931). "Financial control in administration." *Public Administration,* 9, 312–322.

Harris, D. (1996). *Our war: what we did in Vietnam and what it did to us.* New York: Random House.

Harris, G. (1997). "Estimates of the economic cost of armed conflict: the Iran-Iraq war and the Sri Lankan civil war." In J. Brauer and W.G. Gissy (Eds.), *Economics of conflict and peace.* Brookfield, VT: Aldershot, 269–291.

Hartung, W.D. (2003). *The hidden costs of war.* Goshen, IN: The Fourth Freedom Forum.

Hartung, W.D. (2004). "Private military contractors in Iraq and beyond: a question of balance." *World Policy Institute,* July 22. Available from: http://worldpolicy.org/projects/arms/updates/FPIFJune2004.html (Accessed July 3, 2005).

Harvey, D. (2005). *A brief history of neoliberalism*. Oxford: Oxford University Press.

Headlam, C. (Ed.) (1931). *The Milner papers: South Africa 1897–1899*, Vol. I. London: Cassell & Coy.

Headlam, C. (Ed.) (1933). *The Milner papers: South Africa 1897–1899*, Vol. II. London: Cassell & Coy.

Hedges, C. (2003). *What every person should know about war*. New York: Free Press.

Heinl, R.D. (1971). "The collapse of the Armed Forces." *Armed Forces Journal*, June 7, 30–38.

Herf, J. (1984). *Reactionary modernism: technology, culture and politics in Weimar and the Third Reich*. Cambridge: Cambridge University Press.

Herkin, G. (1987). *Counsels of war*. New York: Oxford University Press.

Herr, M. (1977). *Dispatches*. New York: Avon Books.

Hilberg, R. (1972). *Documents of destruction*. London: W.H. Allen.

Hilberg, R. (1980). "The significance of the Holocaust." In H. Friedlander and S. Milton (Eds.), *The Holocaust: ideology, bureaucracy, and genocide*. Millwood, NY: Kraus International Publications.

Hilberg, R. (1985). *The destruction of the European Jews*. New York: Holmes and Meir.

Hilberg, R. (1989). "German railroads/Jewish souls." In M. Marrus (Ed.), *The Nazi Holocaust: historical articles on the destruction of the European Jews*, Vol. 2. Westport, CT: Meckler.

Hilberg, R. (1993). *Perpetrators, victims, bystanders: the Jewish catastrophe*. New York: Harper Collins.

Hinchliffe, L. (1983). *Trust and be trusted: the Royal Army Pay Corps and its origins*. London: Royal Army Pay Corps.

Hitch, C.J. (1969). "Decision making in large organizations." Reprinted in *Planning-Programming-Budgeting: hearing before the Subcommittee on National Security and International Operations of the Committee on Government Operations*, United States Senate, 91st Cong., 1st Sess. 5, 574–581.

Hitch, C.J., and McKean, R.N. (1963). *The economics of defense in the nuclear age*. Cambridge, MA: Harvard University Press.

Hitler, A. (1987). *Mein Kampf*. Boston: Hutchinson.

Hobsbawm, E. (1994). *The age of extremes: a history of the world, 1914–1991*. New York: Vintage Books.

Hoge, C.W., Castro, C.A., Messer, S.C., McGurk, D., Cotting, D.I., and Koffman, R.L. (2004). "Combat duty in Iraq and Afghanistan, mental health problems, and barriers to care." *The New England Journal of Medicine*, 351(1), 13–22.

Hopwood, A. (1983). "On trying to study accounting in the contexts in which it operates." *Accounting, Auditing and Accountability Journal*, 8(2/3), 287–305.

Horngren, C.T., Datar, S.M., and Foster, G. (2006). *Cost accounting: A managerial emphasis* (12th ed.). Upper Saddle River, NJ: Pearson, Prentice Hall.

Hughes, E. (1934). *Studies in administration and finance, 1558–1825*. Manchester: Manchester University Press.

Hughes, S. (2007). *War on terror, inc.: corporate profiteering from the politics of fear*. London: Verso.

Human Rights Watch (2003). *Climate of fear: sexual violence and abduction of women and girls in Baghdad*. New York: Human Rights Watch.

Humphrey, C., and Scapens, R. (1996). "Theories and case studies of organisational and accounting practices: limitation or liberation." *Accounting, Auditing and Accountability Journal*, 9(4), 86–106.

Huntington, S. (1972). *The soldier and the state*. Cambridge, MA: Belknap Press.

Ibrahim, H. (2005). "Gender based violence." War Tribunal on Iraq, June 23–27. Available from: www.worldtribunal.org/main/popup/ibrahim_full.html (Accessed September 15, 2005).

Ilcan, S., and Phillips, L. (2010). "Developmentalities and calculative practices: the millennium development goals." *Antipode*, 42, 844–874.

Integrated Regional Information Networks (2005). "Focus on increase in kidnappings." April 11. Available from: www.globalpolicy.org/security/issues/iraq/attack/consequences/2005/0411kidnappings.htm (Accessed September 10, 2005).

International Committee of the Red Cross (2007). "ICRC report on the treatment of fourteen 'high value detainees' in CIA custody." February 14. Available from: http://wlstorage.net/file/icrc-report-2007.pdf (Accessed March 9, 2012).

Iraq Body Count (2005). *A dossier of civilian casualties 2003–2005*. Oxford: Oxford Research Group.

Isikoff, M. (2009). "The end of torture." *Newsweek*, January 21. Available from: http://thedailybeast.com/newsweek/2009/01/21/the-end-of-torture.html (Accessed June 10, 2013).

Iwan-Muller, E. (1902). *Lord Milner in South Africa*. London: William Heinemann.

Jablonsky, S., and Dirsmith, M.W. (1978). "The pattern of PPB rejection: something about organizations, something about PPB." *Accounting, Organizations and Society*, 3, 215–225.

Jamail, D. (2005). "Iraqi hospitals ailing under occupation." June 21. Available from: www.dahrjamailiraq.com/reports/HealthCareUnderOccupationDahrJamail.pdf (Accessed August 12, 2005).

James, R. (1963). *Rosebery*. London: Weidenfeld and Nicolson.

Jay, P., and Osnos, P. (1971). "Bored GI's turn to fragging, heroin." *The Washington Post*, September 16, A1–A12.

Jensen, D. (2004). *A language older than words*. White River Junction, VT: Chelsea Green Publishing Company.

Johnson, C. (2007). "Otherwise dealt with." *London Review of Books*, 29(3), 7–9.

Johnson, L. (2000). "Transnational private policing: the impact of global commercial security." In J. Sheptycki (Ed.), *Issues in transnational policing*. New York: Routledge, 21–42.

Johnson, L.B. (1969). "Memorandum from the President to the heads of departments and agencies on the government-wide planning, programming, and budgeting system. November 17, 1966." In J.W. Davis (Ed.), *Politics, programs and budgets: a reader in government budgeting*. Englewood Cliffs, NJ: Prentice Hall, 160–161.

Johnson, R.B. (1971). "Testimony from the war's trigger end." *Washington Monthly*, 35, 20–35.

Johnston, D. (2006). "At a secret interrogation, dispute flared over tactics." *The New York Times*, September 10. Available from: www.nytimes.com/2006/09/10/washington/10detain.html?pagewanted=all (Accessed March 27, 2012).

Johnston, D., and Savage, C. (2009). "Obama reluctant to look into Bush programs." *The New York Times*, January 11. Available from: www.nytimes.com/2009/01/12/us/politics/12inquire (Accessed May 30, 2014).

Joseph, P. (1981). *Cracks in the empire: state politics in the Vietnam War*. Boston: South End Press.

Judd, F. (1973). *Someone has blundered: calamities of the British army in the Victorian age*. London: Arthur Baker.

Kallio, N. (2005). "Humanitarian worker in Iraq says things have gotten worse." *Portland Press Herald*, April 6. Available from: www.globalpolicy.org/security/issues/iraq/attack/consequences/2005/0406wprse/htm (September 5, 2005).

Kamiya, G. (2005). "Iraq: the unseen war." *Salon,* August 23. Available from: www. salon.com/news/feature/2005/08/23/iraq_gallery/index_np.html (Accessed September 20, 2005).

Kaplan, F. (1983). *The wizards of armageddon.* Stanford: Stanford University Press.

Katz, F. (1989). "Implementation of the Holocaust: the behavior of Nazi officials." In M. Marrus (Ed.), *The Nazi Holocaust: historical articles on the destruction of the European Jews,* Vol. 2. Westport, CT: Meckler.

Kaufmann, W. (1964). *The McNamara strategy.* New York: Harper and Row.

Keen, S. (1986). *Faces of the enemy: reflections of the hostile imagination.* San Francisco: Harper & Row Publishers.

Kingsolver, B. (1998). "In the belly of the beast." In P.J. Annas and R.C. Rosen (Eds.), *Against the current.* Upper Saddle River, NJ: Prentice Hall, 578–587.

Kirschbaum, E. (2003). "U.S. military upholds TV cover ban on Iraq coffins." *Yahoo News,* November 3. Available from: www.commondreams.org/cgi-bin/ print.cgi?file=/headlines03/1103–09.htm (Accessed August 10, 2005).

Klarsfeld S. (Ed.) (1978). *The Holocaust and the neo-Nazi mythomania.* New York: The Beate Klarsfeld Foundation.

Klein, N. (2007). *The shock doctrine: the rise of disaster capitalism.* New York: Metropolitan Books.

Knorr, K. (1969). "On the cost-effectiveness approach to military research and development." Reprinted in *Planning-Programming-Budgeting: hearing before the Subcommittee on National Security and International Operations of the Committee on Government Operations,* United States Senate, 91st Cong., 1st Sess. 5, 581–586.

Koss, S. (1969). *Lord Haldane: scapegoat for liberalism.* New York: Columbia University Press.

Kruger, R. (1959). *Good-bye Dolly Gray: the story of the Boer War.* London: Cassell.

Kulish, N. (2012). "Court finds rights violation in C.I.A. rendition case." *The New York Times,* December 13. Available from: http://nytimes.com/2012/12/14/ world/europe/european-court-backs-cia-rendition-victim-khaled-el-masri.html (Accessed January 30, 2013).

LaCapra, D. (1994). *Representing the Holocaust: history, theory, trauma.* Ithaca: Cornell University Press.

Laffin, P. (1964). *Tommy Atkins.* London: Cassell.

Langmuir, G. (1980). "Medieval anti-semitism." In H. Friedlander and S. Milton (Eds.), *The Holocaust: ideology, bureaucracy, and genocide.* Millwood, NY: Kraus International Publications.

Latour, B. (1987). *Science in action.* Cambridge, MA: Harvard University Press.

Laurance, J. (2004). "Iraq faces soaring toll of deadly disease." *The Independent,* October 13. Available from: www.globalpolicy.org/security/issues/iraq/ attack/consequences/2004.1013disease.htm (Accessed September 21, 2005).

Le Mesurier, H. (1796). *Commissariat duties in the field 1796.* Reprinted in R. Glover (Ed.), *Peninsular preparation: the reform of the British Army 1795–1809,* Appendix A and B. Cambridge: Cambridge University Press, 1963.

Lifton, R.J. (1992). *Home from the war: learning from Vietnam veterans.* Boston: Beacon Press.

Lifton, R.J., and Falk, R. (1982). *Indefensible weapons: the political and psychological case against nuclearism.* New York: Basic Books.

Lifton, R.J., and Markusen, E. (1990). *The genocidal mentality: Nazi Holocaust and nuclear threat.* New York: Basic Books.

Linden, E. (1972). "The demoralization of an army: fragging and other withdrawal symptoms." *Saturday Review,* January 8, 12–17, 55.

Litz, B.T. (2005). "The unique circumstances and mental health impact of the wars in Afghanistan and Iraq." National Center for PTSD. Available from: www.ncptsd. va.gov/facts/veterans/fs_Iraq-Afghanistan_wars.html (Accessed October 20, 2005).

Locke, R. (1979). "Cost accounting: an institutional yardstick for measuring British entrepreneurial performance circa 1914." *The Accounting Historians' Journal,* Fall, 1–22.

Loft, A. (1986). "Towards a critical understanding of accounting: the case of cost accounting in the U.K., 1914–1925." *Accounting, Organizations and Society,* 11(2), 137–169.

Lovell, A. (1995). "Moral reasoning and moral atmosphere in the domain of accounting." *Accounting, Auditing and Accountability Journal,* 8(3), 60–80.

Lyke, M.L. (2004). "The unseen cost of war: American minds." *Seattlepi.com,* August 27. Available from: www.seattlepi.nwsource.com/local/188143_ptsd27. html (Accessed October 20, 2005).

MacAskill, E. (2009). "Obama releases Bush torture memos." *The Guardian,* April 16. Available from: www.theguardian.com/world/2009/apr/16/torture-memos-bush-administration (Accessed May 30, 2014).

MacAskill, E., and Hirsch, A. (2011). "George Bush calls off trip to Switzerland." *The Guardian,* February 6. Available from: www.theguardian.com/law/2011/feb/06/george-bush-trip-to-switzerland (Accessed June 12, 2014).

Mackenzie, N. (1978). *The letters of Sidney and Beatrice Webb, vol. 2 Partnership 1892–1912.* Cambridge: Cambridge University Press.

Mackenzie, N., and Mackenzie, J. (1977). *The first Fabians.* London: Weidenfeld and Nicolson.

Mackenzie, N., and Mackenzie, J. (1984). *The diary of Beatrice Webb,* Vol. 3. London: Virago.

Mackinder, H. (1907). *Address delivered on the 10th January, 1907, on the occasion of the opening of the class for the administrative training of army officers.* London: HSO.

Magnus, P. (1958). *Kitchener: portrait of an imperialist.* Harmondsworth: Penguin Books.

Markusen, A., and Yudken, J. (1992). *Dismantling the Cold War economy.* New York: Basic Books.

Marriner, S. (1994). "The Ministry of Munitions 1915–1919 and government accounting procedures." In R. Parker and B. Yamey (Eds.), *Accounting history: some British contributions.* Oxford: Clevedon Press.

Mason, T. (1989). "Intention and explanation: a current controversy about the interpretation of National Socialism." In M. Marrus (Ed.), *The Nazi Holocaust: historical articles on the destruction of the European Jews,* Vol. 1. Westport, CT: Meckler.

Matthew, H. (1973). *The liberal imperialists: the ideas and politics of a post-Gladstonian elite.* Oxford: Oxford University Press.

Mathews, M.R. (1997). "Twenty-five years of social and environmental accounting research: is there a silver jubilee to celebrate?" *Accounting, Auditing and Accountability Journal,* 10, 481–531.

Maunders, K., and Burritt, R. (1991). "Accounting and ecological crisis." *Accounting, Auditing and Accountability Journal,* 4(3), 9–26.

Maurice, F., and Arthur, G. (1924). *The life of Lord Wolseley.* London: William Heinemann.

Mayer, J. (2006). "The C.I.A.'s travel agent." *The New Yorker,* October 30. Available from: www.newyorker.com/archive/2006/10/30/061030ta_talk_mayer (Accessed January 16, 2013).

Mayer, J. (2009). *The dark side: the inside story of how the War on Terror turned into a war on American ideals.* New York: Anchor Books.

Mazza, C. (2012). "The Abu Omar case and 'extraordinary rendition.'" *Central European Journal of International and Security Studies,* 6(2), 134–159.

McGuire, J. (Lieut.-Col.) (1918). "Notes on a lecture on army accounting." In War Office Cost Accounting Committee, *Addresses and explanatory remarks to officers and N.C.Os charged with the preparation of cost accounts in certain units, 26th to 29th June 1918,* London: War Office.

McLaren, P., and Giroux, H. (1997). "Writing from the margins: geographies of identity, pedagogy and power." In P. McLaren (Ed.), *Revolutionary multiculturalism: pedagogies of dissent for the new millennium,* Boulder, CO: Westview Press, 16–41.

McNamara, R.S. (1996). *In retrospect: the tragedy and lessons of Vietnam.* New York: Vintage Books.

Medact (2002). *Collateral damage: the health and environmental costs of war on Iraq.* London: Medact.

Medact (2003). *Continuing collateral damage: the health and environmental costs of war on Iraq 2003.* London: Medact.

Medact (2004). *Enduring effects of war: health in Iraq 2004.* London: Medact.

Melville, C. (1923). *The life of General The Right Hon. Sir Redvers Buller.* London: Edward Arnold.

Midleton, Earl of (1939). *Records and reactions 1856–1939.* London: Murray.

Mies, M. (1990). "Science, violence and responsibility." *Women's Studies International Forum,* 13(5), 433–441.

Miller, P. (1990). "On the interrelationships between accounting and the state." *Accounting, Organizations and Society,* 15(4), 315–338.

Miller, P., and O'Leary, T. (1987). "Accounting and the construction of the governable person." *Accounting, Organisations and Society,* 12, 235–265.

Miller, P., and O'Leary, T. (1993). "Accounting expertise and the politics of the product: economic citizenship and modes of corporate governance." *Accounting, Organizations and Society,* 18(2/3), 187–206.

Mitchell, B. (1988). *British historical statistics.* Cambridge: Cambridge University Press.

Mitrany, D. (1918). "The London School of Economics and Political Science." *The Clare Market Review Series,* 1, 5–8.

Moise, E.E. (1985–1986). "The uncounted enemy: a Vietnam deception." *Public Affairs,* 58(4), 663–673.

Moncrieff, G. (Col.) (1909). "Army administration past and present." *Blackwood's Edinburgh Magazine,* 186, September, 377–392.

Morely, J. (1903). *Life of Gladstone,* 3 vols. (2nd ed.). London: Parker.

Morgan, G., and Willmott, H. (1993). "The 'new' accounting research: on making accounting more visible." *Accounting, Auditing and Accountability Journal,* 6(4), 3–36.

Moser, R. (1993). *The new winter soldiers: GI and veteran dissent during the Vietnam era.* New Brunswick, NJ: Rutgers University Press.

Mosher, F.C. (1969). "PPBS: two questions." Reprinted in *Planning-Programming-Budgeting: hearing before the Subcommittee on National Security and International Operations of the Committee on Government Operations,* United States Senate, 91st Cong., 1st Sess. 5, 587–592.

Mosse, G. (1970). *Germans and Jews: the right, the left, and the search for a "third force" in pre-Nazi Germany.* New York: Howard Fertig.

Moussa, H. (2005). "Power shortage drives Iraqis to frustration, fury." Reuters, August 2. Available from: www.vitw.org/archives/973 (Accessed September 17, 2005).

Muller-Hill, B. (1994). "The final solution and the role of experts." In D. Cesarani (Ed.), *The final solution: origins and implementation.* New York: Routledge.

Mumford, L. (1946). "Gentlemen: you are mad!" *The Saturday Review of Literature*, March 2, 5–6.

Murdock, C.A. (1974). *Defense policy formation: a comparative analysis of the McNamara era.* Albany: State University of New York Press.

Murphy, D. (2005). "Iraqis thirst for water and power." *The Christian Science Monitor*, August 11. Available from: www.csmonitor.com/2005/0811/p01s03-woiq. htm (Accessed September 17, 2005).

Napier, C., (1996). "Accounting and the absence of a business economics tradition in the United Kingdom." *European Accounting Review*, 5(3), 449–481.

Nash, H.T. (1980). "The bureaucratization of homicide." *The Bulletin of the Atomic Scientists*, 36(4), 22–27.

National Center for PTSD (2005). "What is posttraumatic stress disorder." Available from: www.ncptsd.va.gov/facts/general/fs_what_is_ptsd.html (Accessed October 10, 2005).

National Priorities Project (2005). "Federal budget tradeoffs." Available from: http://database.nationalpriorities.org/tradeoff (Accessed July 10, 2005).

NBC News Meet the Press (2001). "Transcript for Sept. 16." Available from: www.emperors-clothes.com/9–11backups/nbcmp.htm (Accessed December 15, 2010).

Neikirk, W. (2002). "Critics of Iraq War point to costs." *MaconTelegraph.com*, November 4. Available from: www.macon.com/mld/macon/news/politics/444 0484.htm (Accessed July 2, 2005).

Neu, D. (2000). "Accounting and accountability relations: colonization, genocide and Canada's first nations." *Accounting, Auditing & Accountability Journal*, 13(3), 268–288.

Neu, D., and Graham, C. (2006). "The birth of a nation: accounting and Canada's first nations, 1860–1900." *Accounting, Organizations and Society*, 31, 47–76.

Nofi, A. (n.d.). "Statistical summary: America's major wars." Louisiana State University. Available from: www.cwc.lsu.edu/cwc/other/stats/warcost.htm (July 10, 2005).

Nordhaus, W.D. (2002). "The economic consequences of a war with Iraq." In C. Kaysen, S.E. Miller, M.B. Malin, W.D. Nordhaus, and J.D. Steinbruner (Eds.), *War with Iraq: costs, consequences, and alternatives.* Cambridge, MA: American Academy of Arts and Sciences, 51–84.

Nordstrom, C. (1999). "Requiem for the rational war." In S.P. Reyna and R.E. Downs (Eds.), *Deadly developments: capitalism, states and war.* Amsterdam: Gordon and Breach Publishers, 153–175.

Nordstrom, C. (2004). *Shadows of war: violence, power, and international profiteering in the twenty-first century.* Berkeley: University of California Press.

Novick, D. (1969). "Origin and history of program budgeting." Reprinted in *Planning-Programming-Budgeting: hearing before the Subcommittee on National Security and International Operations of the Committee on Government Operations*, United States Senate, 91st Cong., 1st Sess. 5, 592–599.

Omond, J. (Lieut.-Col.) (1933). *Parliament and the army 1642–1904.* Cambridge: Cambridge University Press.

Openthegovernment.org (2013). "Secrecy report: indicators of secrecy in the federal government." Available from: www.openthegovernment.org/sites/default/files/ secrecy%20Report%202013%20Final.pdf (Accessed June 2, 2014).

Ormsby, T. (Captain) (1908a). "Army finance as a military science part I." *Journal of the Royal United Services Institute*, LII, 836–846.

Ormsby, T. (Captain) (1908b). "Army finance as a military science part II." *Journal of the Royal United Services Institute*, LII, 1532–1540.

Otley, C. (1970). "The social origins of British army officers." *Sociological Review*, 18(2), 213–234.

Padover, S. (1953). *The complete Madison.* New York: Harper and Brothers.

Pakenham, T. (1979). *The Boer War.* London: Weidenfeld and Nicholson.

Palmer, G. (1978). *The McNamara strategy and the Vietnam War: program budgeting in the Pentagon, 1960–1968.* Westport, CT: Greenwood Press.

Panmure Papers (1908). 2 vols. Edited by G. Douglas. London: Hodder.

Parenti, C. (2004). *The freedom: shadows and hallucinations in occupied Iraq.* New York: The New Press.

Parker, L.D. (2005). "Social and environmental accountability research: a view from the commentary box." *Accounting, Auditing and Accountability Journal,* 18, 842–860.

Parker, W. (1982). *Mackinder: geography as an aid to statecraft.* Oxford: Clarendon Press.

PBS (2007). "Mapping the black sites." Available from: www.pbs.org/frontline world/stories/rendition701/map/ (Accessed September 2, 2012).

Pearl, C. (1967). *Morrison of Peking.* Sydney: Angus and Robertson.

Pilger, J. (2002). "Collateral damage." In A. Arnove (Ed.), *Iraq under siege: the deadly impact of sanctions and war.* Cambridge, MA: South End Press, 77–83.

Plumb, J. (1967). *The growth of political stability in England 1675–1725.* Hammondsworth: Penguin Books.

Pois, R. (1989). "The Holocaust and the ethical imperative of historicism." In Y. Bauer (Ed.), *Remembering for the future: the impact of the Holocaust on the contemporary world.* Oxford: Pergamon.

Porter, A. (1980). *The origins of the South African War: Joseph Chamberlain and the diplomacy of imperialism 1895–99.* Manchester: Manchester University Press.

Porter, T.M. (1994a). "Making things quantitative." In M. Power (Ed.), *Accounting and science: natural inquiry and commercial reason.* Cambridge: Cambridge University Press, 35–56.

Porter, T.M. (1994b). "Objectivity as standardization: the rhetoric of impersonality in measurement, statistics, and cost-benefit analysis." In A. Megill (Ed.), *Rethinking objectivity.* Durham: Duke University Press, 197–237.

Porter, T.M. (1995). *Trust in numbers: the pursuit of objectivity in science and public life.* Princeton: Princeton University Press.

Potter, J. (1996). *Representing reality: discourse, rhetoric and social construction.* London: SAGE Publications.

Poundstone, W. (1992). *Prisoner's dilemma: John von Neumann, game theory, and the puzzle of the bomb.* New York: Doubleday.

Priest, D. (2005). "CIA holds terror suspects in secret prisons." *The Washington Post,* November 1. Available from: www.washingtonpost.com/wp-dyn/content/article/2005/11/01/AR2005110101644.html (Accessed August 1, 2012).

Priest, D., and Gellman, B. (2002). "U.S. decries abuse but defends interrogations." *The Washington Post,* December 26. Available from: www.washingtonpost.com/wp-dyn/content/article/2006/06/09/AR2006060901356.html (Accessed November 21, 2012).

Public Accounts Committee (1902). "First, second, third, fourth and fifth reports." *British Parliamentary Papers,* (Cmd.74, 140, 212, 304, 305), V, 1.

Public Accounts Committee (1917–1918). "Appendix 9, use of cost accounts by the War Office (Sir Charles Harris)." *British Parliamentary Papers,* (Cmd.123), III, 1.

Public Accounts Committee (1924–1925a). "First and second reports with proceedings, evidence, appendices and index." *British Parliamentary Papers,* (Cmd.33, 138), V, 1.

Public Accounts Committee (1924–1925b). "Appendix 32 to the report of the Public Accounts Committee; memorandum by the Comptroller and Auditor General (F. Phillips) in regard to the proposed change in the form of army estimates and accounts." *British Parliamentary Papers,* (Cmd.196), VI, 820.

Public Accounts Committee (1924–1925c). "Appendix 33 to the report of the Public Accounts Committee: paper by Sir Charles Harris, notes on the proposed changes in the form of army estimates and accounts." *British Parliamentary Papers,* (Cmd 196) VI, 826.

Quinn, B., and Cobain, I. (2011). "Mundane bills bring CIA's rendition network into sharper focus." *The Guardian,* August 31. Available from: www.guardian. co.uk/world/2011/aug/31/cia-rendition-flights-cost?intcmp=239 (Accessed September 9, 2011).

Quinn, G. (1994). "The Iraq conflict (1990–)." In M. Cranna (Ed.), *The true cost of conflict.* London: Earthscan Publications, 25–54.

Raskin, M.G. (1970). "The Kennedy hawks assume power from the Eisenhower vultures." In L.S. Rodberg and D. Shearer (Eds.), *The Pentagon watchers: students report on the national security state.* Garden City, NJ: Doubleday and Company, 65–97.

Raskin, M.G. (1979). *The politics of national security.* New Brunswick, NJ: Transaction Books.

Raskin, M.G. (1991). *Essays of a citizen: from national security state to democracy.* Armonk, NY: M.E. Sharpe.

Ravetz, J.R. (1990). *The merger of knowledge with power: essays in critical science.* London: Mansell Publishing Limited.

Read, D. (1972). *Edwardian England 1901–15: society and politics.* London: Harrap.

Redway, G. (Captain) (1902). "Complexity in army accounts." *The Journal of the Royal United Services Institute,* XLVI, 1259–1275.

Reid, A. (1911). *Memoirs of the Crimean War.* London: MacMillan.

Reitman, J. (2004). "Apocalypse now {pay later}." *Rolling Stone,* 962, 58–66.

Report from the Commissioners Appointed to Inquire into the Practicability and Expediency of Consolidating the Different Departments Connected with the Civil Administration of the Army (Howick Commission) (1837). *British Parliamentary Papers,* XXXIV, part I, 1.

Report from the Select Committee on Military Organisation (1860). *British Parliamentary Papers,* Vol. VII, pp. 1–23.

Report of the Committee on the War Office Reconstitution (Esher Committee) (1904). *British Parliamentary Papers,* VIII, 1.

Report on Educational Training in the British Army (1920). *British Parliamentary Papers* (Cmd.568), XXVIII, 301.

Report on the Organisation of the Permanent Civil Service (1854). *British Parliamentary Papers* (Cmd.439), XVII, 375–376.

Reprieve (n.d.). "Renditions, Inc." Available from: www.reprieve.org.uk/investigations/rendition (Accessed August 12, 2013).

Research Unit for Political Economy (2003). "Behind the war in Iraq." *Monthly Review,* 55(1), 20–49.

Richmor Aviation, Inc. v. Sportsflight Air, Inc. (2011). "New York Supreme Court, Appellate Division, Third Department." Colombia County Clerk's Index No. 2171/07.

Richmor.com. (n.d.). "Air charter company still flying high after forty years." Available from: www.richmor.com/news1.php (Accessed February 11, 2013).

Rickover, H.G. (1969). "Cost-effectiveness studies." Reprinted in *Planning-Programming-Budgeting: hearing before the Subcommittee on National Security and International Operations of the Committee on Government Operations,* United States Senate, 91st Cong., 1st Sess. 5, 599–608.

Riverbend (2005). *Baghdad burning: girl blog from Iraq.* New York: Feminist Press at the City University of New York.

Roberts L., Lafta R., Garfield R., Khudhairi J., and Burnham, G. (2004). "Mortality before and after the 2003 invasion of Iraq: cluster sample survey." *Thelancet.com,*

October 29. Available from: http://image.thelancet.com/extras/04art10342web.
pdf (September 15, 2005).

Robinson, S.L. (2004). *Hidden toll of the war in Iraq: mental health and the military.* Washington, D.C.: Center for American Progress.

Rome, J. (2009). "Italian court finds CIA agents guilty of kidnapping terrorism suspect: world's first 'extraordinary rendition' trial ends: twenty three Americans sentenced in absentia." *The Guardian*, November 5, 24.

Rose, J. (1914). *Pitt and the Great War.* London: Bell.

Rose, J. (1986). *The Edwardian temperament, 1895–1919.* Athens: Ohio University Press.

Rose, N. (1991). "Governing by numbers: figuring out democracy." *Accounting, Organizations and Society,* 16(6), 673–692.

Rosenberg, A. (1983). "The philosophical implications of the Holocaust." In R. Braham (Ed.), *Perspectives on the Holocaust.* Netherlands: Springer.

Ross, A.M. (1968). "Overblown affinity for numbers." Reprinted in *Congressional Record: proceedings and debates of the 90th Congress,* 2nd Session, Vol. 114, Part 15, 20382–20383.

Rowen, H.S. (1969). "Bargaining and analysis in government." Reprinted in *Planning-Programming-Budgeting: hearing before the Subcommittee on National Security and International Operations of the Committee on Government Operations,* United States Senate, 91st Cong., 1st Sess. 5, 609–613.

Royal Commission Appointed to Inquire into the Civil and Professional Administration of the Navy and Military Departments and the Relation of Those Departments to Each Other and to the Treasury (Hartington Commission) (1890). *British Parliamentary Papers,* (Cmd.5979) XIX, Report with Appendices, 1.

Royal Commission Appointed to Inquire into the Civil Establishments (Ridley Commission) (1887). *British Parliamentary Papers,* Vol. XIX, First Report, 1.

Royal Commission Appointed to Inquire into the Military Preparations and Other Matters Connected with the War in South Africa (Elgin Commission) (1904). *British Parliamentary Papers,* (Cmd.1789) XL, Report, 1.

Royal Commission Appointed to Inquire into the Supplies of the British Army in the Crimea (McNeil and Tulloch Commission) (1856). *British Parliamentary Papers,* Vol. XX, First Report including Appendix, 497.

Royal Commission into Transport and Supply Departments (Strathnairn Committee) (1867). *British Parliamentary Papers,* XV, 343.

Royal Commission on War Stores in South Africa (1906). "Report with appendices of Messrs. Annan, Kirby, Dexter & Co., chartered accountants." *British Parliamentary Papers,* (Cmd.3130) LVIII, 1, 73.

Ruddick, S. (1990). "The rationality of care." In J. Bethke Elshstain and S. Tobais S. (Eds.), *Women, militarism and war: essays in history, politics and social theory.* Savage, MD: Rowman & Littlefield Publishers, 229–254.

Rumsfeld, D. (2003). "FY 2003 emergency supplemental appropriations: testimony as prepared for delivered by Secretary of Defense Donald H. Rumsfeld, Senate Appropriations Committee and House Appropriations Committee—Subcommittee on Defense." U.S. Department of Defense, March 27. Available from: www.defenselink.mil/speeches/2003/sp20030327-secdef0102.html (Accessed July 1, 2005).

Russell, W. (1858). *The British expedition to the Crimea.* London: G. Routledge and Co.

Saar, J. (1970). "You can't just hand out orders." *Life,* October 23, 30–37.

Sanders, R. (1973). *The politics of defense analysis.* New York: Dunellen.

Santoli, A. (1981) *Everything we had: an oral history of the Vietnam War by thirty-three soldiers who fought it.* New York: Ballantine Books.

Sapolsky, H.M. (1972). *The Polaris system development: bureaucratic and programmatic success in government.* Cambridge, MA: Harvard University Press.

Sarup, M. (1993). *An introductory guide to post-structuralism and postmodernism.* Athens, GA: The University of Georgia Press.

Scally, R. (1975). *The origins of the Lloyd George coalition: the politics of social imperialism, 1900–1918.* Princeton: Princeton University Press.

Scarry, E. (1985). *The body in pain: the making and unmaking of the world.* New York: Oxford University Press.

Schell, J. (1982). *The fate of the earth.* New York: Alfred A. Knopf.

Schelling, T. (1971). "PPB and the complexities of foreign affairs." In A.F. Westin (Ed.), *Information technology in a democracy.* Cambridge, MA: Harvard University Press, 383–394.

Scherer, F.M. (1964). *The weapons acquisition process: economic incentives.* Boston: Harvard University Press.

Schlesinger, J.R. (1974). *Selected papers on national security, 1964–1968* (RAND Corporation Rep. No. P-5284). Santa Monica, CA: RAND Corporation.

Schneir, W., and Schneir, M. (1984). "The uncounted Viet Cong: how the military cooked the books." *The Nation,* May 12, 570–576.

Schweiker, W. (1993). "Accounting for ourselves: accounting practice and the discourse of ethics." *Accounting, Organizations and Society,* 18(2/3), 231–252.

Searle, G. (1971). *The quest for national efficiency.* Berkeley: University of California Press.

Select Committee into Army and Ordnance Expenditure (1849). *British Parliamentary Papers,* IX, 1.

Select Committee on Army and Navy Expenditure (1887). "First report." *British Parliamentary Papers,* Vol. VIII.

Select Committee on National Expenditure (1902). "Memorandum by Lord Welby: the control of the House of Commons over public expenditure." *British Parliamentary Papers,* (Cmd.387), VII, Appendix No. 13, 228–231.

Select Committee on National Expenditure (1918). "First to tenth reports." *British Parliamentary Papers,* (Cmd.23, 30, 59, 80, 92, 97, 98, 111, 121, 132), IV, 95.

Semmel, B. (1960). *Imperialism and social reform.* New York: Anchor Books.

Shane, S., Mazzetti, M., and Cooper, H. (2009). "Obama reverses key Bush security policies." *The New York Times,* January 22. Available from: www.nytimes.com/2009/01/23/us/politics/23obama.html?pagewanted=all&_r=0 (Accessed June 10, 2013).

Shapiro, M.J. (1988). *The politics of representation: writing practices in biography, photography, and policy analysis.* Madison: The University of Wisconsin Press.

Shapiro, M.J. (1989). "Textualizing Global Politics." In J. Der Derian and M. Shapiro (Eds.), *Postmodern readings of world politics, international/intertextual relations.* Lexington, MA: Lexington Books, 11–22.

Shaw, G. (Brevet Lieut.-Col.) (1939). *R.A.Q.C. supply in modern war.* London: Faber and Faber Ltd.

Sheehan, N. (1988). *A bright and shining lie: John Paul Vann and America in Vietnam.* New York: Vintage Books.

Siems, L. (2011). *The torture report: what the documents say about America's post-9/11 torture program.* New York: OR Books.

Singh, A. (2012). "European court of human rights finds against CIA abuse of Khaled el-Masri." *The Guardian,* December 13. Available from: www.guardian.co.uk/commentisfree/2012/dec/13/european-court-human-rights-cia-abuse-khaled-elmasri (Accessed January 30, 3013).

Skidelsky, R. (1983). *John Maynard Keynes,* Vol. 1. London: Macmillan.

Slessor, A. (Captain) (1900–1901). "The universities and the army." *United Services Magazine,* 22, October–March, 516–526.

Sombart, W. (1913). *The Jews and modern capitalism.* London: T. Fisher Unwin.

Speer, A. (1971). *Inside the Third Reich.* New York: Spheer Books.

Spencer, H. (1960). *The man versus the state.* Ohio: Caxton.

Spiers, E. (1992). *The late Victorian army, 1868–1902.* Manchester: Manchester University Press.

Stanmore, Lord (1906). *Sidney Herbert: Lord Herbert of Lea, a memoir,* 2 vols. London: John Murray.

Stark, E. (2004). "The coffins Bush won't let you see." Rocky Mountain Peace and Justice Center, January 28. Available from: www.rmpjc.org/2004/CoffinsBush WontLetYouSee (Accessed August 10, 2005).

Steinbruner, J.D. (1981–1982). "Nuclear decapitation." *Foreign Policy,* 45, 16–28.

Stephenson, Sir Frederick (1915). *At home and on the battlefield: letters from the Crimea, China and Egypt 1854–1888.* London: John Murray.

Stevens, R.W. (1976). *Vain hopes, grim realities: the economic consequences of the Vietnam War.* New York: New Viewpoints.

Stone, C. (1987). "Elite distemper versus the promise of democracy." In G. Domhoff and T. Dye (Eds.), *Power elites and organisations.* Newbury Park: Sage Publications.

Streim, A. (1989). "The tasks of the SS Einsatzgruppen." In M. Marrus (Ed.), *The Nazi Holocaust: historical articles on the destruction of the European Jews,* Vol. 2. Westport, CT: Meckler.

Stubbing, R.A. (1986). *The defense game.* New York: Harper and Row.

Sweetman, J. (1971). "Uncorroborated evidence: one problem about the Crimean War." *Journal of the Society for Army Historical Research,* XLIX(200), 194–198.

Szymanski, G. (2005). "Mom, who lost son in Iraq, talks about disgusting White House private meeting with Bush." *Lewis News,* July 5. Available from: www. lewisnews.com/article.asp?ID=105971 (Accessed August 22, 2005).

Talmon, J.L. (1989). "European History: seedbed of the Holocaust." In M. Marrus (Ed.), *The Nazi Holocaust: historical articles on the destruction of the European Jews,* Vol. 1. Westport, CT: Meckler.

Taxpayers for Common Sense (2002). "Cost of Iraq invasion severely underestimated; tens of billions have been ignored." Available from: http://www.taxpayer. net/TCS/Press Releases/2002/11–01–02iraq.htm (Accessed July 15, 2005).

The Pentagon Papers (1971). *The Defense Department history of United States decision making on Vietnam,* Vols. II, III, IV (The Senator Gravel Edition). Boston: Beacon Press.

The Rendition Project. (n.d.). "Rendition and human rights." Available from: www. therenditionproject.org.uk/the-issues/rendition-and-hrs.html (Accessed July 18, 2013).

Tinker, A. (1980). "Towards a political economy of accounting: an empirical illustration of the Cambridge controversies." *Accounting, Organizations and Society,* 5, 147–160.

Tinker, T., Lehman, C., and Neimark, M. (1991). "Falling down in the hole in the middle of the road: political quietism in corporate social reporting." *Accounting, Auditing and Accountability Journal,* 4(2), 28–54.

Trachtenberg, M. (1991). *History and strategy.* Princeton: Princeton University Press.

Trevelyan, C. (1856). *Memorandum on the civil administration of the British Army by Sir C.E. Trevelyan, written in May 1855, with observations by Commissary General Sir Edward Coffin.* London: HMSO.

Trevelyan, G. (1922). *British history in the nineteenth century and after 1782–1919.* London: Longmans.

Trevelyan, G. (1960). *The English revolution 1688–1689.* London: Oxford University Press.

Trevelyan Papers (CET). Robinson Library, University of Newcastle upon Tyne.

Turner, E. (1956). *Gallant gentlemen: a portrait of the British officer 1600–1956.* London: Michael Joseph.

Tyler May, E. (1989). "Explosive issues: sex, women, and the bomb." In L. May (Ed.), *Recasting America: culture and politics in the age of cold war.* Chicago: The University of Chicago Press, 154–170.

Udall, S.L. (1994). *The myths of August: a personal exploration of our tragic Cold War affair with the atom.* New York: Pantheon Books.

Ureibi, S. (2005). "Quieter than bombs: Iraq's foul water also kills." *UT San Diego,* July 11. Available from: www.globalpolicy.org/security/issues/iraq/attack/consequences/2005/0711foul.htm (Accessed October 5, 2006).

U.S. House of Representatives (1962a). "Hearings on military posture and H.R. 9751 to authorize appropriations during fiscal year 1963 for aircraft, missiles, and naval vessels for the armed forces, and for other purposes: hearings before the Committee on Armed Services, House of Representatives." 87th Cong., 2nd Sess.

U.S. House of Representatives (1962b). "Department of Defense Appropriations for 1963: hearings before a Subcommittee of the Committee on Appropriations, House of Representatives." 87th Cong., 2nd Sess.

U.S. Senate (1961). "Organizing for national defense: hearings before the Subcommittee on National Policy Machinery of the Committee on Government Operations, United States Senate." 86th Cong., 1st Sess.

U.S. Senate (1967a). "Planning-Programming-Budgeting initial memorandum: prepared by the Subcommittee on National Security and International Operations (pursuant to S. Res. 54, 90th Cong.) of the Committee on Government Operations, United States Senate." 90th Cong., 1st Sess. 1.

U.S. Senate. (1967b). "Planning-Programming-Budgeting: hearings before the Subcommittee on National Security and International Operations of the Committee on Government Operations, United States Senate." 90th Cong., 1st Sess. 2.

U.S. Senate. (1968a). "Status of U.S. strategic power: hearings before the Preparedness Investigating Subcommittee of the Committee on Armed Services, United States Senate." 90th Cong., 2nd Sess. 1.

U.S. Senate. (1968b). "Planning-Programming-Budgeting: hearing before the Subcommittee on National Security and International Operations of the Committee on Government Operations, United States Senate." 90th Cong., 2nd Sess. 3.

Van Creveld, M. (1985). *Command in war.* Cambridge, MA: Harvard University Press.

Velayutham, S., and Perera, M. (1996). "The influence of underlying metaphysical notions on our interpretation of accounting." *Accounting, Auditing and Accountability Journal,* 9(4), 65–85.

Ventris, C. (2000). "New public management: an examination of its influence on contemporary public affairs and its impact on shaping the intellectual agenda of the field." *Administrative Theory & Praxis,* 22, 500–518.

Vietnam Veterans Against the War (1972). *The winter soldier investigation: an inquiry into American war crimes.* Boston: Beacon Press.

Von Lang, J. (1983). *Eichman interrogated.* London: The Bodley Head.

Wallsten, S., and Kosec, K. (2005). "The economic costs of the war in Iraq" (Working paper 05–19). Washington, D.C.: AEI-Brookings Joint Center for Regulatory Studies.

War Office Cost Accounting Committee (1918). *Instructions relating to experimental cost accounting in selected units*. London: War Office.

Ward, S. (1957). *Wellington's headquarters: a study of administrative problems in the peninsula 1809–1814*. Oxford: Oxford University Press.

Watt, D. (1988). "The London University class for military administrators, 1906–31: a study of British approach to civil-military relations." *LSE Quarterly*, 2(2), 155–171.

Webb, B. (1975). *Our partnership*. Edited by B. Drake and M. Cole. London School of Economics and Political Science: Cambridge University Press.

Webb, S. (1903). *Twentieth century politics: a policy of national efficiency*. Fabian Tract No. 108. London: The Fabian Society.

Weber, E. (1980). "Modern anti-Semitism." In H. Friedlander and S. Milton (Eds.), *The Holocaust: ideology, bureaucracy, and genocide*. Millwood, NY: Kraus International Publications.

Weedon, C. (1987). *Feminist practice & poststructuralist theory*. Cambridge, MA: Blackwell.

Weissman, D. (2012). "The North Carolina connection to extraordinary rendition and torture." University of North Carolina School of Law, January. Available from: www.law.unc.edu/documents/clinicalprograms/finalreditionreportweb.pdf (Accessed January 13, 2013).

Weizenbaum, J. (1976). *Computer power and human reason: from judgment to calculation*. San Francisco: W.H. Freeman and Company.

Wellers, G. (1978). "Reply to the Neo-Nazi falsification of historical facts concerning the Holocaust." In S. Klarsfeld (Ed.), *The Holocaust and the neo-Nazi mythomania*. New York: The Beate Klarsfeld Foundation.

Wells, H.G. (1934). *Experiment in autobiography: discoveries and conclusions of a very ordinary brain (since 1866)*. London: Victor Gollancz.

White, A. (1901). *Efficiency and empire*. London: Macmillan.

Whitlock, C. (2009). "Italy convicts 23 Americans: message sent on rendition CIA operatives, colonel were tried in absentia." *The Washington Post*, November 5, A14.

Wiesel, E. (1988). "Some questions that remain open." In A. Cohen (Ed.), *Comprehending the Holocaust*. Frankfurt am Main: Peter Lang.

Wiggins, J. (1964). *Freedom and secrecy*. New York: Oxford University Press.

Wildavsky, A. (1967). "The political economy of efficiency: cost-benefit analysis, systems analysis, and program budgeting." In F.J. Lyden and E.G. Miller (Eds.), *Planning, programming, budgeting: a systems approach to management*. Chicago: Markham Publishing Company, 371–402.

Wildavsky, A. (1978). "Policy analysis is what information systems are not." *Accounting, Organizations and Society*, 3, 77–88.

Williams, E. (1965). *A documentary history of England*. Harmondsworth: Penguin Books.

Wilson, J. (1973). *CB: a life of Sir Henry Campbell-Bannerman*. London: Constable.

Wilson, J. (1995). *British business history 1720–1994*. Manchester: Manchester University Press.

Winston, D. (1980). "Pagan and early Christian anti-Semitism." In H. Friedlander and S. Milton (Eds.), *The Holocaust: ideology, bureaucracy, and genocide*. Millwood, NY: Kraus International Publications.

Wohlstetter, A. (1969). "Statement of Dr. Albert Wohlstetter to the Senate Committee on Armed Services." April 23. Reprinted in *Planning-Programming-Budgeting: hearing before the Subcommittee on National Security and International Operations of the Committee on Government Operations*, United States Senate, 91st Cong., 1st Sess. 5, 667–670.

Woodham-Smith, C. (1977). *Florence Nightingale*. Glasgow: Fontana.

World Health Organization (2002). *World report on violence and health*. Geneva: World Health Organization.

World Health Organization (2004). *The economic dimensions of interpersonal violence*. Geneva: World Health Organization.

Wright, F. (1956). "The British army cost accounting experiment 1919–1925." *The Australian Accountant,* November, 463–470.

Young, H. (Captain) (1906). "Practical economy in the army." *Journal of the Royal United Services Institute,* L, 1281–1285.

Young, M. (2000). *Army Service Corps 1902–18*. London: Leo Cooper.

Young, M.B. (1991). *The Vietnam Wars: 1945–1990*. New York: Harper Perennial.

Index

For Product Safety Concerns and Information please contact our EU
representative GPSR@taylorandfrancis.com
Taylor & Francis Verlag GmbH, Kaufingerstraße 24, 80331 München, Germany

www.ingramcontent.com/pod-product-compliance
Ingram Content Group UK Ltd.
Pitfield, Milton Keynes, MK11 3LW, UK
UKHW021608240425
457818UK00018B/440